A *New*
BEGINNING

A *New* BEGINNING

The Compelling True Story

of One Man's Journey

Against Overwhelming Odds

ALFRED LANGER

With Gene Church

LANGDON STREET PRESS

Minneapolis

Langdon Street Press
212 3rd Avenue North, Suite 290
Minneapolis, MN 55401
612.455.2293
www.langdonstreetpress.com

ISBN - 978-1-934938-85-0
ISBN - 1-934938-85-8
LCCN - 2010920146

Cover Design & Typeset by Kristeen Wegner

Printed in the United States of America

LANGDON
STREET
PRESS

DEDICATION

A NEW BEGINNING is dedicated to the more than fifteen million brave ethnic Germans from Sudetenland, Pomerania, Prussia, and Silesia who, in 1945 and 1946, were viciously expelled from their homeland, forced without mercy into abject poverty, endured hardship beyond imagination, and valiantly expressed heart, courage, and determination to overcome virtually insurmountable obstacles and create new beginnings in distant and foreign lands.

ONE

ALFRED SAT ACROSS THE KITCHEN TABLE FROM HIS MOTHER and picked unenthusiastically at his breakfast. His face mirrored hers—both full of emptiness, remorse, and sadness.

The two were alone on this morning, as the other family members were involved in their own pursuits—Alfred's older sister was at work, his father was toiling in the nearby fields, and his brothers had either moved away or were in the army

"You should eat," Elsa quietly offered, her voice trembling slightly. "You'll need your strength."

He nodded politely, slowly raising a forkful of summer sausage to his mouth. It would be a very long time before he and his mother would share another meal.

They stared at each other in silence until Elsa glanced at the clock on the wall and sighed deeply. "It's time," she whispered.

Alfred nodded again, biting the inside of his lip to prevent the tears from spilling onto his cheeks. He rose from his chair and walked slowly to the door, reaching for his suitcase and touching his mother's hand as she reached for the bag at the same time. She wanted to carry it for him, he knew—he could tell by the warmth and affection that was clearly written on her face—and so he nodded his acknowledgment as he forced a smile, hoping to appear brave. He looked fondly around the living room and kitchen, capturing each image in his mind as if it were a photograph; these were images that would have to last him for many years.

Finally, reluctantly, Alfred opened the front door and stepped out onto the porch. Elsa slipped her free hand into his and together, they walked slowly down the front steps and toward the sidewalk that would lead to the train station. He could sense her struggling with the weight of the suitcase, but he knew that she didn't want to be denied this last chance to express her love and affection.

After all these years of doing her very best to raise all of us and steer us in the right direction, he thought, *she wants to make this last sacrifice for me.*

After walking for several blocks, Elsa finally broke the silence. "Don't forget to say your prayers."

"Every night," Alfred promised, smiling warmly at her.

"And every morning," she reminded him.

"Yes, and every morning."

They each wished desperately that they could have prolonged the five minutes it took to reach the Selbitz train station. Overwhelmed and feeling nostalgic, Alfred noticed and appreciated everything along the way: the neighbors' houses; the fresh summer scent of the trees, shrubbery, and abundance of flowers; children romping joyfully in their front yards; and the myriad sounds of the city. The familiarity of these seemingly ordinary things was something he knew, without question, that he would greatly miss.

Upon reaching the boarding area of the two-and-a-half-story train station, Elsa finally set the suitcase on the ground, as Alfred checked once more that he had all the necessary tickets and documentation. A few others waited for the train—he overheard their conversations as they spoke of traveling to nearby towns or villages. Such was not the case for Alfred; he was going to the end of the line.

Several strangers looked at their watches, seeming impatient for the train's arrival. Alfred and Elsa, however, savored these last moments together. He took his mother's hand in his once more as they each thought, *Perhaps the train will be late. Perhaps we'll have a few more precious moments together.*

The train whistle broke their reverie, sounding a shrill reminder of Alfred's imminent departure. Soon the iron giant came into view, bellowing black smoke into the clear, blue summer sky as it rounded the bend and approached the station. Elsa looked deeply into her son's eyes, and as the train lumbered to a stop, her tears began to flow. Alfred drew his mother into a firm embrace, neither wanting to let go; neither wanting this separation to become a reality.

Within moments the conductor shouted the words that mother and son both had been dreading: "All aboard!" Their collective tears became uncontrollable, though the train's insistent whistle drowned out their sobbing. Alfred stroked his mother's hair and whispered in her ear, "I love you, Mama."

With great difficulty, she softly replied, "God speed," as she wiped away her tears with the white handkerchief he'd given her as a Christmas gift.

He boarded the train at the last possible second, just as it began pulling away from the station. He watched from the doorway of the railcar as his mother—along with the family and life he had known—slowly disappeared into the distance.

Now, his old life was behind him, and the new one lay ahead—virtually halfway around the world. Alfred wiped away his own tears with the sleeve of his jacket, and when he looked up, the station was no longer in sight.

Elsa Langer stood on the platform for a few more minutes, staring wistfully down the track as the train sounds grew softer. She replayed her own last words to her son, over and over, *God speed*. She bowed her head, closed her eyes tightly, and whispered, "Dear heavenly Father, please watch over and protect our precious young son. Give him strength and guidance and wisdom. And in all things, Thy will be done. Amen."

Elsa's heart was overflowing with both pride and fear—pride that Alfred was man enough and strong enough to deal with any circumstance or challenge that might present itself to him, yet fear that perhaps the cruel and uncertain world outside their small town might contain insurmountable odds and pitfalls that he would not be able to endure.

She made her way off the train platform and began her walk home, noticing that the morning's clear blue sky on that August 16, 1961, day had become filled with puffy white clouds. The afternoon's weather would be uncertain, Elsa realized, much like the future. Still, as she walked, she reflected on the remarkable experiences that had led her family to this totally unexpected and memorable point in their lives.

* * *

Quaint—that was the best description for the small town of Hermannstadt, a charming yet isolated farming community in the Sudetenland in Germany. Picture-postcard perfect, Hermannstadt was comfortably nestled in the far northeastern part of the country and was relatively protected from the outside world. The town had only two primary roads, one referred to as the Old Road and the other, stretching barely five kilometers from end to end, as the Main Road. With the exception of a small business district, both roads ran along lush, rolling fields that were dotted with farmhouses.

The majestic Altvater mountain range, home to the highest point in the Sudetenland and standing twelve kilometers outside the town, provided the perfect background for this peaceful and picturesque setting. In summer, hikers trekked to the fifteen-hundred-meter mountain peak, and during the long winter months, countless cross-country skiers found a perfect playground in the deep, powdery snow. In the heavily forested surrounding area, it was common to see lumberjacks hauling newly cut logs on horse-drawn sleds to larger cities, where they would be processed in lumber mills.

In September 1939, as their own country was invading neighboring Poland and beginning a world war, Hermannstadt had a population of just over two thousand people residing in slightly fewer than five hundred homes. Perhaps predictably for the community, the majority of Hermannstadt's residents, even those who owned businesses, were farmers of one sort or another. And because there was a limited number of residents—and virtually all of them attended Maria Hilf Catholic Church—nearly everyone in town knew everyone else. Many could boast relatives who had lived there—in peace and relative prosperity—for generations, and the town enjoyed such a degree of safety and security that only a few houses had unnecessary and seldom-used locks on their doors.

During the Christmas season of 1939, the women of small and intimate Hermannstadt had a special reason to be joyous—they were excited and abuzz with the recently learned news that at some point that following summer, the population of their town would increase by one.

*   *   *

Rudolf Langer paced the floor of the combination living room and kitchen, wringing his calloused hands and mopping the sweat from his brow—unusual behavior, given that he previously had fathered three healthy children. This was one of the extremely rare days that he was not working in his fields, taking care of his livestock, or attending to the small forest he owned.

As the oldest son of Franz and Antonia Langer, Rudolf had inherited the family property after returning home, following two years' service in the German Wehrmacht after World War I. The Langer family had owned the farm and its land for generations, and the tradition—for as long as anyone could remember—was to pass ownership to the oldest son. As children, Rudolf, his sister, and his brothers all had lived in the same house in which Rudolf now resided as an adult and in which his own children were born. Rudolf worked the same land that his father and forefathers had worked for hundreds of years.

Today, however, Rudolf had helpers performing his usual chores. Today, Rudolf Langer was understandably preoccupied.

Gerti, Rudolf's nearly four-year-old daughter, watched with childlike fascination as her father paced the floor like a caged animal. "Tata," she said, "when will the new baby come to our house?"

"Soon, I hope," he replied quietly, running his hands through his dark brown hair, then nervously lighting a new cigarette from the one he had just finished. "It takes time." It was uncommon to see him in such a state of agitation, but Gerti casually accepted his answer and returned to playing with a handmade doll, cradling it gently in her lap. Upstairs in their cribs, Rudolf Junior, known as Rudi, age three, and Willie, eighteen months, slept peacefully, unaware of the controlled chaos of the house.

Frieda Bannert, the Langers' middle-aged live-in maid, appeared briefly on her way to the kitchen. Rudolf placed his hand gently on her shoulder as she passed. "Frieda, is it time?" She shook her head and offered an understanding smile. "Rudolf, the baby will come when it's time for it to come." A loud moan was heard from the upstairs bedroom, and Rudolf's head jerked involuntarily in that direction. Frieda patted his hand. "It's normal," she calmly reminded him. "You know that. Have a schnapps. I need to get some more hot water."

For Rudolf, the following minutes seemed like hours. He continued to pace as the moans emanating from the upstairs room became louder, more frequent, and more insistent. Finally, late on that muggy Thursday afternoon, July 11, 1940, the town midwife, Hanke Alexandra, appeared at the top of the stairs holding a small bundle wrapped in white. Rudolf looked up, his face filled with anticipation. "It's a fine, healthy boy," she said.

Rudolf beamed and proudly announced, "And his name will be Alfred."

Hanke, also beaming, informed him, "Elsa says you can call him Fredi."

Rudolf's smile faded momentarily. "Is Elsa—?"

Hanke waved away his concern. "Elsa is fine. Come and hold your new son."

Gerti, full of excitement, rushed over to her father. "Can I see him, Tata?"

"Of course you can." Rudolf took his daughter's hand and helped her up the stairs to where Hanke was waiting with the baby. The midwife handed Rudolf the small bundle, and he leaned down so Gerti could see her new brother.

The little girl cocked her head to one side, studying the sleeping baby. "He's so small. And so red."

"Just like you used to be," Rudolf responded with a loving smile.

"Can I touch him?" Gerti asked. When Rudolf nodded, she gently placed her finger to the baby's cheek. She looked up into her father's eyes. "And he's soft, too."

Before the sun set that evening, the entire town had learned of the new member of the Langer household. In many ways, the town functioned as an extended family—the residents all looked after each other and had a strong sense of community—and the Langers' pride in their new baby was shared by all who lived in Hermannstadt.

On that warm July evening in 1940, with the moon's phase waxing crescent and one new addition to the population, the residents of Hermannstadt slept in peace, harmony, and security.

* * *

Such was not the case in other parts of Europe. The Third Reich, Adolf Hitler's unstoppable war machine, had already invaded Poland and recently had claimed northern and western France; within a few short months, it would bring Britain to its knees, as it violently and rapidly swept its way through country after country.

The majority of those living in Hermannstadt, however, were unaffected and, in many cases, completely unaware of the turbulence and turmoil of the escalating war—yet their innocence was understandable. At the time, no railroad tracks ran through—or even near—their town, which meant they had no understanding of the vast, nonstop troop and equipment movement of the Third Reich, as well as the fact that any source of information was severely limited. No one in their small town owned an automobile or a truck, so twice a week, one of the townsmen would drive a horse-drawn cart six kilometers to the train station, which was located in Würbenthal, where he would deliver and pick up mail, farming supplies that were not available locally, and the newspaper that offered information on events in and around the state of Sudetenland. The trip took the better part of a day, and once completed, the townsman would spend the next two days delivering the mail by bicycle and then, weather permitting, begin the trip again.

The newspaper—usually from Zuckmantel in Czechoslovakia—carried stories of one-sided victories and successes, as dictated by Josef Göbbels, Hitler's brilliant and masterful Minister of Propaganda. The news was received in tiny Hermannstadt with relative indifference; because of the town's isolation, few within the small population were affected in any way by the developments in the war.

With all government funds directed toward the war effort, however, none was available to provide the once-promised electricity or telephone service for the community. Instead, a generator in the basement of the small City Hall was started every morning to produce power for that building, as well as providing electricity for the school and the doctor's office. The generator also supplied enough wattage to operate the one radio in town, which was located at City Hall. The only information available on the single channel that the town received was of local weather reports and continuing stories of victories relating to the war.

On extremely rare occasions, someone would receive a letter from a friend or relative that mentioned the horrors of the various conflicts and the joy of victories. On even rarer occasions, a stranger traveling through Hermannstadt would stop for the night and share stories of his own experiences. Still, those in the tiny town seemed unaffected by any news of the outside world. In Hermannstadt, life carried on as usual.

* * *

The women of Hermannstadt could barely contain their excitement when they learned of the newest member of the Langer family—everyone wanted to visit and to get a chance to hold baby Fredi. Frieda Bannert was busier than usual, as she tended to her usual chores in the Langer household while also helping to care for Fredi and ensuring that Elsa wasn't overwhelmed by visitors.

Frieda was firm but polite in her response to requests to see Elsa: "She needs to rest," she would tell those who came calling. "Perhaps tomorrow she'll be able to come downstairs." She kept to herself the fact that this birth had been more difficult than the previous three—Frieda was well known for her loyalty and discretion. Initially, Elsa objected to Frieda's sending visitors away—she wanted to spend time with her friends—but she finally conceded that the protective Frieda knew best.

Although Frieda kept the visitors from Elsa's room, she was happy to bring Fredi downstairs to meet the other members of the community. As he was passed around the room from one woman to another—each cooing at him and saying that he was adorable—Gerti would stand in front of each visitor, point at the infant, and proudly exclaim, "That's my brand new baby brother!"

The morning after Fredi's birth, like all others, Rudolf gently milked their two cows, spread fresh straw in the stable, and provided food for the other livestock—two work horses, an ox, five goats, four pigs, six rabbits, several chickens, and a few ducks. Then Rudolf climbed into his ox-drawn wagon and returned to his fields, which were about one kilometer away. "Congratulations!" a neighbor called out as he passed Rudolf on the road. Rudolf waved back with a smile as big as all outdoors and continued on his way. As always, there was much to do.

* * *

Within a few days the Langer household returned to its normal routine. Elsa was strong-willed and independent, the result of having grown up in the strict and repressive environment of an orphanage in Einsiedel. Since marrying Rudolf and moving to the farm, she'd become even stronger, both physically and in character.

Following his early morning chores, Rudolf returned home to check on his recuperating wife; he found her reading the family Bible. He sat gently on the edge of the bed and traced the outline of her face with his finger. "You're an attractive woman, Elsa," he offered tenderly.

She shook her head demurely. "And you must be losing your eyesight."

"I've never been more serious. You're more attractive now than the day I first saw you." He smiled at her appreciatively. "How are you feeling?"

"Well enough to get back to work," she replied, throwing back the covers and getting out of bed. Although Rudolf protested that she still needed to rest, Elsa got dressed and carefully tucked her brunette hair into its usual bun. Stepping out into the hallway, she called out, "Time to get up, Gerti!" Gerti, already awake, peeked out her bedroom door, her hair still tousled from sleep. "There are many chores to be done this morning," Elsa informed her only daughter—and then she tempered her words with one of her electrifying smiles, the kind that could light up any room.

Rudolf assisted Elsa down the stairs, and Gerti followed, rubbing sleep-filled eyes. "I'm not old enough to do any chores," Gerti objected. "I'm only four!"

"It's time you learned," her mother insisted. "You can be my little helper."

Upon entering the kitchen, Elsa found Frieda already hard at work, baking bread and preparing breakfast. "How are you feeling?" Frieda asked with concern.

Elsa slipped a bib apron over her now-trim frame. "Less fat!"

Rudolf chuckled along with the two women, but he issued his wife a stern warning as he kissed her cheek: "You take it easy today." Then, pointing a finger at Frieda, he added, "And you make sure she does. I'll see you both at supper." With that he was out the back door.

Before Frieda could speak, Elsa assured her, "I know. I know. I'll take it easy. But today I'm going to have a helper."

Frieda looked puzzled, then smiled with fondness at Gerti as the child entered the kitchen and announced, "Okay, Mama. Teach me some chores."

Elsa knelt down to Gerti's level. "If it's all right with Frieda, I'll show you how to pick vegetables in the garden." With an approving nod from Frieda, the two of them went outdoors to the large, fenced-in garden, which produced tomatoes, carrots, onions, beets, radishes, rhubarb, celery, lettuce, and chives. Much of the garden, however, was given over to potatoes, as potatoes were a staple for the family. Elsa often served them boiled or baked or used them to make potato salad or potato dumplings.

Now, Elsa pointed toward the ground where leafy shoots were exposed. "Those are potatoes. When the leaves on top are bright green, that means the potatoes are ready to be pulled up. Can you find some that are ready?"

Gerti rolled her eyes. "Of course I can. I'm four years old." After receiving basic instruction, Gerti pulled up three large potatoes—just enough for their evening meal. Elsa smiled proudly at her daughter as they went back into the house with Gerti's small harvest.

After delivering the potatoes to Frieda, Gerti worked with her mother, cleaning the first floor of the house—a large open area that consisted of the kitchen, living room, and dining room. The first floor also housed Frieda's bedroom; the other bedrooms—one for Rudolf and Elsa, and another for the children—were on the second story, each containing feather beds and a freestanding wardrobe closet. A staircase led from the first floor down to the cellar, which remained cool enough throughout the year to store vegetables, as well as the meat they acquired when they butchered livestock—usually a pig or goat—which was then preserved in air-tight wooden barrels.

The house itself was formally identified as number 78 and was located on the Old Road. Constructed of local stones and adobe and painted a fresh white, its thick walls helped to provide warmth during the harsh winter months and coolness during the summer. The home's furnishings were rather primitive, constructed as they were of hewn wood—efficient yet comfortable. The flooring was finely polished wooden planks.

Because of the Langers' profound faith, which they practiced daily, the walls were adorned with religious pictures and an eight-inch by twelve-inch crucifix—a treasured gift from Rudolf's father—was prominently displayed in the living room. Each time Elsa passed the crucifix, it was her habit to touch the feet of Jesus, offer a small prayer for the safety of her family, and give thanks for the blessings they had received. She did this so frequently that the bronze finish on the feet of Jesus was worn away.

Now that the housecleaning was finished, Gerti watched as her mother and Frieda kneaded dough for bread. Elsa had carefully explained each step in the bread-making process, and finally, she allowed Gerti to help pat the dough into round shapes. Just before setting the loaves on the pan, Elsa scored three small crosses on the bottom of each loaf. She did this every time she made bread—a subtle yet effective reminder of her and her family's faith in God and the blessings they had received.

Then Elsa smiled at Gerti and explained, "Now it's ready for the oven. It's important that the bread is left in the oven for just the right amount of time—that's how we get the crust to be crispy and brown."

The oven used for baking was one that had been installed by Rudolf's father—it also helped to heat the house in winter, along with the wood-burning stove. Made of fire-resistant bricks, the baking oven stood nearly six feet high. It resembled an igloo, with a flat top, and it was set against a wall with a chimney behind it. Inside, there were two separate compartments—the lower compartment held the glowing, red-hot kindling, and the upper compartment was used to bake bread and assorted cakes.

Like the rest of the town, the Langers' house had no electricity. Lighting was provided by oil lamps, and as the day grew longer and shadows started to fill the kitchen, Frieda left the bread-baking to Elsa and Gerti and began to light the lamps. She walked through the downstairs rooms, removing the glass cylinders on the top of the oil lamps and touching a lit match to the wicks. Then she adjusted the brightness of the lamps by raising or lowering the wicks, and by the time Rudolf returned from his work in the fields that evening, the rooms all offered a welcoming glow.

On this night, Rudolf had a special surprise when he arrived home. He'd found a mixed-breed puppy wandering around one of his fields. Judging by the dog's shaggy brown fur, Rudolf guessed that he was part sheepdog, and because he was clearly undernourished, Rudolf also surmised that the dog didn't have a home. Fritzl, as the puppy later was named, was warmly accepted, and the little dog soon showed himself to be a quick learner. Within a short time, Fritzl became adept at herding the goats out to a nearby pasture to graze and then gently nudging them along on their return trip home. Although Fritzl was allowed inside the house, he preferred to sleep in the barn, as if he were protecting the other animals from any predators during the night. The whole family loved Fritzl, and he became an integral part of the Langer household.

TWO

SPRINGTIME ARRIVED IN HERMANNSTADT AND BROUGHT with it renewal, refreshment, and regrowth. The warm spring air was a welcome change after the cold winter. Fredi had been baptized just a few weeks earlier, when the snow was still deep on the ground, and the family had braved freezing temperatures and tall snow drifts to make their way to Maria Hilf Church, about one kilometer from their home.

Now, an abundance of shrubbery, trees, and flowers began blooming, and the town and surrounding area saw myriad brilliant and glorious colors. The shade trees that stood tall along both sides of the Old Road seemed to meet at their tops, fashioning a canopy under which the residents would walk.

Spring also signaled the annual planting season. Each morning, before the sun rose and after the cows were milked, Rudolf would put a harness on one of the horses, hitch him to the plow, and lead him to the nearby fields to prepare the fertile ground. Rudi, now nearly four years old, would drive the cows and goats to a pasture where they would spend the day grazing, with Fritzl, as always, assisting.

The planting of the fields was a communal event, with the neighbors willingly assisting Rudolf in planting the barley, hay, oats, and wheat, just as Rudolf reciprocated their generosity whenever he could. Elsa, in her own way, was part of the process. After fixing breakfast for her growing family, she and Frieda would scurry about, preparing a lunchtime meal for the workers in the fields. Lunch usually consisted of cold cuts and bread or leftovers from the previous day's meal, along with fresh milk or coffee. Once it was ready, she would take it to the barn, place the food securely on their wagon, hitch the wagon behind the other horse, and send him out to meet the workers—on his own. It was uncanny that the horse knew exactly where to go, without any direction or guidance. Occasionally, the children were allowed to join their father, and they would sit in a circle with the workers and enjoy a hearty lunch. Fredi, not quite one year old, was bundled warmly and joined his siblings on this exciting trip.

On rainy days, when he couldn't work in the fields, Rudolf always had an abundance of chores that needed to be accomplished. Dressed in denim pants with suspenders, a wool shirt without a collar, laced-up leather boots, and a hat that always had a brightly colored feather in its brim, he would make repairs to the house, barn, stable, or fences, or he'd split wood into kindling for the stove and oven.

Once the spring planting was completed, all those who'd assisted were invited to a grand celebration, held in the Langer barn. Usually, a couple of the men would bring along an accordion and a harmonica to provide entertainment. The bright, up-tempo music urged the guests to dance waltzes and polkas and join in the singing of happy German folk songs. The pleasant evening also would include the drinking of schnapps, which, although it was readily available, was always appreciated by the guests.

Conversations on these evenings generally revolved around life in their community—the women discussing children or church activities and sharing recipes; the men discussing the planting and their hope for a full and fine harvest. Politics and the war effort were seldom—if ever—topics of conversation, as those subjects were of little concern to anyone in the community.

Children were included in the festivities as well. The older ones often would venture into the hayloft, jumping wildly about and playing games of tag. This year, Fredi was in his carrying basket near Elsa. He smiled widely as the music played and the happy guests sang along—and the evening was not complete without the communal singing of one song in particular, "Lili Marlene," which was based on a German poem written in 1915. The song told of a soldier longing to see his sweetheart when he returned to

his hometown—it was as close to the topic of war as the residents of Hermannstadt ever got.

* * *

"Hurry, Elsa," Rudolf said, a little louder than normal. "It's time to
leave. We'll be late for the service."

"I'm dressing them as fast as I can!" Elsa called from the upstairs bedroom. With Frieda's help, Elsa was hurriedly clothing the four Langer children in their very finest outfits. The children always wore fine clothes to
attend church each Sunday, but today was extra-special—it was Easter
Sunday, one of the two most holy days (along with Christmas) of the entire year. For the residents of Hermannstadt, Easter services were held at
Maria Hilf Chapel, located directly behind the Langer house.

While the main church was located in the middle of town, the chapel
was at the top of a hill, overlooking the peaceful and serene valley below.
The chapel, built in the early 1900s, had been renovated in 1929 and 1930,
thanks to the tireless efforts of volunteers, including the local priest. They'd
formed a bucket brigade—a long line of helpers, winding down to a creek
in the valley below—and diligently and tirelessly transferred water to the
top of the hill. Once there, the water was used to make cement, not only
used to repair the chapel but also to create a small tower on the roof that
held a brand new bell. Inside the chapel, a new altar had been installed,
and a large painting featuring St. Isador of Seville, a bishop who had died
in 636 and who was the patron saint of farmers, was hung with pride on
one of the walls.

The Langer children finally were ready, and the family left their house
and joined nearly everyone in town as they took part in the annual Easter procession up the hill to Maria Hilf Chapel. Gerti proudly wore her
dirndl—a traditional German dress for a young girl of the region—the
only article of clothing that Elsa had purchased. With Frieda's assistance,
Elsa had made all the other clothing. The older boys wore their Sunday-
best lederhosen (leather trousers with suspenders), leather shoes, and their
special jackets with edelweiss embroidered on their lapels. Fredi was dressed
in the same attire he had worn for his baptism—it was made of fine linen,
trimmed with tucks and lace, and had a matching bonnet.

The procession seemed to go on forever, each family enjoying the joy and holiness of the day, singing hymns of praise as they made their trek. Once they all reached the top of the hill, the congregation was blessed with an outdoor Mass on this holy ground, and their spirits, in glory and unison, were lifted.

Following the Mass was a wonderful time for communal conversation. Feelings expressed about the war and Hitler were positive, in general. It was the commonly held belief that when Hitler's promises came to fruition, their isolated town would benefit, at least to the extent that electricity, telephones, and plumbing would be installed.

The residents of Hermannstadt were not aware that all available funds in the entire country were being expended toward the war effort—an effort that would eventually result in monumental defeat and moral bankruptcy. On that Easter Sunday, as the families of the tiny farming community gathered together, they were blissfully unaware of the serious matters that were taking place just beyond their borders. The serenity, calm, and joy of that Easter service was in stark contrast to explosive events to come. For Rudolf, Elsa, and their children—and for all their neighbors—life in peaceful Hermannstadt would soon be very, very different.

* * *

Although Hermannstadt remained essentially the same as it had for centuries, the outside world was experiencing the trauma of dramatic change. When boys were ten years old, they were encouraged to join the Hitler Youth. There was prestige in wearing identical brown shirts, learning to march in formation, and attending special closed meetings—meetings that were designed to develop unquestioning loyalty to the Führer. Members were expected to stand straight and tall, with their chests out and chins tucked in whenever they were addressed by adults. Members also were instructed that they were never to be caught with their hands in their pockets, which was seen as a sign that they were slackers.

The school in Hermannstadt had three classrooms—one for the first, second, and third grades; one for the fourth, fifth and sixth grades; and one for the seventh and eighth graders, who were instructed by Adolf Seidel. He and the two other teachers strongly believed in the new Führer and enthusiastically shared their faith and opinions that he would bring about change for the better. Now, in addition to reading, writing, arithmetic, nature, and the history of the region in which they lived, the children also were indoctrinated in the glory of the Third Reich and, more specifically, in admiration of Adolf Hitler. It was decreed that before each school day began, the children would stand outside in a circle, raise their arms in a "Heil Hitler" salute, and pledge allegiance to their Führer and their country.

Still, most residents of Hermannstadt continued their daily routines, tending to their crops and livestock. The town continued to receive only limited news of the outside world and the escalating war, and even then, it was always of a positive nature that brought hope and promise to their country. The constant propaganda spouted by public officials encouraged the population to be proud Germans and believe in the success of the new order.

Reports repeatedly explained that the march toward world domination was going exceedingly well. Country after country fell to the superior power and force of the unstoppable German war machine. Citizens were certain that their lives would be bettered by these efforts. The common feeling was that when the dust settled and the war was finally over, life would simply carry on as it had before and during the conflict.

* * *

Franz Langer, Rudolf's father—now in his mid-seventies—lived at number 162, about a kilometer up the Main Road and on the other side of the business district. He and Rudolf's mother, Antonia, had moved into number 162 when Rudolf married Elsa, passing the family home to his son and new daughter-in-law, just as Franz' father had done for him.

Franz owned a building in the business district, where he constructed a baking oven—this one considerably larger than the one he'd built in Rudolf's house—and with the new and improved oven, Franz became the town's baker. From early each morning until late into the night, he prepared baked goods that he sold to the residents of the town. Eventually, he expanded his bakery to include a complete assortment of produce, provided by the local farmers, and various groceries that were delivered twice a week from larger cities.

When his grandchildren were old enough, they would walk or ride their bicycles to his market, where they were always treated to pieces of chocolate, lollipops, or sugar candies. The children never officially worked at the store, but they were always very willing to help their grandfather—Antonia had passed away a few years earlier—whenever he needed help with cleaning the floors and straightening the groceries.

Franz was a frugal person—as was his son Rudolf—and an excellent businessman. Hermannstadt had no bank or savings institution; people generally didn't need money, as bartering was the usual form of payment between buyer and seller. Still, both Franz and Rudolf wisely saved the money they had in the form of gold and silver coins, which they hid in their houses.

* * *

As the Langer children grew older, they each were assigned various chores, an exercise in learning the value of hard, honest work and responsibility. Gerti was now in charge of cleaning the hardwood floors, as well as hanging the freshly washed clothing on the outside clothesline. This, in addition to helping in the kitchen, kept her extremely busy.

Rudi and Willie helped to clean the barn and stable, feed the livestock, and drive the goats and cows out to the pasture to graze. They brought firewood into the house and pumped water into a bucket, which was brought into the house and used for cooking and bathing.

After their chores were completed, the children often played with the farm animals, chasing the ducks around the yard or teaching Fritzl new tricks. They'd pick blueberries in the nearby forest and have an occasional game of soccer with other neighborhood kids—none of them had toys purchased from a store; they didn't need them. They played hide-and-seek and made their own bows and arrows and slingshots.

In winter, dressed in boots, long pants, thick sweaters, and jackets, they constructed small snow forts and engaged in rousing snowball fights with their friends. Fredi also loved sledding, enjoying the feeling of the chilling winds that swept across his rosy-red cheeks as he flew down the hill in front of the chapel on a homemade sled. Fritzl raced along at his side, and his brothers enthusiastically cheered him on. Occasionally, the Langer children hiked to the base of the nearby mountain range and watched with curiosity and envy as cross-country skiers glided gracefully from one town to another.

When the weather turned warm again, they especially enjoyed fishing in the Goldoppa River behind their house, using a technique that was somewhat unique—a well-guarded secret that Rudi taught to Fredi when Fredi was four years old.

"Lie down here," Rudi instructed his brother, "and turn your hands over, palms up." Fredi didn't understand so Rudi, somewhat impatiently, positioned himself on the riverbank and demonstrated to Fredi how he should hold his hands. "Now lower them into the water," Rudi continued, "really slow, so you don't make a splash."

"Why?" Fredi asked innocently.

"So you don't scare the fish, silly," Rudi said.

After a heavy rain the stream was abundant with rainbow trout. Fritzl, nearby, as always, watched with interest as Fredi slowly lowered his hands into the water.

"Now be really still," Rudi whispered. "Don't move."

After a short time, the trout grew accustomed to the new object in its path and would swim directly over Fredi's hands—at which time Rudi would instruct his brother to catch it! After a few failed attempts and much patience, Fredi jerked his hands upward, caught a trout, and threw it over his head and onto the grass. That afternoon, he eventually caught enough trout to make a delicious meal for the entire family.

Although the children usually were able to occupy their time in acceptable ways, on rare occasions some of the more adventurous children would challenge one another to crawl over a neighbor's fence, steal some plums, pears, or apples from a tree, and return to the group to share their spoils. Such mischief-making did not exclude the Langer boys.

On this day, the three boys stood at attention in the barn, staring at the floor, their faces drawn. Elsa, while the perfect example of a loving, caring mother, was also the family disciplinarian and was responsible for administering punishment on those extremely rare occasions when it was necessary. "Were any of you in the Decker orchard this afternoon?" she calmly asked.

Without hesitation, Fredi softly but quickly answered, "It was me, Mama. I took the apples."

"And that means you broke which Commandment?"

"Not to steal," Fredi replied.

The boys were familiar with the Ten Commandments, and they were also quick to admit their actions—Rudolf and Elsa had ingrained in them that they should never tell a lie, and telling a lie to one's parents, in particular, was a sign of disrespect that could not be tolerated. So even though Fredi understood that he would be punished, he did not lie to his mother about taking the apples.

Elsa took a sturdy leather strap from the wall and sighed heavily.

Fredi turned around and bent over, preparing himself for the coming pain.

Elsa frowned as she looked at Rudi and Willie. "You two turn around as well."

Rudi feigned disbelief. "Why us?" he asked. "We didn't do anything."

"I think it's unlikely," Elsa said, "that your brother would have gone over the fence and stolen their apples without your encouragement. Please correct me if I'm wrong."

Silently, Rudi and Willie slowly turned around and bent over. The reprimand was delivered as one solid strike on the rear end. While the pain was short-lived for the three of them, the lesson of telling the truth was one that would last a lifetime.

* * *

Rudolf used a tree stump in the backyard to chop kindling for the stove and oven. He would place a log on the stump, hold it with one hand so it wouldn't fall over, and then rapidly bring down his ax, pulling his hand away from the log at the very last second. Years of experience brought a degree of expertise in this potentially dangerous activity.

Fredi often watched his father chop kindling and was amazed by his accuracy. One day, when Fredi was four years old and motivated by curiosity, he decided to attempt the task himself. He convinced Willie to be his helper by promising, "I can do it!"

"But what if you can't?" Willie asked, the concern clear on his face.

"Don't be such a baby," Fredi taunted his older brother.

It was an insult that Willie could not ignore. Cautiously, he picked up a log and placed it on the stump.

Fredi, using every ounce of his strength, raised the heavy ax above his head, and glanced briefly at his older brother. "Make sure to let go when I swing."

"I will," Willie weakly replied. "Just do it."

With his confidence swelling, Fredi brought the ax down as hard as he could, fully expecting Willie to pull his hand away at the last second, just as he had observed their father do hundreds of times.

The scream that exploded from Willie's mouth was ear-shattering. Blood gushed from his wound as the youngster clutched his hand and rolled on the ground in pain. Fredi stood frozen in shock, fearing he had cut off one of Willie's fingers; wishing he would somehow awake from this bad dream.

But the nightmare was a frightening reality. Willie's screams brought the entire family running into the backyard. Rudolf's stern glare brought tears to Fredi's terrified eyes, as Elsa and Frieda quickly rushed Willie inside, washed off the wound, and applied bandages. Fortunately, the wound was superficial—some skin had been sliced off his right forefinger, but it would heal quickly.

As soon as the bandages were applied and the tears all dried, Elsa turned to Fredi. Her voice was firm as she held her thumb and forefinger as close together as possible without touching them. "You came *that close* to cutting off your brother's finger."

Fredi stared at the floor, shuffling his feet from side to side, filled with anguish but relatively certain of what was to come next. He turned to his brother and, as tears reappeared, sincerely offered, "I'm sorry, Willie. I really am."

To everyone's shock and surprise, Willie softly replied, "It was my fault, too. I should have pulled my hand away." He looked at Fredi, shrugged, and then turned his gaze to their mother. "I guess we should both go to the barn for our punishment."

Fighting back tears, Elsa gently patted them both on the head. "I think there's been enough pain for one day."

That night, Elsa joined her children in their bedroom to read a passage from the Bible and say prayers, as was their nightly ritual. Because of the depth of their religious convictions, Elsa read from the Bible on a regular basis, and prayers were a part of their daily lives. Before each meal, Rudolf always offered a blessing, and the family would all reverently bow their heads, as they listened to Rudolf's words: "*Lieber Herrgott sei unser Gast, und segne die Gaben die Du uns bescheret hast.*" ("Dear God, be our guest at this table and bless the food You have given us.")

That night, after they'd all recited the Lord's Prayer and Elsa was about to leave the children's room, Fredi quietly asked if he could mention something. The older children often would take turns during this time to offer their own prayers for their entire family, but this was the first time that Fredi had made that request.

"Of course you can mention something," Elsa replied quietly.

Fredi cleared his throat and, his voice quivering, said softly, "Lord, I'm sorry for what I did to Willie today, and I hope he'll be all right. I also hope that someday you'll be able to forgive me."

His mother placed her hand gently on his shoulder and offered, "Your brother is going to be just fine, and I know you've already been forgiven."

* * *

Each autumn, several neighbors would join Rudolf in his fields to help harvest the crops. Tall grass, which had been cut earlier, was rolled into rows and left to dry in the sun, where it would become hay, stored in the barn, and provide food for the livestock during the winter months. The work was arduous and all done by hand with scythes. Trip after trip was made in the ox-drawn wagon between the fields and the barn, delivering the crops and returning for another load. The older children assisted by piling the crops onto the wagon and then unloading them in the barn. At first, it seemed like a game, but after a few trips, they discovered that it was difficult labor.

The wives of the workers also put in a full day of hard work. Sitting in a circle in the barn, they plucked feathers off chickens and geese, which would be the centerpiece of the evening's festive meal. In addition to preparing other food, they also used a Bundt pan to bake dark whole-grain Komiss bread.

Once the fields were cleared and the crops gathered, there was still work to be completed. Three or four of the men who had assisted Rudolf participated in a ceremony referred to as *Weizenklopfen* (beating the grain with a flail), considered a highly skilled job. They stood in a circle and, in sequence, began to strike the kernels of wheat, using two sturdy wooden sticks connected by a strong leather strap. This separated the kernels from the stalk; the kernels then were picked up and moved aside. The men got rid of the chaff by tossing the material into the air, a process called winnowing. The chaff blew away, and the heavier grain fell to a canvas spread out on the ground.

After this strenuous exercise was finally completed and as the evening sun was setting, the celebration began. Makeshift tables held the abundance of food prepared by the women, along with several bottles of schnapps. Before eating, a prayer was offered, thanking God for the fine crop He had provided, for the safety of all their families, and for the blessings they had received during the past year.

After dinner, the entire group gathered around the large baking oven in the kitchen to continue sipping their schnapps as they engaged in conversation. The children crawled up and sat on top of the flat-topped oven, which was still warm from the day's baking. Although conversation on other occasions were usually lively and animated, on this night, the children noticed something different, something unusual that they were still too young to clearly understand.

"The newspaper doesn't seem to be reporting as many stories about the war," one neighbor commented absently, between bites of the Komissbrot.

"Mr. Von Kronen got a letter from his son-in-law," another offered, his voice devoid of emotion. "Said the war wasn't going as well as it was in the beginning."

"Yesterday, the innkeeper told me a traveler mentioned several battles were being lost to the Russians," said a third, stretching his arms and yawning.

The children were not so nonchalant. "What does all that mean?" Rudi asked from the stovetop, his voice trembling with concern.

"It doesn't mean anything," Rudolf answered with confidence, calming his son's fears. "Whatever is happening won't affect us in any way. History has certainly proven that."

* * *

At age four, Fredi shared a special affinity with Fritzl. As the youngest child, he probably had the most time to play with the shaggy dog—his older siblings had more chores to attend to than he did—and soon Fredi and Fritzl became inseparable. They played together throughout the day, and when it was time for Fredi to go to bed, Fritzl would follow Fredi into the house before going back outside to sleep in the barn.

Sometimes Fredi's best friend, Pepi Thurmer, would join him and Fritzl on their daily explorations. The two boys—always accompanied by Fritzl—would venture into the nearby woods to pick wild berries, or they'd visit neighboring farms, where they would watch others hard at work, or they'd spend lazy hours by the stream, catching trout with their bare hands.

Like many of the residents in Hermannstadt, Fredi had never seen a motorized vehicle or a train, never heard a radio or phonograph, never seen a motion picture, and never traveled more than five or six kilometers from his home. This was the entire world as he knew it, and even though he'd heard seemingly outlandish tales of faraway places and machines capable of performing unbelievable feats, he had no interest in ever leaving the safety and tranquility of his little town.

This peaceful sense of security, however, was destined to change overnight.

THREE

DINNER AT THE LANGER HOUSEHOLD FOLLOWED A PREDICT-able routine. While enjoying their meal, Rudolf would ask Gerti, Rudi, and Willie about the things they'd learned at school that day. Fredi, eager to share as well, might tell the others that he'd spent the afternoon teaching Fritzl to play fetch.

On this night, however, Rudi altered the subject matter when he turned to his father and asked, "Tata, why did all the soldiers leave today?"

"Leave where?" Elsa asked, surprised by his question.

"Leave our town," Rudolf answered as he finished another bite. "I ran into Mr. Siebert in the field this afternoon. He'd heard the same thing."

Elsa was intrigued. "Where did they go?"

Rudolf shook his head. "No one seems to know. Apparently, no explanation was offered for their sudden departure."

Ever since the war had begun in September 1939, there had been a small contingent of German soldiers in or around Hermannstadt. They seemed to serve no particular purpose and seldom, if ever, bothered anyone. They were just there, offering no sense of either threat or protection. But on that particular fall morning in 1944, they had mounted their horses and, without any comment or justification to the mayor or any city officials, just rode away.

Rumors now began to circulate that the German Army was suffering defeats on several fronts and for the first time, the demise of the Third Reich was whispered as a distinct possibility. News broadcast from the town radio changed from boasting of major victories to concern over the heavy losses of men and materials. Still, few residents of Hermannstadt considered this as much of an issue—they were isolated, insulated, and far away from the reality of war. In their small town, life continued on as usual.

Soon after that day, Fredi noticed a strange occurrence on the Old Road. He rushed into the kitchen, looking for his mother, and found her standing at their front window, also witnessing the bizarre scene. Horse-drawn wagons, both covered and open, were traveling down the road in an endless procession. The people in the wagons had a look of desperation—even a look of fear.

Flüchtlinge moving through town

"Who are all those people, Mama?" Fredi asked.

Elsa shook her head as she continued to stare out the window. "I have no idea."

"There are so many of them. Where are they going?"

The sight was unlike anything she had ever seen. "Maybe your father will have some answers when he gets home."

Frieda joined them at the window, and they watched in amazement as the wagons continued to roll past. Occasionally, one would stop, and some of the men and older children would frantically remove items from the rear of the wagons, dumping the discarded possessions along the side of the road.

Fredi, always eager to investigate, said enthusiastically, "Let's go see what they're doing."

Elsa shook her head again. "I don't think that's a good idea." In truth, she was concerned for his safety. "We'll wait until your father gets home. I want you to stay inside."

"But I want to play with Fritzl," Fredi protested.

"He can come inside, and you can play here."

"He likes it better outside."

Elsa pursed her lips, then forced a smile—she didn't want to appear too concerned. "I'll get him a treat. He'll like that, and the two of you will have plenty of room to play in here."

Out in the fields, a neighbor had joined Rudolf and told him about the procession of wagons. Together, they returned to the Old Road and not only watched but also approached one of the families as they were removing various items. The two men spoke briefly with the family, and the information they received was not encouraging.

Elsa and Frieda both were surprised when Rudolf returned home that evening much earlier than usual. Fredi was pleased that his father gave him permission to go back outside with Fritzl, although Rudolf warned, "Just make sure you stay in the yard."

Rudolf and Elsa sat at the kitchen table as Frieda poured each of them a cup of coffee. Before either woman could ask a question, he explained, "The people in the wagons are Germans from eastern regions, such as Pommern, Ostpreussen, and Oberschlesien. They already are feeling the effects of the war."

"Where are they going?" Frieda questioned.

"They left their homes as the German Army was retreating—they were trying to escape the advancing Russians." He sadly shook his head. "According to them, Germany is on its last leg of the war, and those poor people were right in the middle of the conflict because of nearby railroad tracks, which transported troops and equipment. They're desperate," Rudolf continued, "and are trying to make their way to western Germany and what they hope will be safety."

"Why are they coming through Hermannstadt?" Elsa asked.

"They thought that coming through our town provided the shortest route." Rudolf took a deep breath and looked into the distance. "They told us some horror stories—stories the children shouldn't hear."

"Like what?" Elsa whispered, almost fearful of hearing the stories herself.

"Stories about innocent people being rounded up sent to the east and forced into hard-labor camps."

There was a long moment of silence, broken when Frieda finally asked, "Did they say why they were leaving things alongside the road?"

Rudolf nodded. "To lighten their loads so they can travel faster. They're leaving family heirlooms, crates of fine china, expensive silverware, portable stoves, sewing machines, even furniture. They're terrified, running for their lives, and are willing to sacrifice anything they have and everything they own so they can escape."

After another period of silence, Elsa quietly asked, "What about us?"

Rudolf softly touched her hand. "No one knows." It was all the answer he would offer at that time; he kept the balance of the information to himself. One of the men on the wagons had told Rudolf that the rapid exodus was really due to the events that had taken place in small border towns in East Prussia. One town he mentioned was Nemmersdorf.

Well-founded rumors circulated that when the Russian Army stormed through the picturesque town, they committed a series of unspeakable atrocities. Women were randomly raped, and that was followed by a full-scale massacre. Old men, women, children, and even babies were murdered in cold blood, some killed by blows from shovels or the butts of rifles, and the balance shot at close range. There was talk about people having been nailed to barn doors. The entire town was decimated.

In time, the name Nemmersdorf was, to many Germans, a symbol of war crimes of the Red Army—an example of the Russians' worst and most vile behavior.

* * *

The other Langer children had also seen the long row of wagons, and when they arrived home from school, they were filled with questions. Rudolf carefully explained what he could, leaving out the rumors of people being sent to forced-labor camps. The children were more intrigued with the items that had been left along the road—they wanted to look through them and see if there was anything they could keep for themselves.

"We have all that we need," Rudolf said firmly.

Elsa's tone was more compassionate. "You should never take advantage of others' hardships."

Several of the Langers' neighbors, however, did not share their principles, and they ravaged through items left behind by the travelers.

Later that evening, Rudolf attended a gathering with a few of his neighbors. They discussed the travelers, the news that had been shared, and what—if anything—they should do.

"Maybe we should leave as well," one suggested, "before the Russians get here."

"Remember that before the Great War, Czechoslovakia was an independent country. Sudeten Germans resented Czech dominance. Just a few years ago—in the late 1930s, if you recall—Germans were actually encouraged by Hitler to demand self-rule. After German troops invaded Czechoslovakia in '39, the Czech government surrendered to Hitler and became a part of German-occupied territory."

"Thank you for the history lesson," one of the men snapped impatiently, "but what does this have to with our current predicament?"

The old man's pipe had gone out, and he slowly relit it as the others waited for him to continue. "Now we've been told that when the Germans again occupied Czechoslovakia, they brought along widespread suffering, not only to those in labor camps but also with mass slaughter. I think the folks passing through Hermannstadt have understandable reason to fear for their lives."

"But doesn't that make the point that we should leave as well?" one of the younger men asked.

"I don't believe the rumors," another one interjected. "I'm not about to give up everything I've worked my whole life for!"

A chorus of voices quickly agreed. Collectively, the group determined that although the Russian military was indeed approaching, the residents of Hermannstadt had lived through such a situation before, and this time should not prove to be any different.

* * *

The ground began to shake violently. The windows all rattled as if they were going to explode. Poor Fritzl trembled uncontrollably. Elsa, Frieda, and Fredi were dumbstruck, frozen where they stood, afraid to move. When someone began pounding on their back door, Fredi cautiously went to see who was there.

It was his friend Pepi Thurmer, his face filled with wonder and amazement. "Have you seen them?" Pepi asked.

"Seen who?" Fredi responded.

Pepi shook his finger in the direction of the road, frustrated because he couldn't find the words to explain what he'd seen. He finally pushed past Fredi and ran swiftly to the front window in the living room, blurting out, "*Look!*"

Elsa and Frieda stood behind the two boys at the window, still completely unaware of what was happening. What they saw was beyond their comprehension. Great machines, unlike anything they had ever seen, were rumbling down the road. It was an endless line of tanks and trucks, propelled by wood-burning engines that caused them to belch black smoke into the sky. They left deep ruts in the road, and their deafening noise caused buildings in the area to shudder.

The boys referred to the immense vehicles as "iron horses" and were totally captivated by the sight. Occasionally, one of the huge tanks would pull off to the side of the road so other vehicles could pass it, but there was no courtesy in their movement. The tanks destroyed everything in their path, including the picket fence in front of the Langer house, mowing it down as if it were little more than a row of toothpicks.

The Russians were on the move, and the Old Road was being used because the Main Road was also filled with similar equipment. Some were closed trucks and some open; some pulled large pieces of artillery, and others were filled with soldiers. While the road through Hermannstadt was certainly not the widest or in the best shape, it was the most direct route from the eastern region of Stalingrad to the German border.

Curiosity turned to caution and then to fear. The boys wanted to go outside for a closer look at the smoke-belching beasts, but Elsa forbade it. Several times, the wood-burning trucks would stop for fuel, usually in the form of kindling. Troops would leave their trucks, go anywhere they wanted, and take whatever firewood they needed. An abundant supply was available along the road, as most families had begun storing wood for the approaching winter.

Schools closed earlier than usual on that day, and the Langer children ran home, fascinated as they passed the convoy. Rudolf, like all the other farmers in the area, left his field and returned to his house and family. Pepi was sent back to his own home and instructed to go through backyards and avoid contact with any of the soldiers.

The Langer family and Frieda huddled together, watching the "iron horses" as the convoy went on and on. Dinner that evening was eaten in silence. The children understood that the adults were concerned, and it was a feeling they'd never known the grown-ups to exhibit. Sleep that night came slowly—the constant sound of the trucks kept them awake. In time, following considerably more prayers than usual, the children managed to drift off to sleep.

Such was not the case with the adults. They sat at the kitchen table, their conversation whispered. "What do you think we should do?" Frieda asked.

"Wait," Rudolf answered, still watching as the machines rolled past the front of their house.

"What did the others say?" Elsa wanted to know, her eyes riveted on her husband.

Rudolf tried his best to sound convincing. "The general feeling is that nothing will happen. They'll pass through town and just be gone. They have no reason to stay here and cause us any trouble." But for the first time in his life, Rudolf wished he had installed locks on their doors.

The convoy continued, nonstop, throughout the night and half the next day. Finally, although they continued to roll during the following weeks, the number of tanks and equipment in the convoy seemed to lessen a little. The school remained closed, as did most businesses, and the farmers stayed at home—they were concerned about leaving their families and did not attend to the customary plowing of the fields in preparation for the spring planting. Food would be severely diminished the following year because of this, yet the farmers were helpless to do anything about it. Hermannstadt and countless other small towns in the Sudetenland were at the mercy of the personnel and equipment moving along their roads.

Residents had reason to be afraid of leaving their houses—rumors ran rampant of unprovoked violence and vicious rapes committed on innocent younger women and girls. Those who absolutely had to leave their houses would disguise themselves, hoping to be overlooked. The females would disguise themselves as old women, walking stooped over with a shawl covering their heads and faces. The men would wear their oldest clothing and walk with a cane and a limp, hoping to avoid harassment or unnecessary punishment.

The Russian objective was clear: to secure all the towns in the convoy's path as they pursued the German Army and to make absolutely certain that no one would be left behind to join or form a resistance movement and attack them from the rear.

The Russians commandeered the courthouse and used that as their headquarters in order to exercise complete control over the citizenry.

While most of their troops continued to pass through the town, a contingent stayed behind to assure their intention. These soldiers were hardened and battle-tested, weary from years of war, and deeply incensed by the deaths of their fallen comrades; they were capable of instant retribution and viciousness beyond anyone's comprehension.

* * *

The front door of the Langer home burst open and three scruffy-looking soldiers, pistols drawn, stormed into the living room. The entire family and Frieda immediately froze in place, the children clutching their parents. Elsa closed her eyes, silently praying.

"Give us your weapons," the obvious leader commanded in a flat and menacing tone, his eyes glaring at them wickedly.

Rudolf drew himself up to his full height and said calmly yet firmly, "We have none."

The German, Czechoslovakian, and Russian languages are close enough in pronunciation and meaning that most people of the region had a basic understanding and comprehension of all three. The leader moved two steps closer to Rudolf, his dark eyes glowering. "If you lie to me, you'll be punished severely." He waved his pistol toward the rest of the family. "And so will they."

Rudolf raised his right hand. "As God is my witness, there are no weapons in this house."

Not satisfied with the response, he held them at gunpoint while motioning for the two other soldiers to search the house. Even though the front door had been left open and the cold wind blew through the house, Rudolf, Elsa, and Frieda all felt perspiration collecting on their brows and trickling down their backs.

After what seemed an eternity, the two soldiers returned to the living room and reported that they had found no weapons. The leader continued to stare menacingly at Rudolf.

"You will display a white flag outside your house so others will know this place is clear of weapons." And with that, the three soldiers turned around and strode out of the house.

Rudolf exhaled loudly, and Elsa turned to Frieda. "You and I will make the flag immediately." She looked at Rudolf. "We'll have it up right away. Then they won't bother us again."

Rudolf nodded, then turned his attention to the children, who still had not spoken. He patted each one gently on the head. "You all did fine. You were very brave. I'm proud of each of you."

Unlike many of their neighbors who had weapons in their houses for hunting or to protect their livestock from predators, the Langers never owned weapons—they'd never felt the need. Yet the emotions he now felt were mixed. On one hand, there was a sense of relief that there was no weapon for the soldiers to find. But on the other hand, Rudolf held a lingering wish that he did possess something—anything —to protect his family and preserve their way of life.

Less than a week later, even though their white flag was in clear view in front of their house, three more soldiers burst through the front door and marched into the Langers' living room. Rudolf jumped up from his chair and quickly explained, "We have the white flag! We've already been searched. There are no weapons here."

The soldier narrowed his eyes and offered a sardonic smile. "We know. Sit back down."

Rudolf did as he was told, and the children, again terrified, scurried behind their father's chair. Elsa and Frieda stood in the kitchen, afraid to make a move.

The soldier barked at the women, "You two! Come in here where I can see you."

Elsa and Frieda quickly moved to the side of Rudolf's chair, both doing their best to conceal the children.

The soldiers began to search the house again, but this time their quest was not for weapons. They yanked drawers open, taking whatever possessions they wanted—including the silverware that had been in the Langer family for generations. Rudolf knew without looking at her that Elsa was about to speak, so he held up his hand, warning her to remain silent.

One of the soldiers glared at Elsa. "Where's your jewelry?"

Elsa tried to control her trembling—a combination of fear and rage— as she spoke clearly. "I have no jewelry."

"You're lying!"

The hair bristled on the back of her neck. She stood just a little taller and defiantly returned the stare. "I don't lie. I never have. Not even to you."

The soldier glared at her as the other two men continued their pilfering through cupboards and shelves, taking anything of value for themselves. One of them noticed the crucifix on the wall with rosary beads hanging from the feet of Jesus. He reached for it, just as another soldier carrying a clipboard entered the room. Rudolf surmised that he was an officer—he had silver bars on his uniform. The officer immediately saw what was happening and spoke loudly and with authority to the man reaching for the crucifix. "Don't touch that!"

The three soldiers instantly stopped what they were doing and snapped to attention. The officer glared at each of his men, finally holding his gaze on the one who clearly had something in his pocket. "What is that?" the officer demanded. "Show it to me." The soldier slowly removed a handful of silverware and held it in front of him. "Is that yours?" the officer asked, taking a step.

"No, sir" came the quick response.

"Are you a common *thief?*" the officer sneered.

"No, sir," the soldier replied softly, sucking in his chin and sticking out his chest.

The officer's tone was one of a parent reprimanding a child. "If that's not yours, and you're not a common thief, I want you—all of you!—to return everything you have taken from this house." The soldiers followed his orders without hesitation; then they resumed standing at attention. "Return to your posts, and report to me this afternoon," the officer instructed.

The soldiers quickly saluted their superior, then marched out of the house. The officer studied the clipboard he was carrying before addressing Rudolf. "This is the Langer house?"

"That is correct," Rudolf replied.

He lowered the clipboard and in a slow and reserved voice, he explained, "The Russians are honorable people, filled with pride but decimated by the horrors of war. Sometimes, actions are difficult to comprehend, although understandable for what many of us have experienced. I apologize for what my men did and assure you that it will not happen again." With that, he offered a slight bow and left the house.

The family looked at each other in confusion. "Will ... we be safe now?" Elsa asked hesitantly.

"I don't know," Rudolf replied softly. "As long as that officer is here, I don't think they'll bother us again." He looked at the floor. "But you can never be sure."

Rudi tugged on his father's sleeve, his eyes wide. "What do they want, Tata?" he whispered.

Rudolf patted his son's head reassuringly. "I think they probably want the same thing we do. They want the war to be over so they can return to their families and live in peace."

"Will the trucks ever stop so we can go outside and play?" Willie asked.

Elsa walked over to the crucifix and softly touched the feet of Jesus, as Rudolf sighed and answered Willie. "Eventually. They can't go on forever." In his own thoughts, however, he could not erase the realization that until the tanks did stop rolling, he and his family were prisoners in their own home.

* * *

With the first snowfall came additional hardships. Snow, ice, and slush slowed the troop and equipment movement to the point that several times, the convoy got bogged down and was unable to continue. When this occurred, it was not uncommon for some of the troops to take over the Langer household, forcing the family to sleep in the barn. While inconvenient, it was, at least, somewhat comfortable, as the heat emanating from the baking stove provided adequate warmth. *We're still prisoners in our own home*, Rudolf thought.

And then, one day, the trucks were gone, and the military movement appeared to be over. For the first time in months, people felt they could leave their houses in relative safety. Some of the businesses in town re-opened, but supplies were at a bare minimum. Rudolf gathered with his neighbors to discuss what they thought might happen next. Plans were made to reopen the school and even resume working in the much neglected fields.

Suddenly, a thundering noise in the distance grew louder and seemed to be coming in their direction. Everyone returned to their homes as quickly as possible, praying desperately that it wasn't the return of the tanks. Soon, it became clear that the thundering sound was not caused by Russian tanks but by horses' hoofbeats—hundreds of horses. Rudolf and Elsa watched in amazement as the animals galloped past the house. They realized at that moment that the townspeople would not be able to act on their plans to reopen the school and to resume working the fields. The riders, dressed in colorful uniforms with warm overcoats, rode in a long column and sat tall in the saddle, looking proud.

The column then broke into smaller groups and rode into the yards that had barns behind their houses. One of the groups entered the Langer backyard and dismounted in well-trained unison. The family watched apprehensively through their kitchen window, until one of the men, obviously the commander of the group, walked up to the back door and knocked. Rudolf and Elsa looked at one another in disbelief—no soldier had ever exercised the politeness of knocking on the door. Cautiously, Rudolf opened the door and stared into the eyes of the tall, clean-cut stranger.

The man smiled slightly and announced in a clear, controlled baritone voice, "We are called the White Russians, from the Ukraine. We are following the main troop movement. My men and I would like to feed, water, and rest our horses here and perhaps find some food for ourselves."

Momentarily speechless, Rudolf could only gape at the man, but then he said, "Come in."

The man entered the kitchen, and as he noticed the children standing close to their mother, he smiled and reached into his coat pocket. The children trembled, fearful that he was reaching for a pistol, but instead, he pulled out several pieces of hard candy. He took a step toward the children, but they took a step backward.

"Here," he said, extending his hand. "This is for you. It tastes good."

They looked up at Elsa, who nodded her assent, and they each took a piece of candy.

"What do you say?" Elsa prompted them.

"Thank you," the children replied in unison.

"You're very welcome," the man said. Then, turning toward Elsa, he smiled. "Your children are very polite. Very well behaved."

"Thank you," she replied cautiously.

The man attempted to calm her. "Ma'am, I want to assure you that we mean you no harm. What I mentioned to your husband is all we seek. Nothing more."

Rudolf slipped his arm protectively around Elsa's waist as he addressed the White Russian. "You and your men are welcome here. We will provide what we can. If you'd like, I believe there's room in the barn for you to keep your horses."

"Would it be possible for my men to sleep in your hay loft?" the man asked.

"Absolutely," Rudolf assured him. "They'll be comfortable there; an oven keeps the barn warm."

The White Russian nodded and smiled again. "That would be very much appreciated. We've been riding for several days without the pleasure of any warmth."

Over the next several weeks, the Russians showed themselves to be true to their word. In return, Rudolf ensured that their horses were well fed, well rested, and well tended to; and Elsa invited the commander and several of his men into the house, where they shared food and warmth. The Russians reciprocated by offering some of their field rations and Komissbrot.

During several conversations, the Langers discovered that even though the Russians ostensibly were their enemies, on an individual basis the men were human beings with families of their own; men who had been forced into an untenable situation with which none of them was pleased. Ascertaining that peace was a common goal created a new insight for many of the adults in Hermannstadt. Now, even the prospect of losing the war didn't seem so bleak, if it meant that perhaps the life they had grown used to would someday return.

When the Russians eventually mounted their horses and moved off toward the west, Rudolf and Elsa were filled with mixed feelings. They were concerned for their new acquaintances, who were going back into battle, where lives would probably be lost; they also were deeply troubled by the final piece of news they were given—the White Russians would soon be replaced by the Czechoslovakian Army, Russia's new ally in the war.

* * *

The Langer family did not formally observe anniversaries and birthdays—Easter and Christmas were the two days they celebrated, with Christmas the larger of the two celebrations. As Elsa thought back on last year's celebration, it was almost impossible to comprehend that barely a year ago, life had seemed so perfect and so normal.

Last year, Rudolf had attached runner blades to the bottom of the wagon, converting it into a sleigh, and then hitched it behind one of the horses to take the children on a peaceful ride into his forest through the drifting snow. Bundled warmly against the wintry winds, the children had excitedly spent that entire morning searching for the perfect evergreen tree that then became the centerpiece of their living room for the Christmas season.

Rudolf let the children think that the ideal tree had been their own choice, but he had offered subtle suggestions to ensure that the one chosen would be acceptable to all. The tree was cut and brought back to their house, where the family decorated it with tinsel and attached thin taper candles to its branches. Fresh apples, which had been stored in the cellar, were placed underneath the tree. It was the Langer family tradition that the fruit would be the only gift for the children—and the children considered it a delightful treat on Christmas Day.

For Elsa and Frieda, Christmas Day began well before the sun rose. Working diligently by the light of their oil lamps, the two women prepared a very special meal that consisted of a roasted duck, stuffing, potato dumplings, sauerkraut, and gravy. After stoking the kindling in the baking oven, they also formed several loafs of bread, along with an assortment of delicious cakes. When Gerti woke up, she immediately joined her mother and Frieda in the kitchen to assist with the various kitchen duties.

The captivating aromas that filled the house soon woke up everyone else, and they all eagerly volunteered to sample the food—to make sure everything was right! Elsa playfully slapped at the many young hands as they tried their best to grab a taste. As the abundance of food slowly cooked to perfection, the family dressed in their finest attire and attended Christmas Mass at Maria Hilf Church. As always, the church was filled to capacity with fellow worshipers on this, their holiest of days.

Following the service and Christmas greetings to friends and neighbors, the family made a brief stop at the Hermannstadt cemetery on their way home. Rudolf's father, Franz, had passed away the year before and was buried beside his wife, Antonia. The family solemnly paid their respects and offered a silent prayer in front of one of the largest gravestones in the cemetery, one that had white marble angels carved on each side.

Once back within the warmth and comfort of their home, the women continued their kitchen duties, as Rudolf, seated in his favorite chair, read the newspaper, and the boys played games with each other and Fritzl, trying to keep themselves occupied until the meal preparations were completed and the feast would begin.

When they finally sat down at the finely decorated table, Rudolf offered the prayer. Following that, each of the children provided a prayer of his or her own, giving thanks for their parents and the blessings they all had received.

But that was last year, seemingly forever ago and now little more than a fleeting memory. This year, there would be no trip to the forest to pick out the perfect tree, and there were far fewer Christmas greetings exchanged with friends and neighbors. The Christmas meal, while acceptable and delicious, was nowhere near the type of feast to which the family was accustomed for their Christmas celebrations.

This year everything was completely different. Christmas, which had once been filled with celebration and excitement, was now a day filled with concern, anxiety, and fear of the unknown.

FOUR

THROUGHOUT 1945, THE RESIDENTS OF HERMANNSTADT remained on edge, walking an invisible tightrope without a safety net. Uncertainty continued to reign, as they wondered what the Czech Army would bring to their once-peaceful little town. The more than three million German citizens who lived in the Sudetenland had resented Czech dominance since the region was ceded to Czechoslovakia after the Great War ended in 1918, and they were pleased to follow Hitler's advice of demanding self-rule for themselves. Rumors circulated that the powerful German war machine now occupied Czechoslovakia and was merciless in its domination. Allegedly, tens of thousands of Czechs had been viciously murdered, and countless thousands more were sent to slave-labor camps, where death was a certainty. But the unanswered question remained: after the way the Germans had treated the Czechs, how would the Czechs respond, now that they had the upper hand? This question was answered in short order.

* * *

In early spring, another convoy of military vehicles stormed into Hermannstadt; the Czechs had arrived. Because the white flags still were posted in front of every house, the army knew immediately the residents were unarmed and unable to offer any resistance—and the Czechs looked and acted considerably more menacing than the Russians. Although the main body of troops and artillery rolled swiftly along, several stayed behind to establish a headquarters in the City Hall and set up well-manned and armed outposts on each end of town. Without a single shot being fired, the Czech Army instantly controlled and secured the entire town of Hermannstadt and the surrounding area. They had free rein to terrorize the German population in a land that, prior to 1939, had been theirs.

Unfortunately for the Langer family, one of the Czech outposts was established in their yard. The family watched, helpless and terrified, as a truck filled with soldiers pulled behind their barn. Attached to the rear of the vehicle was a large cannon, a menacing-looking piece of artillery that they later would learn was called a Howitzer, a remarkably powerful and devastating weapon.

The soldiers, acting as military police, had the authority to go anywhere they wished and do anything they desired. The first day, the family watched with concern as the soldiers in the yard busied themselves by setting up the cannon and turning the barn into a temporary headquarters.

The second day proved to be not as calm.

Without warning, the kitchen door burst open and four Czech soldiers stormed in. The family was spread throughout the house, doing various chores, but they all heard one soldier bark, "Everyone in the house will come to the kitchen!"

Elsa was upstairs cleaning one of the bedrooms when she heard the voice. As she rushed down the stairs, she instinctively removed her wedding ring and placed it in her mouth. Frieda, alone in the kitchen, stared at the floor, afraid to make eye contact with the intruders. Rudolf, seated in the living room, quickly placed his pocket watch inside his boot before joining his terrified family in the kitchen.

The soldiers were gruff-looking, dirty, and unkempt. The one who seemed to be in charge had a stubble of beard and a nasty-looking scar across his right cheek. His raspy voice was stern. "Give us your money. Your coins."

Rudolf shook his head. "We have none. They've already been taken from us."

Without warning, the soldier slapped Rudolf across the face. The impact was so strong it caused his knees to buckle. "Your coins," the soldier repeated.

"I told you," Rudolf said, rubbing his cheek. "We have *none.*"

Gerti began to cry, and Elsa held her close to her side. The soldier hit Rudolf again, this time with even more force. The man's blow left a scarlet imprint on Rudolf's face.

"We are poor farmers," Rudolf insisted. "Everything we had already has been taken by the Russians."

The soldier narrowed his eyes momentarily, then nodded, as if understanding, but with clenched fist viciously hit Rudolf again, this time knocking him to the floor. Elsa gasped, and the rest of the children began to cry. As Rudolf slowly got to his feet, the soldier drew back his hand a fourth time, but Elsa quickly intervened. "Stop!" she pleaded. She walked to a nearby shelf and emptied a jar containing six gold coins, which she handed to the intruder.

He stuffed the coins into his pocket, then demanded, "Now your jewelry."

"I have none," Elsa replied with calm resolve.

"Show me your hands!" he commanded.

When she held out her hands for the soldier's inspection, Rudolf noticed her ring was missing. *She's hidden it somewhere,* he thought, proud of her defiance but still greatly concerned for their safety.

The soldier emitted a guttural, almost feral sound as he pointed at Gerti and announced, "We'll take the little girl. My men will enjoy the pleasure she can offer."

Gerti began to tremble and clutched Elsa's dress. Rudolf stepped quickly in front of Gerti and, with all the courage and inner strength he could muster, said, "She's my daughter. You'll have to kill me first."

"I have killed many men," the soldier said matter-of-factly. "One more will not bother me in the least."

Elsa squared her shoulders as she moved beside her husband. "She's my daughter as well. Have you also killed many women in cold blood?" With piercing eyes that could melt cold steel, the soldier stared at the defiant woman, his face contorted by abject hate. Elsa stood her ground, returned the stare, and calmly asked, "How would you feel, deep down inside your own heart, if someone murdered your mother, or your wife, or your sister, or your daughter for no reason?"

The soldier continued to glare at husband and wife without speaking. Then, quite unexpectedly, he turned on his heel and marched out the kitchen door, his men following.

The family collectively held their breath for a few seconds, then expelled a huge sigh of relief that was followed by numerous hugs. Rudolf looked into his wife's eyes and quietly said, "Your wedding ring ..."

Elsa opened her mouth as if she was about to speak but instead, she removed the ring from under her tongue and returned it to her finger. The corners of Rudolf's mouth twitched, and he couldn't hide his smile as he reached down into his boot and produced his pocket watch. Elsa returned the nod and the smile.

Then she shuddered, as the events of the last few minutes raced through her mind. She put some cool water on a cloth and gently wiped Rudolf's reddened face, doing her best to ease his pain. Then Elsa took the children, still trembling from the ordeal, to the comfort of their bedroom upstairs and, in a soft, calming voice, read stories from the Bible to them.

* * *

Hermannstadt was under martial law. The remaining Czech soldiers on regular patrol, up and down both roads, told the residents what to do and when to do it. Several innocent people were severely punished for failure to comply with the simplest orders, and a ten o'clock curfew was strictly enforced each night. The newly installed Czech mayor, a cruel man named Blazek, commanded that no one was to give away or sell anything without permission. If it was discovered that someone had hidden or buried valuables, that person would be put to death.

The farmers were told which crops to plant in their fields and when to plant them. For generations, the planting season had been an exhilarating rite of spring and rebirth, an exciting time for celebration, with friends and neighbors gathering to sing and dance to the anticipation of the coming crop; now, it had become drudgery. Public gatherings of any kind and for any reason were forbidden, and the farmers had become mere workers for their vicious and resentful Czechoslovakian occupiers. The once-proud farmers and land owners knew that most of their crops would go to others, who had done nothing to help produce them.

Although Rudolf continued to lament the fact that they were prisoners in their own home, one small but relevant fact was that at least the majority of Hermannstadt's residents still had their own homes. That became remarkably important and offered ongoing hope that, in time, the Czechs would leave and things would return to normal. It was apparent, however, that it wasn't going to happen soon.

Several able-bodied men and teenagers from the town and surrounding area were taken by force to the nearby mountain range and forced into back-breaking hard labor, working twelve hours a day in the burgeoning copper mines. These mines originally had been planned to help in the eventual modernization of Hermannstadt—monetary allotments were to be distributed to the towns in Sudetenland—including paved roads, electricity, running water, a larger school, better communication, zero unemployment, health care for everyone, and transportation that would connect them to the outside world. Now, the spoils of their efforts would flow directly into the coffers of the Russians and the Czechs.

Pepi's father was relegated to the copper mines. "Why did the soldiers take Pepi's father away, Tata?" Fredi asked.

"To work in the mines," Rudolf answered sadly.

"When will he come back home?"

"No one knows, son. All we can do is pray for his safe return."

The children were confused by the events of the occupation, but the adults were no better able to understand why they being punished so severely—they had done nothing to harm anyone. The great man named Hitler had promised them a life of peace and prosperity, electricity and telephones, zero unemployment and health care for everyone,

Hitler had built the Autobahn, the most sophisticated highway system in the world. He transformed an enormous network of railroads and ensured that trains ran on time and were completely reliable. He created a nation of full employment, building great cities in the process. He was responsible for achieving unbelievable strides and improvements in developing guns, tanks, jet aircraft, and even rockets. And now, his maniacal quest for world domination was toppling like a house of cards.

The remarkable highway and the railroad tracks were now used to transport advancing armies toward Berlin and Munich and other major cities, as the Germans continued their retreat. Great masses of people were transferred out of relatively safe factory jobs and forced into military service, and with little training available, there was heavy loss of life. Families were devastated, as rumors persisted that the number of casualties from the ongoing war totaled in the millions—a figure beyond anyone's comprehension.

* * *

Initially, it was a series of far-off, muffled thuds—subtle, noticeable, yet indescribable. Rudolf and most of his neighbors came out into their front yards, trying to discern the cause.

"What is it?" Rudolf called to his neighbor across the road.

"I don't know" came the response.

As the thuds grew louder, Rudolf's concern grew greater. Suddenly, the bell from Maria Hilf Chapel behind the Langers' house started to toll. It wasn't Sunday; it couldn't be a call to church. "What *is* it?" Rudolf repeated, growing more fearful as the thuds and the pealing of the church bell competed for his attention.

A man on horseback came galloping down the middle of the road, screaming at the top of his voice, "They're bombing us! The Russians and the Czechs are bombing us! Run to the forest and hide!"

Rudolf looked with alarm at the Czech soldier who was still standing nearby at his outpost. The soldier nodded, confirming the rider's warning.

Quickly, Rudolf ran back inside the house to alert the family, trying not to panic.

"Let's go into the cellar," Frieda suggested as she ran toward the door.

Rudolf stopped her. "If a bomb hits the house, it would crush the cellar. Grab some jackets and blankets, and we'll go to the forest."

The thuds became louder, seeming to come from all directions, surrounding them. Elsa hastily threw some food into a wicker basket; Rudolf, thinking rapidly, collected some important papers: wedding, birth, and baptism certificates and ownership papers for the house and farm. Frieda and the children gathered clothes and blankets. Within minutes, they were out the back door, running for their lives toward the nearby forest, with

Fritzl leading the way.

Once they were reasonably settled deep within the woods, with several other families nearby, whispered conversations questioned the continued bombing. Someone suggested that the bombs were exploding in or near towns such as Jägerndorf, Zuckmantel, and Würbenthal—all towns with railway lines running through them.

The children trembled and clutched their parents. "Why are they doing this?" Fredi whimpered.

Elsa hushed him, explaining, "We have to keep our voices as quiet as possible. We don't want anyone to discover us here in the woods." She gently stroked Fredi's hair and held him close as she answered, "I don't know why they're doing this."

Sundown was upon them, and the temperature in the forest had turned chilly. A voice in the distance whispered, "Why don't we build a fire?"

"No!" another whispered harshly. "That is a bad idea—it would give away our hiding place and perhaps make us targets as well."

As darkness fell around them, Rudolf, Elsa, and Frieda bundled the children in extra jackets and blankets. Rudolf assured the children that everything was going to be all right, but the continuing thuds did little to allay their fears—or Rudolf's. Though they were shielded by the trees, they still could see the illumination in the sky—the bombers were dropping ignited magnesium strips attached to tiny parachutes, which floated slowly downward, lighting the way, and helping the bombers to see their eventual targets.

Few of those gathered in the forest slept during that long night, but when the sun rose, the bombing finally ceased, and the group decided—with some trepidation—that it was safe to return to their homes.

As Rudolf had suspected, the Czech troops, which had remained in Hermannstadt and other small towns, posed no military threat; they were used to direct bombing raids. This brought little relief to the residents. Although the bombs clearly caused enormous devastation, the true devastation—and moral outrage—came from within the city limits.

The Czech soldiers struggled to move the position of the cannon. Instead of toward the Old Road, it was now pointed toward the hill beyond the Langers' backyard. Watching in silence through their window, the family was confused by the soldiers' actions. *What on earth are they doing?* Rudolf wondered, as he watched two of the soldiers remove a huge shell from the back of a wagon and insert it into the cannon. His question was immediately answered. The enormous report from the weapon shook the ground as well as the house. The windows rattled and items fell from shelves and shattered on the wooden floor. The family fell to their knees, huddling together, as their livestock made bellowing sounds and tried to escape from their pens. As the family rose up and looked through the window again, they realized the object of the Czechs' obsession.

BERGKLOSTERKIRCHLEIN HERMANSTADT 1930 genant SCHWEDENKIRCHE

Das Kloster-Bergkirchlein, auch Schweden-Kirchlein.

The cannon shell had exploded barely twenty-five yards from Maria Hilf Chapel. Elsa's heart plummeted. How could the Czechs be so callous as to try to destroy that holy place? Another shell was inserted into the cannon and fired, followed by more shaking, more rattling, more bellowing from the animals. This time, the explosion was less than ten yards from their beloved chapel. Rudolf and Elsa both wanted to scream at the soldiers to stop the unholy travesty they were perpetrating. But they knew that such an encounter would only result in harm to their family and themselves. Another large shell was inserted; another shot was fired—this one, a direct hit. Maria Hilf Chapel, where the Langer family and their neighbors had spent so many Sundays in Mass and prayer, where they'd all enjoyed the traditional Easter procession, was now completely destroyed. Elsa and Rudolf were speechless as tears of anguish rolled down their cheeks. No words could express their sense of devastation and loss. For the Czech soldiers, it was just another day at work, another day of doing their job, another day of following orders ... another day of destroying people's hopes and dreams. In shocked silence, Elsa, Frieda, and Gerti began picking up the items that had been broken. Rudolf absently rolled a cigarette, lit it, and exhaled thin smoke, letting it obscure his vision of the senseless devastation that lay up the hill behind their house.

Later that afternoon, the soldiers left their posts and were seen walking toward the business district. Rudolf and the boys cautiously ventured outside to check their property. The concussion caused by the cannon had lifted the barn door off its hinges. Hesitantly, they approached the weapon and lay their hands on it. It was still warm, as if it were a living thing.

Just before sundown, the siren in the middle of town began to blare. It was another signal to the residents to evacuate their houses and find solace in the forest. The Langers were better prepared this time and had everything ready to take with them, although with a growing sense of uncertainty and despair. Just before they left the house, Elsa stopped to remove the crucifix from the wall. She tucked it safely under her arm, running her fingers across the rosary beads.

The siren signaling evacuation to the forest continued on a daily basis for the next three weeks. Then, just as quickly as it had begun, it abruptly halted. For the first time in nearly a month, the families in Hermannstadt were able to sleep in the comfort of their own beds—although they realized they still were not safe.

On the May 1, 1945, word began to rapidly circulate that the Füh-rer had committed suicide. Adolf Hitler—the man who had promised so much to so many, the man who had caused so much devastation and death—ended his own days on this earth with a single pistol shot to the head. To many, Hitler's death meant that the war would soon be over and that order and peace would be restored. Half their hopes came to fruition on May 7, when Germany unconditionally surrendered to the Allies.

There followed a period of relative calm, during which time everyone simply waited to see what would happen next. Czech soldiers remained at their posts but seemed to take no particular interest in continuing their heavy-handed ways with the residents—although they were very much in control of the town, they exhibited an unidentified sense of restraint. This changed on June 5, however, when the Allies—the Americans, the British, and the Russians—divided Germany. The Czechs were now officially in charge. While many residents of Hermannstadt clung to the belief that this new development would be only temporary, they were proven remark-ably wrong. It took about a month for the Czechs to completely reorganize their plans, but once they did, what followed was total oppression. They continued to dictate which crops the farmers were to plant, and more men and teenager boys were forced into hard labor in the nearby copper mines. The residents of Hermannstadt and many other towns in the region were little more than slaves, and goods and services dried up as the Czechs took food for themselves. The Czech soldiers seemed to spend most of their time eating and getting drunk, as well as chasing the women and young girls to perpetrate sexual abuse, and occasionally catching and torturing a German soldier.

* * *

While the circumstances in Hermannstadt were remarkably diffi-cult, other nearby towns were treated to a different brand of brutality. In Jägerndorf, a prosperous city in Sudetenland with rich German cultural heritage, residents were chased out of their houses with whips. Czech sol-diers marched up and down streets, shouting, "Tomorrow you will all be transported to army barracks where you will receive official resident pa-pers! After that, you will be able to return to your homes! It will not be necessary to bring anything with you!" The next day, thousands of residents lined up along the street to get their documents. Everyone was anxious to get through this ordeal and return home. Once confined in the barracks, however, they waited for days on end without any word of what was going on. Two weeks passed, during which time they received only lukewarm potato soup, coffee, and some bread to sustain them. There was no distinction between young and old, male and female; everyone was treated the same disrespect and cruelty.

Loudspeakers blared the continued announcement that those who might try to escape would be shot. During the night, soldiers circled the barracks, firing rifles into the air, making it impossible for anyone to sleep. Those who were suspected of being sympathizers of the Nazi Party or who were members of the Hitler Youth were dragged outside by the camp guards and beaten with braided whips, while others were forced to count the remarkably painful strokes, usually between twenty and twenty-five lashes. Those who did not voluntarily give up all the possessions they had with them were beaten. Every two days there was a body search, and punishment for having anything considered to be contraband was swift and ruthless. One man was punished severely for wanting to keep a small pocketknife, which he argued was needed to cut the bread. Two men, fearing the pain of the whip, committed suicide; their bodies were thrown into a ditch. The Czechs then erected a provisionary toilet over their bodies, and the people in the barracks were forced to use it.

After two weeks, the former residents of Jägerndorf were forced to leave the barracks and walk to Würbenthal, thirty-six kilometers away, without being given any food or water. Completely exhausted when they arrived in Würbenthal after the two-day trek, the people were forced to sleep on the concrete floor of an abandoned factory. Before sunrise, they were gathered on the street outside and pushed to continue the march to Freiwaldau. Along the way, four people collapsed along the side of the road; the Czech soldiers quickly shot them for holding up the others. Women and children, wailing for their murdered husbands and fathers, were beaten until they were silenced. The soldiers forced nearby farmers to dig graves for the fallen men or face execution themselves. After arriving in Freiwaldau, the people still were not given anything to eat. The majority spent the night on a hillside near a factory, the inside of which could provide accommodations only for a chosen few. Rain drenched those outside, chilling them to the bone. Although completely exhausted, the pouring rain made it impossible for most of them to sleep.

The next day brought little relief, but the people at least were offered a slice of bread and malt coffee before continuing the march toward Altstadt. Once there, they found more barracks and finally received a decent night's sleep. Early the next morning, their fifth day, they marched on to Grulich, where they were taken to a railway station and forced into open railway cars—these normally were used to haul huge amounts of coal to the west but now were used to transport countless Germans westward. The train moved slowly, day and night; no one—not even the children, who wailed plaintively—received any food or water. Another heavy rain drenched them as they rode in the open car and, when mixed with the dust from the coal, made each traveler filthy. At last the train arrived in the Czech border city of Teplitz-Schoenau and from there it crossed over into Germany. Their homeland had been taken over by Czechoslovakia; it became isolated behind the Iron Curtain. None of the Sudeten Germans ever received any restitution, nor were they allowed to go back.

When accounts of such treatment reached Hermannstadt, the residents actually felt a mild sense of relief—even though they were under the complete control of the Czechs, they had not been treated so brutally. They still had their houses; they still had their farms; they still had their livestock. Some even held out hope for better days ahead, when they would once again enjoy freedom.

The hopeful residents of Hermannstadt, however, did not have the slightest idea of what was coming for them and their entire town.

FIVE

A THICK LAYER OF TENSION HUNG OVER THE SUDETENLAND like an ominous black cloud, blocking out hope for a better life; for a better future. Daily life continued as normal as possible, but tasks were carried out by rote, without the usual calm to which the residents had grown accustomed. The crops were harvested in the fall, but there was no celebration or gathering to rejoice in the occasion. There was no singing or dancing, as there had been before the occupation. No sweet sounds of the poignant song "Lili Marlene" filled the rafters of the Langer barn after the traditional Weizenklopfen was completed. Concerned parents prevented their children from playing in the streets or fields. People seemed to be moving in slow motion, as if in a mire, their hearts and minds consumed by an unseen haze of uncertainty.

During rare late-night gatherings, some of the men would quietly express their frustrations: *The war is over. Why don't they leave us alone? Why do they still guard us as if we were prisoners? Why must they still take the majority of our crops?* Their emotions became more heated and their anger rose as they spoke of somehow fighting back and reclaiming their independence. After all, they had done nothing to anyone; in fact, for all practical purposes, they'd had no involvement with anything concerning the war.

For centuries, Hermannstadt, even when surrounded by war and conflict, had remained a peaceful, self-sufficient town—a haven in the midst of disorder and mayhem, never directly involved with or affected by any of the turmoil that went on around it .

On May 8, 1946, that peaceful existence ceased to exist.

* * *

A Czech policeman pounded on the front door, but Rudolf opened it with caution. The man in the ill-fitting, rumpled uniform shoved a piece of paper into Rudolf's hand, turned around, and marched away. Rudolf slowly closed the door, staring at the paper.

"What is it?" Elsa asked, her voice trembling slightly.

"I'm not sure," he replied.

"Read it to us, Tata," Rudi suggested.

Frieda, Elsa, and the children all gathered around Rudolf, anxious to hear the news. Rudolf took a long, deep breath, inwardly fearing the worst, and softly read:

ACHTUNG!
ALL THOSE PEOPLE WHO HAVE BEEN DESIG-
NATED TO BE TRANSPORTED MUST LEAVE
THEIR HOMES WITHIN THE NEXT THREE DAYS
AND LEAVE THEIR HOMES IN THE BEST POSSI-
BLE CONDITION.
YOU ARE ALLOWED TO TAKE WITH YOU POS-
SESIONS THAT WEIGH NO MORE THAN 50 KI-
LOGRAMS.
IF THE WEIGHT EXCEEDS THE SPECIFIC ALLOW-
ANCE, THE POSSESSIONS WILL BE CONFISCAT-
ED, REGARDLESS OF WHAT THEY MIGHT BE.
EVERYTHING ELSE MUST BE LEFT IN THE HOUSE.
YOU MUST LEAVE WINDOW COVERINGS, CAR-
PETS AND RUGS, LAMPS, NO FEWER THAN TWO
TOWELS, ALL BED MATTRESSES, LINENS, AND
AT LEAST ONE PILLOW AND COMFORTER. ALL
ITEMS ARE TO BE FRESHLY WASHED.
YOU MAY NOT STOW OR CARRY POSSESSIONS

WITH YOU WRAPPED INSIDE RUGS OR COM-
FORTERS.
ALL YOUR POSSESSIONS WILL BE CHECKED. IF
THESE DIRECTIVES ARE NOT FOLLOWED THE
RESPONSIBLE PERSON WILL NOT BE TRANS-
PORTED BUT WILL BE SENT TO THE EAST TO
HARD LABOR.
WHOEVER DOES NOT REPORT AT THE DES-
IGNATED PLACE IN FRONT OF THEIR HOUSES
THREE DAYS AFTER RECEIVING THIS ORDER
WILL BE ARRESTED BY THE POLICE.

Rudolf lowered the paper, but his eyes continued to stare straight ahead. An eerie, desperate silence filled the room. Finally, Elsa placed her hand on Rudolf's arm. "I ... don't understand," she said. "They're making us leave?"

Rudolf read the notice again, this time to himself. He nodded slowly. "That's what it appears to say."

"Where are they making us go?" Rudi questioned.

Rudolf shook his head slowly. "I don't know."

"But I don't want to leave!" Fredi cried.

"None of us does," his father replied quietly.

Gerti thought for a second and then said, "Three days. Won't that be Pentecost?"

Elsa looked at the crucifix on the wall and softly answered, "Yes, dear. It will be."

Although the children asked more questions, Rudolf and Elsa could not answer them—they were as confused by this pronouncement as the children were. All that any of them could do was spend the rest of the day in perplexed silence. That evening after the prayers—several more prayers than usual—and when the children were asleep, Rudolf suggested that Elsa begin to choose what they would take with them. But she sat motionless, staring blankly into the distance, as if she didn't hear the words. Rudolf nodded and gently patted her shoulder. He understood her fear and sense of helplessness and didn't press her to begin the task.

Later that evening, Rudolf met with several of their neighbors.

"I'm not leaving," one of the younger men announced determinedly.

Another man waved the notice in his face. "You and your family will be killed."

"We'll hide in the forest," the young man replied.

"And while you're hiding, they'll burn your house and barn."

In truth, there were no options. The Czech police were well aware that the residents were gathering to discuss the notice, but they did nothing to prevent or disrupt the meeting—they knew the residents had no other choice but to follow the directive. Ultimately, with sadness, Rudolf and his neighbors came to the same conclusion; to do otherwise would be tantamount to committing suicide.

As the men returned to their homes from the meeting, they each felt a personal sense of failure that they had been unable to protect their families and the land they so loved and cherished. Everything they had worked their entire lives for was being taken away, with no promise or even indication they would ever be allowed to return. *We are still prisoners*, Rudolf thought, *only now we'll be prisoners somewhere else.*

Elsa was still seated motionless at the kitchen table when Rudolf came through the back door. He closed it quietly and looked at his wife, shame and embarrassment consuming his heart. Speaking softly, he asked, "Have you given any thought to what we'll need to take with us?"

She stared straight ahead, her eyes seeming glazed over and lifeless.

"Elsa," Rudolf said.

Without looking at him, she asked, "Are they really going to make us leave?"

Rudolf sighed heavily, wishing he could say something to soothe her pain. "Yes. We have no choice. If we stay ..." He was unable to complete the sentence. To do so would only have added to her already overwhelming grief.

The next morning brought the same sense of helplessness and numbing pain. Rudolf went into the barn with several pieces of wood, a hammer, and some nails. When the children heard the hammering, they went to see what their father was doing, stopping briefly at the stable to tend to the livestock.

"Who will take care of them when we leave?" Rudi asked.

"What will they eat?" Willie asked.

Fredi looked down at Fritzl, always at his heels, and his eyes filled with tears.

The boys entered the barn and watched as Rudolf constructed a sturdy wooden box. There was something different about the box, but Rudolf didn't explain; he only said, "Boys, let the cattle, horses, and sheep into the pasture so they can spend the day grazing." Without questioning, they immediately did as they were told.

The wooden box that Rudolf was constructing had a false bottom, a place where they could keep valuables—mostly gold coins—that had been safely hidden from the Russians and the Czechs. No matter where they went or where they ended up, gold could always be used as a form of currency. It was the family's safety net and had to be protected at any cost. When Rudolf returned to the house, he found the living room filled with a huge assortment of items. Elsa was preparing great piles of everything that she wanted to take with them—she had no concept of how quickly these possessions would exceed the weight limit of fifty kilograms. She wanted to take pictures, the tapestry from the wall, cooking utensils, china, blankets, and clothing. Rudolf softly touched her arm. "We can't take all this. We can only take what we absolutely need." She turned away, unable to speak, as tears spilled onto her cheeks.

Seeing her mother in tears caused Gerti to start crying as well. When the boys came inside, they became alarmed—they had seldom seen their mother cry. Words of consolation provided no relief for her, and that troubled them even more. Then Rudolf entered the room, pulling the wooden box. It was about two feet wide by three feet long, set on wheels—taken from the old baby stroller—with a handle attached to one end. He pulled the box down to the middle of the living room and explained, "This will hold the things we'll be able to take with us."

The entire family looked on with astonished, stunned disbelief. How would it be possible for everything the six of them owned, used, or had worn to fit inside this small box? They suddenly were faced with the clear realization that they were being forced to make choices—choices that would be difficult. Rudolf turned to Frieda, "I'm supposing that as far as they're concerned, you're not technically a part of our family, so you'll be allowed to take your own fifty kilograms worth of belongings."

Frieda stared at the floor and quietly replied, "I'm not leaving."

Elsa and Rudolf stared at her, their mouths agape. Then Elsa said, "You *must*. We all must leave."

"I'm not leaving," she repeated. "Like all of you, I have lived here my entire life. I can't leave."

Rudolf tried to reason with her. "Do you have any idea of what they'll do to you if you stay?"

Frieda shook her head. "No. But there's no reason for them to hurt me. While I won't like it, perhaps I can be of assistance to whoever stays behind. People, whoever they are, will still need maids and cooks. I'm not afraid."

The children began to sob—they all had grown up with Frieda acting as their nanny. She had been their protector and their playmate. It was impossible for them to imagine their lives without her. They begged her to come with them, but she was politely adamant in her refusal. She hugged the children tightly, whispering in their ears that she would always love and care for each of them. Frieda's reasoning and personal justification for staying was much deeper than she had expressed. She knew that regardless of their unknown destination, it would be difficult for the six of them to survive. Rudolf and Elsa most definitely didn't need another mouth to feed or another person for whom they felt responsible. Although her heart was breaking, she made the firm decision, knowing this would be the best for them—her thoughts and concerns were for the family, not herself.

The next morning the boys dressed more slowly than usual, as if willing the day not to begin, and then they tended to their chores with the animals for the last time. Fredi gave a lot of thought to asking his father if they could bring Fritzl with them, but he already knew the answer. Upstairs, Rudolf pulled a suitcase out from under the bed, hoping they might be able to take that along as well. Suspecting otherwise, he packed the case with second-tier items, mostly clothing for Elsa and Gerti—things they'd like to keep but that weren't completely essential.

Clothing took up so much space within the small box that Elsa sorted out layers of different things for everyone to wear. That evening they each tried on the various pieces, each one thicker than the last. It was the beginning of summer, and some of the heavier clothing was uncomfortable and very warm. Still, Elsa knew that in time, these would be articles of clothing they would need. Rudolf and the boys continued to try on clothing, and

Elsa and Frieda—with Gerti's help—went into the kitchen to prepare what would be, in all probability, the last dinner they would share in this home they all loved. As they sat down at the table, their faces were solemn and silent. Fritzl, lying nearby, rested his face on the floor, somehow seeming to be aware that something ominous was in the air.

Rudolf offered the traditional prayer as the family bowed their heads. "Dear God, be our guest at this table and bless the food you have given us." Everyone remained silent, and then he added, "And we ask Your blessings and guidance for our family and Frieda as we face tomorrow and all that it will bring." Unlike the hundreds of dinners that had preceded this one, all of which had been celebrations of family and togetherness, the meal tonight highlighted the ambiguity and insecurity of their lives, a feeling that was magnified with each passing second.

Sleep that night came with extreme difficulty. Tomorrow, as they joined other residents from their beloved town of Hermannstadt, they would be homeless, shipped away to an unknown destination, as if they were little more than livestock. Rudolf tossed back the blanket and quietly left the comfort of their warm bed. He went downstairs, where he paced the floor for the remainder of the night. *Where we will be sleeping tomorrow night?* he wondered. He also worried for the livestock. Who would take care of them? How would they survive? And then he experienced the saddest thought of all: *Who will be sleeping in our bed tomorrow night?*

Just before dawn, as was normally the case, Elsa and Frieda efficiently prepared a hearty breakfast, along with various food items that they would carry with them. The children, seated at the table wearing the numerous layers of clothing, picked at their food. "You have to eat," Elsa cautioned. "You'll need your strength." On this morning, after three days of contemplation and prayer, she had accepted their fate and knew she must be strong for the rest of the family. She was the disciplinarian, the family rock.

Fredi left the table and went out to the back porch, where he knelt down to gently pet Fritzl. The beloved dog was a part of their family, and Fredi could not comprehend why Fritzl couldn't come with them. Fritzl looked up at the youngster with sad eyes, almost as if he were pleading. Fredi petted him softly and holding back tears explained, "You will be all right, fella. Everything's going to be fine. We'll be back some day, and things will be just like they are now."

"It's time, son," Rudolf said quietly from the back door. He fought to hold back tears as he watched his youngest son say good-bye to his dog. The family gathered in the front room of their fine house and in silence, each turned slowly, studying the walls and the furniture and the family pictures—things that were impossible for them to carry—trying to create memories that would, perhaps, have to last them a lifetime.

Holding his chin high and showing his bravest face, Rudolf put all the valuable family papers inside the pocket of one of the jackets he was wearing. Elsa, following his example, carefully took the crucifix and her precious rosary beads down from the wall, wrapped them in a fine linen tablecloth that had been in her family for years, and tucked them under her arm. With one final look around the room where so much love had been shared, their new journey began.

Frieda went outside with them and, after an emotional hug with each family member, watched from the front porch as the Langer family walked across the lawn to the spot where they'd been ordered to wait. Almost immediately, an ominous rumbling filled the air as three open trucks thundered down the road. These trucks, which would provide what was referred to as "a humane and orderly transfer," was, in truth, a Russian travesty perpetrated by the Czechs. The first truck, filled with families and their belongings, passed in front of the Langers' home and came to a halt. Just as the sun rose over the horizon, the second truck lumbered to a stop in front of their house. It was nearly filled with their neighbors, their faces drawn and ashen. Many were shedding quiet tears as their eyes focused on the floorboard. A Czech policeman, carrying a rifle, exited the cab of the truck, lowered the tailgate, and indicated that Rudolf and his family should board. The family lifted their meager belongings into the rear of the truck and then, one by one, each climbed aboard.

Fredi winced as he heard a loud grinding of gears, and the truck began to slowly move forward. He looked back at his house and could see Fritzl sitting in their front yard, making no attempt to chase the truck. The dog's head was cocked slightly to one side, and he barked softly—not nearly as loudly as when he was playing with the children or chasing a small animal in their yard. Then he sat quietly and stared at the truck, and Fredi stared back, knowing in his heart that his words spoken earlier on that dark morning would, sadly, never come to pass.

And then the truck lumbered slowly around a corner, and Fritzl, Fredi's old and dear friend, was no longer in sight.

* * *

As the convoy traveled down the road, the passengers noticed several plumes of smoke rising into the sky behind them. Elsa and Rudolf seemed confused by it, but a man seated across from them softly explained, "Some of the elderly townsmen heard rumors that we were going to be relocated deep into Russia. They chose to not follow orders. Not to leave. They knew if they stayed, it meant death."

Rudolf pointed at the smoke. "What is that?"

"Rather than leave, they set their farms on fire and took poison. They're already dead."

As the trucks moved farther away from Hermannstadt, more plumes of smoke filled the air, choking out the crisp mountain air in the countryside. Rudolf and Elsa trembled, watching in disbelief and horror as their once peaceful and tranquil town self-destructed. And husband and wife both wondered: *Are we destined for Russia? For labor camps? For our own death?*

* * *

Unknown to any of the passengers on the trucks, their fate had been determined long before the beginning of their ride that morning.

Some eight hundred years earlier, Germans emigrated east and established numerous towns in an area known as Bohemia. Over the following centuries, that region was conquered by different countries and subsequently controlled by different rulers. In 1918, at the conclusion of World War I, Sudetenland, along with other German-populated areas, was made a part of Czechoslovakia. In the 1930s, at Adolf Hitler's encouragement, Sudetenland demanded self-rule. But after Hitler's forces invaded Czechoslovakia in 1939, Sudetenland once again became a part of German-occupied territory. Then, when Germany surrendered to the Allies in 1945, Czechoslovakia became an independent country and expelled all ethnic Germans.

The Soviet support of Czechoslovak plans for the post-war expulsion of the Germans from Czechoslovakia was not at all exceptional—in fact, it was expected. Further, in Czech president Benes' eyes, the British confirmed the same understanding and expression. The non-stop rhetoric became reality between July 16 and August 2, 1945, at the Potsdam Conference held in Germany. The primary attendees were Josef Stalin from the Soviet Union, Winston Churchill from the United Kingdom, and newly elected president Harry Truman from the United States. Collectively, they determined and agreed that Sudeten Germans would have to leave Czechoslovakia. President Benes stated: "The defeat of Germany will provide a unique, historical opportunity to cleanse our state of the German element in a radical way. Take everything from them except a handkerchief so they can wipe away their tears."

President Benes issued a number of decrees—143 in all—with regard to postwar Czechoslovakia. The murders and expulsions of the large German population began in earnest when Benes' "reslovakization" program started in 1945. All the pent-up rage at the war was directed at women and children and old men in a gruesome, genocidal mix of punishment. On March 18, 1946, the Czechs mandated that all German civilians were collectively presumed guilty and must be stripped of their property. They began the most barbarous persecution and oppression of German citizens humanly imaginable: deportation, expulsions, internments, and kangaroo-court verdicts. Many expelled German civilians were sent to concentration camps, where they were murdered by poisoning, intentional starvation, and unchecked disease. Benes decree No. 115 declared that all acts against Germans, including the rape and murder of children, were "justified acts of retribution" that could not be prosecuted. Simply put, it was fully legal to kill Germans.

The property of virtually all Sudeten Germans was confiscated by Czechoslovakia and claimed to be a part of war reparations. During the organized phase in 1946, a total of 2,232,544 people were driven out of the Sudetenland: two-thirds of them to the west, the American sector; and one-third to the east, the Soviet sector.

At least fifteen million ethnic Germans were mercilessly driven out of their homes in Central and Eastern Europe as a result of an agreement between the Allies to "transfer" ethnic Germans from areas ceded to the Soviet Union and its satellites, Poland and Czechoslovakia. The driving out of the East German and the Sudeten Germans was the largest mass exile in human history.

None of this information, as tragic and detrimental as it was, was available to the Langer family or to the other former residents of Hermannstadt on the trucks in the convoy. They continued to slowly trudge northward toward an unknown destination.

SIX

THE CONVOY TRAVELED THROUGH OBERGRUND, ZUCKMAN-tel, Salisfeld, and then finally began to slow as they neared the outskirts of Nicklausdorf. The uncomfortable thirty-kilometer trip had lasted from sunup until sundown. Nicklausdorf was a farming town much like Hermannstadt, except that it had considerably more commerce. Most important, Nicklausdorf had a major railroad station.

No one knew how long they'd remain there; no one knew where they'd be staying that night. But beyond those concerns was another that seemed more worrisome. The rail tracks from the station ran east and west. Continuing on a westward route meant more uncertainty and probable hardship, knowing that their destination—if, in fact, they were transported to western Germany—would be a place of severe devastation caused by five years of war. A trip eastward, however, would take them to Russia's Siberia—a frightening thought for all.

The soldiers began to shout at the passengers to exit the trucks. Once on the ground, everyone was thoroughly searched for any valuables they might have in their possession. Unfortunately, one of the soldiers discovered Rudolf's gold watch and chain inside one of the coats he was wearing. The man flashed a sardonic smile as he stuffed the watch into his own pocket.

Another soldier ripped the embroidered linen tablecloth from Elsa's hands. "This will be a fine addition to my wife's table," he said contemptuously.

Elsa tried to remain calm as she bravely replied, "I would be appreciative if I could keep what's inside the cloth." The soldier unfolded the tablecloth, revealing the crucifix and the rosary beads. He held them for a long moment, determining their worth, and then handed both pieces back to Elsa without further comment. As had been her habit for many years, she touched the feet of Jesus and then clutched the crucifix closely to her side.

All boxes and suitcases were opened and carefully examined, the soldiers taking whatever they wished for themselves. A few blankets and items of clothing were taken from the box that Rudolf had constructed. Once the soldiers were satisfied that they had stolen everything of value, the unwilling passengers from the three trucks were forced at gunpoint into the train station. Once inside, the doors were locked behind them, and other soldiers with guns were posted as guards. The room contained a few wooden benches and—most fortunately—an indoor restroom, but other than that, the station was desolate and empty.

The imprisoned passengers all knew each other, and as a result, whispered conversations rustled throughout the room. One question continued to dominate all conversations: would they be sent east or west? Many of the women, especially the elderly, sat softly crying in small groups, their tears born of fear and hopelessness. The younger children played with each other—something they had been unable to do for many months—but the older children seemed more like the adults, in that they, too, wondered what their future would bring.

Soon, it was apparent that they would be spending the night in the station. None of them had eaten anything since breakfast, and now, lack of food became a serious concern. Those who had dared to bring food with them—defying the strict instructions—had it confiscated either in front of their houses before they left or at the train station when they arrived.

People began to settle in on the cold concrete floor, huddling together to stay warm. Elsa removed some blankets from their box and gave them to her children to soften their resting place. "Keep all your clothes on," she instructed. "They'll keep you warm and also make the floor a little more comfortable."

"What about our prayers," Fredi asked innocently.

Elsa hesitated a moment before replying. "Tonight, we'll all just say prayers to ourselves, in silence. God will still hear you." Then, after tenderly kissing each of her children and patting them softly on the head, she ran her fingers over the rosary beads and offered a silent prayer of her own.

Before the children dropped off to sleep, they were given an unexpected and pleasant surprise—Rudolf quietly distributed a small piece of Elsa's homemade bread to each of them.

"Where did you get this?" Elsa whispered.

"It doesn't matter," he whispered back. "Let's just say I was lucky." In truth, his "luck" was a matter of preparation. Rudolf had placed a few loaves of bread in the false bottom of the box, exactly for a situation such as this. The children gratefully ate the bread and thanked their father. While not nearly enough to adequately satisfy them or stifle a gurgling stomach, it was, at least, enough to ease their hunger for a little while.

The next morning, the doors of the train station burst open and several soldiers entered. They carried open boxes of stale sliced bread and a few pails of water. They placed the items on the floor, turned, and left without a word, locking the doors behind them. Those on the floor sprang to life and ran toward the meager nourishment. Initially, there was some pushing and shoving as a few tried to take more than their share.

Rudolf walked briskly toward the crowd, speaking loudly and firmly. "People! We are all neighbors. Friends. We all know each other." The crowd ceased their scrambling and grabbing, embarrassed when they stopped to realize what they'd done. Rudolf continued, "Have we not always shared with each other?" No one spoke, and several men hung their heads in shame. "Should we all not do the same thing now, rather than becoming like the animals who guard us?"

Heads nodded in agreement, as an orderly line was formed to distribute the bread and water. The elderly were served first, then the children, then the adults. As Rudolf walked back toward his family, a neighbor— one who had been part of the fray—stopped him and said quietly, "Sorry, Rudolf. You were right to say that." He put out his hand, and Rudolf shook it.

"We'll stick together," Rudolf said, "just as we always have."

"And just as we always will," the neighbor replied.

* * *

The mid-May temperatures and mass of humanity caused the heat level inside the railway station to rise considerably. It was so uncomfortable that Elsa finally gave the children permission to remove two layers of their clothing. Elsa sat on the box and kept an eye on the clothing piled before her as the children amused themselves by visiting with others they hadn't seen for months.

Because of the rising heat, one of the men opened a window, allowing fresh air to enter the stifling room. A soldier outside slammed the window shut and glared at the man, as if challenging him to try again.

During the day, the noise of passing trains made any form of rest virtually impossible. The Langer family and their neighbors dealt with it as best as they could, as well as coping with the lack of food and water, and the stifling heat, which only abated in the cool of the evening.

With each passing train, they wondered if that was the one destined to carry them elsewhere. Several men stood in a corner of the room, smoking cigarettes but without conversation—there was nothing more to say. All their words had been spoken, and they knew that none of their questions would be answered.

That evening, the children put on the clothing they'd removed earlier, and said their prayers in silence. Once again, Rudolf treated them to another small piece of bread, for which they expressed quiet thanks.

The following day was the same as the one previous, filled with hunger and thirst; filled with growing anxiety over where they would be sent—and when.

* * *

The next morning, before sunrise, the doors burst open again, but this time there was no bread or water. This time, the soldiers shouted for everyone to get up, collect their belongings, and move to the platform outside. Those who did not move quickly enough to satisfy the soldiers were shoved with the butt of a rifle in their ribs. Mild panic and great disorganization ensued, as people moved in all directions to avoid being prodded by the soldiers, who continued their incessant screaming; families became separated. Elsa quickly packed their blankets and clothing into their box, as Rudolf instructed Gerti and Rudi to hold on to his coat and for Willie and Fredi to hold on to Elsa's dress. "Take a hold and don't let go, no matter what," he said firmly. The children, although confused, followed their father's direction without question, just as they always had done.

The people exited the building in an orderly fashion, hoping to avoid the soldiers and their weapons. Once outside, and still in semi-darkness, they saw the train—a huge engine billowed black smoke and was attached to a long series of wooden cars, called "cattle cars" because they were once used to carry livestock from the country towns to the markets in the larger cities. Unknown to the former residents of Hermannstadt, these were the same cattle cars that recently had transported incalculable numbers of Jewish people to various concentration camps ... and their eventual deaths.

The soldiers continued shouting directions, commanding the people to enter the cars as quickly as possible. Their instructions were followed without dissent, as the passengers climbed into the foul-smelling enclosures. Rudolf pulled the box behind him and lifted it inside the cattle car. The soldiers kept loading the people into the cars until they were so stuffed with people and their sparse belongings that there was barely room for anyone to sit on the floor. Then the soldiers lifted another box of bread and three pails of water into the car, and slammed the doors shut with a mighty crash. Those inside could hear locks being snapped shut. *Prisoners.*

A few people began to softly weep; others were heard reciting prayers. Most were in a state of shock and utter disbelief—although that did not prevent them from devouring the meager food supply as quickly as possible. Then they became silent, listening intently, but the only sound was that of the engine that was taking them to their final destination. Finally, there was another sound—metal on metal. The wheels of the engine were beginning to gain traction on the tracks below, moving them ever faster forward.

The floor of the car was covered with straw and in one corner was a hole to be used as a toilet—the call of nature took precedence over any desire for privacy. Small slits near the roof of the railcar were too high to allow anyone to see outside, but they let in a small amount of fresh air, although it was not enough to eliminate the stench surrounding them. The train began to move a little faster, and everyone's hearts began to collectively beat a little faster. *Which direction?* It was the question on everyone's mind.

As the sun rose higher in the sky, those who were able to discern its position in the sky announced, with great relief, that the train was heading west, away from Russia. All the adults expelled a huge sigh of relief; then there was silence, followed by more prayers of thanks that—at least for the time being—they had been spared. As the train picked up more speed and rocked rhythmically from side to side, Rudolf smiled at Elsa and nodded—perhaps they were going to be all right after all.

The train began to slow down. Could it be? Could they have arrived at their destination after traveling for less than half a day? Concerned looks were exchanged, and more questions filled their minds. The train had pulled off onto a railway spur and came to a full stop to wait as another train roared past. After a few moments, the wheels beneath them began to churn again, and the train lurched forward.

Rudolf, Elsa, and the other passengers soon became accustomed to the stopping and starting of the train, which never traveled for more than two hours at a time before it pulled over to the side to let another train pass. So many other trains were moving in the opposite direction that it seemed as if all of Europe was moving from one place to another.

By that afternoon, just as it had been within the confines of the train station, the heat in the cattle car began to rise. The stench, however, became more unbearable—it was foul and offensive, burning eyes and nasal passages. Several people became nauseated and, having no other option, vomited onto the straw, which only added to the vile odor and caused others to become ill as well. The one hole in the floor of the corner of the car was in constant use. Tempers grew short, and arguments erupted quickly, although they ended as abruptly as they'd begun. The train continued to stop, then start; stop, then start—all day long. At sundown, the train pulled off onto another spur and came to a halt for the evening. The one slice of bread and one drink of water that each of the passengers had been given before sunrise did little to quell their hunger. They were crammed so tightly into the car that it was impossible for anyone to lie down. Some sat on their possessions or on the floor. It made little difference, however, that no one was able to lie down—trains traveling in both directions throughout the night continued to interrupt their sleep.

Rudolf looked with loving concern into the eyes of his children—eyes understandably filled with apprehension and unbridled fear. With a slight nod, he instructed his family to hold hands and bow their heads. Once that was accomplished, he lowered his own head and whispered with passion, "Dear Heavenly Father, we thank You for the blessing that our family is still together. While meager, we thank You for the food You have provided. While unknown to us, we thank You for the future You have planned, whatever it may be. We place our lives in Your hands, knowing You will be with us through this time of trial. Our trust and faith is with You because "Thy will be done. Amen."

* * *

The railcar door slid open the next morning with a deafening bang, and soldiers handed in the box of bread and pails of water. People shouted, "Where are we?" "Where are we going?" "We need more food!" "People are sick!" The only response to their cries was the door slamming shut. Even though people scrambled for the food and water, their movements were slower than on the previous day—they were weakened and dehydrated. People who'd never had to go hungry in their entire lives were now teetering on the brink of starvation. The sound of the metal on metal began anew as the train moved forward, jerking the passengers. The bread and water was handed out, and those directing the effort made sure that everyone received a share.

The sun rose higher in the sky, the heat intensified, the increasingly foul odor caused more people to become ill. A man seated in the corner jumped to his feet and began to violently scratch his legs. As he pulled up his trousers, he discovered he was covered with fleas that had bred in the straw on the floor. Soon, several others were similarly afflicted, causing them to scratch at their legs so hard that they bled.

The train came to another stop. More people called out, begging for assistance; none was offered. After another train passed them, they started up again. The same cycle continued throughout the entire day, just as it had the day before. Stop, go. Stop, go. The flea infestation worsened. The next morning again brought the same pattern: bread, water, no assistance. The door slammed shut. Stop, go; stop, go. The heat intensified. People passed out, or vomited, or scratched themselves raw from the fleas.

How long will this go on? Rudolf wondered. *How will we ever survive?*

A child began to scratch his head considerably more than would be measured as normal, a questioning, frightened look on his face. "Stop," his mother said emphatically. "You'll hurt yourself."

"I can't," the boy replied, continuing to scratch. "There is something on me."

She looked closer, spreading his hair apart, and discovered head lice. Desperately, she brushed his head as hard as possible without hurting the child, but it was to no avail. The little boy began to cry. His tears were as infectious as the head lice.

Three more days and three more nights continued in the same way— stop, go. Heat, fleas, lice, hunger, and thirst. Unbearable stench. Three people died. Even when the doors were opened in the morning, the soldiers refused to allow the dead to be removed. The screaming had stopped, replaced by pain-filled silence. Everyone was numb from the odors and the sounds and the hunger. Most of them became zombie-like—weak and unable to function, move, or think rationally. They had been in virtual darkness for five days and as a result, when the train door finally opened—and stayed opened—and the sun shone in on them, the people had to shield their eyes. The Czech soldiers began to scream, "*Alle raus, raus ihr Deutschen Schweine!*" ("Everyone out, you German pigs!") The passengers barely had the strength to move—some were afraid that the instruction was some sort of evil trick. After a brief hesitation, followed by further commands, they finally began to slowly exit the railcar. Once on the ground, most of them found their legs were unsteady, the result of not being able to move or walk around for nearly a week. Those who exited first helped the others, until the rancid-smelling enclosure was empty … with the exception of those who had died during the trip.

The Langer family huddled together, glad for this slight degree of freedom; glad for a glimpse of the sun and trees; glad to be alive. Their prayers had been answered.

"Do we have any more bread, Tata?" Fredi whispered.

"No, son," Rudolf quietly replied. "It's been gone for two days."

"But I'm hungry," Gerti said.

"We all are," Elsa observed with compassion. "Perhaps we'll have some food soon." It was an optimistic remark but one that was not truly believed.

Several other trains were at the station, all emptying the cattle cars filled with people who looked much the same as the Langers did—dead tired, half-starved, barely able to stand or walk. Their eyes were dark, and their cheeks were sunken. Hundreds of people milled about, in a daze, confused and disoriented. They were all kept in a confined area on the railway platform and closely guarded by the soldiers. When the final car was emptied of its passengers, a soldier, who appeared to be in charge, belted out in a menacing voice, "You will form a line and follow me!" Then he turned and began to walk away from the station.

The people, guarded by soldiers on both sides, followed the soldier in charge. Rudolf was glad that he'd thought to put wheels on their box. Carrying it now, in his weakened state, would have been impossible. As they walked along, Fredi looked up at his father and asked, "Where are we, Tata?"

Rudolf looked up at a sign hanging from the roof and replied, "Prague."

"Where's that?" Rudi questioned.

Rudolf wearily shook his head. "I'm not sure, son," he answered. And then he sadly thought, *I'm not sure of anything at all.*

SEVEN

THEY FOLLOWED THE SOLDIER DOWN A WIDE STREET PAVED with bricks, the likes of which most of them had never seen, past huge buildings that towered high into the sky. Prague was a very different place from Hermannstadt—a different world filled with motorcars and finely dressed people who stared at them with intense disdain. The slow-moving convoy of tattered, filthy, exhausted souls numbered close to six hundred, all of whom were starving, weak, and confused. Many had to be assisted by others, too spent to walk on their own.

Rudolf was firm as he spoke to the children. "Remember what I told you. Hang on to your mother and me, and don't let go for any reason." The children, although they were as hungry and tired as any of the others, followed their father's instruction. Still, they were in awe as they passed between the huge buildings, as if they were traversing through a canyon composed of mortar and steel. After walking for about one and one-half kilometers, the large group was herded into a warehouse, where they were met by people wearing long white smocks, resembling medical attire. A pungent aroma filled the air, strong enough to make them gasp.

"What is that smell, Mama?" Gerti asked, suppressing a cough.

"I don't know, dear," Elsa replied. "Just hold on tight."

Before either of them could say any more, a soldier announced, in a voice booming with authority, "The men and the women will separate. The men will form a line over here"—he pointed to his right—"and the woman and children over here." He pointed to his left.

Willie and Fredi looked up at their father. "Just don't let go of my coat," Rudolf reminded them in a hushed voice. The young boys nodded, beset by fear and confusion.

"*Raus! Schnell!* Now! Faster!" the soldier shouted.

The group slowly followed the orders. Rudolf leaned down to his sons and quietly said, "It will be better if you stay with your mother. Go hold on to her. Don't let go."

The boys were hesitant at first but then moved with the milling crowd until they reached Elsa. She pulled her children close to her, as they all followed the instructions barked by the soldier. The groups of men and women were formed into orderly lines and then instructed to remove all their clothing and place them into a container with a number on its side. Elsa hesitated. Had her ears deceived her? Had she misunderstood? To be naked in front of not only her neighbors but also total strangers was a thought so vile, she could barely comprehend it. Everyone around her seemed similarly hesitant, but when the soldiers took menacing steps closer, everyone began to comply. The children looked up at Elsa, their eyes wide and uncertain. She looked at the rifles the soldiers were brandishing and then slowly nodded at her children. With their eyes trained squarely on the floor, Elsa began to remove her clothes, as did the other people in both groups. As instructed, they placed their clothes in the numbered containers, which were then deposited on a series of long tables.

Soon the room was crammed with naked bodies—all trying their best to cover themselves with their hands. The children, without their mother's clothing to cling to, huddled as close as possible to Elsa, none of them looking at the other. Shame and embarrassment filled their hearts as the soldiers looked on with smug, derisive smiles.

Both groups were forced forward until they reached a station, where several people dressed in white, with surgical masks covering their faces, used automatic clippers to shave everyone's heads until they were completely bald. Although this caused additional embarrassment, the action also removed the head lice that had been prevalent among the ragged group. Following the head-shaving, the people were forced into an area with shower heads on the walls. Here, they trudged under the streams of water with a heavy scent of kerosene—obviously some type of disinfectant. Most found this tolerable, in that it removed the foul odor from their bodies—the result of being packed together for the past week—and offered them a degree of cleanliness. Next, they were directed between several high-powered fans that blew hot air to dry them off. At the next station they were sprayed with a white powder, which had a foul smell and left several people gasping for air. The entire ordeal took about twenty minutes, during which time their clothing also was disinfected with the white powder.

At the final station, a group of men that Elsa assumed were doctors conducted an examination of each person, poking and prodding each body, looking in each mouth, and concluding the examination by jabbing each person with a hypodermic needle for a reason that was never explained. Rubbing their arms from the sting of the injection, the naked line of humanity waited impatiently for their clothing to be returned. When it finally appeared, Elsa quickly clothed herself and helped the children put the layers of clothing back on in the reverse order from which it had been removed. Once everyone was clothed, Elsa looked around at the other women in shock and disbelief at their appearance—most of the women desperately searched for scarves to cover their shaved heads. The men were still in a separate group on the far side of the room. Elsa craned her neck, trying to locate Rudolf, but he was completely out of sight. Both groups were ordered to exit the building and, once outside, discovered they were on another railway platform.

But the size of the group had increased considerably. Others were already standing on the platform—thousands of people, all strangers, all waiting nervously for the continuation of their unknown journey. Elsa kept the children at her side as she tried to find Rudolf. She pushed through masses of men, women, and children, shouting his name and growing more anxious that she wouldn't find him. Then she saw him, about fifty feet away—he was frantically searching for them as well, calling her name repeatedly. "Rudolf!" she called back. He heard her voice over the cacophony of the others that separated them and immediately snapped his head in her direction. Their eyes locked with a great sense of relief. Moving as quickly as possible through the throng of people, Rudolf finally was able to gather Elsa is a warm and grateful embrace, with the children gathered closely at their sides.

A long train with numerous cars was directly in front of them, and soldiers were forcing those nearest to it on the platform to board. As soon as the train was filled to capacity, it steamed out of the station, and the crowd waiting on the platform was urged forward. Within moments, another train arrived, and the restless crowd was pushed forward again, until each car was packed to the maximum. Within fifteen minutes, that train was filled and another one took its place—it seemed an unending procession.

For an instant, Fredi let go of his mother's dress, just long enough to wipe his nose. But in that brief moment, a man, his wife, and three children were shoved between Fredi and Elsa. Fredi glanced up to see that he was being separated from his family, but as he tried to move back toward them, more and more people came between them. Within seconds, he could no longer see them. "Mama! Tata!" he cried out, but his small voice was lost in the constant buzz of the crowd.

Elsa looked down when she no longer felt Fredi's small hand on her skirt. Her eyes widened, and she screamed in alarm, "Rudolf! Fredi's gone!"

The family searched together in all directions, calling out Fredi's name. But Fredi was confused and disoriented, and the noise from the mob of people prevented his hearing the family crying out for him. He pushed his way through the crowd, hoping to find someone from Hermannstadt who could help him, but he only found himself immersed in a sea of strangers. The family, while still clinging desperately to one another, continued to move slowly through the crowd, calling Fredi's name. Then Fredi saw a wooden box, just like the one his father had constructed. He forced his way through the throng of people moving toward the train, desperate to get back to his family, but when he reached the box, he discovered it was being pulled by a total stranger.

Fredi broke down in tears, but no one stopped to assist the terrified five-and-a-half-year-old; they had their own worries. Fredi thought that if he somehow could get above the crowd, he might be able to see his parents, so he made his way to one of the trains and climbed up the steps. His idea—really more of a gut reaction than clear thought—proved not only unsuccessful but frightfully close to disastrous. The soldiers began pushing people toward the steps where Fredi stood. His eyes widened as the great mass moved closer and closer to him. At the last second, he jumped to the ground, just barely escaping the oncoming crowd, which certainly would have pushed him back inside the train car to a permanent separation from his family. As waves of people continued to press forward, Fredi saw that his only escape was underneath the train itself. He ducked his head, crawled under the train, and came out on the other side.

Now he was completely alone. No other people were in sight, although he could hear strange voices and screaming, the sound growing in intensity and causing him to be even more confused. He had no idea which way he should run; he had completely lost his bearings. He approached the train, which was filling with passengers, and looked up into the windows, searching desperately for his family. The faces that looked back at the young boy were blank, strange, and unwilling or unable to offer any help. Tears blurred his vision as he kept moving, begging God to help him; he had no idea where he was going or what would become of him. As he reached the end of the train car, he looked underneath the coupling between the cars and to his amazement, he finally saw his family, moving closer and closer to the train. He ducked underneath the coupling and ran to his mother, hugging her tightly and weeping uncontrollably. "I'm so sorry!" he kept repeating. "I couldn't find you."

Elsa and Rudolf both enveloped the little boy in their arms, comforting him and drying his falling tears. "It's all right," Elsa said reassuringly. "God has returned you to us." One of Elsa's hands held Fredi tightly to her side; the other gripped the crucifix that had adorned and blessed their home. The reunited family kept moving forward, and seconds later, they were pressed onto the train. The interior of the train car was remarkably different from the one on which they had spent so many torturous days.

This one had wooden benches on each side and an open aisle down the middle. While it certainly was not comfortable, it was at least a place to sit, with room to move around if they wished. The car even had windows that could be opened to let in fresh air. Rudolf took some blankets out of the box he so carefully continued to protect and gave them to the family to sit on. This slight degree of comfort, however, did nothing to erase their hunger.

Fredi closed his eyes tightly and prayed harder than he had ever prayed before. He thanked God for returning him to his family and remembered the special words from the prayer he offered each night before sleep. "Thy will be done ..."

* * *

The train lurched into motion, leaving others moving forward on the platform, waiting for the next transport. *Where are we going?* Rudolf wondered. *Where are we all going?* As the train picked up speed and began to rock back and forth, the only thing Rudolf knew for certain was that the train was old and in poor condition. The railcar squeaked and screeched with each movement, as if the wood itself would splinter and fall apart at any moment. Rudolf and Elsa looked at each other, sharing a nod and a slight smile—although everything else they once had was lost, at least the family was still together. That thought alone gave them some comfort. Rudolf looked around the car and realized he didn't recognize anyone. No one from Hermannstadt was riding with them.

It seemed that just as the train reached maximum speed, it began to slow down—the same experience they'd had on the other train for the better part of a week. The train pulled off the main track and onto a spur so that a larger and faster train could pass by. Rudolf was dispirited by the thought that this same thing might occur for an indefinite period of time, but he was pleasantly surprised when the door at the end of the car opened and three people entered. One carried a box of sliced bread, with margarine on each slice, and the others carried two pails of water, with ladles that they dispersed at various points. It was not much food, but at least it was something to ease their growling stomachs. Even so, the faces of the riders remained drawn, spent, and seemingly lost in doubt.

When darkness fell, the wind blew chill and unrestricted through the open slats on the walls and the floor of the car. The Langer family shifted their positions and pulled their blankets more tightly around themselves, hoping to provide protection from the falling temperature. *How long will we travel this time?* Elsa wondered. She hoped it would be long enough for her children to get some sleep—the constant stopping and starting of the train made it difficult for anyone to truly rest. Unfortunately, sleep was again interrupted as the train pulled over onto a spur, waited, and then lurched forward again.

The following morning, the strangers on the train began exchanging information with each other—where they were from; how long they'd been traveling; how the Russians had treated them before the mass transport began. Their stories differed considerably—some had experienced extreme violence and brutality in their towns and villages, while others were guarded by military forces but basically allowed to conduct business as usual. In hushed tones, they painfully reflected on the promises Hitler had made concerning their future and the greatness they would all enjoy. Prosperity. Peace. Security. Now, it was all lost, and their personal toll had been great—countless thousands of deaths; and for the survivors, the end of the life they had known.

Stop, go. Bread, water. Sleep, boredom. Hot, cold. People paced aimlessly up and down the aisle, stretching out cramps in their unused muscles; then tried to find comfort on the wooden benches that seemed to grow harder with each mile. The boredom was inevitable and unavoidable during the five long days and nights they spent on the train, and it eventually caused irritability, with harsh words exchanged among the passengers. Finally, the doors were opened, and all were ordered to exit the train.

They were in Bayreuth in West Germany, a large city in the northern part of Bavaria. As the people left the confines of the railcar, they were ushered, under armed guard, down a narrow street, past buildings that were pockmarked with bullet holes. They soon found themselves in a refugee receiving camp, located in a huge building. Again, the men were separated from the women and children, but there was a different feeling here—an indescribable sense that somehow, this place was not as degrading as their previous, unpleasant stop.

The attendants here were all members of the German Red Cross. Their attitude and actions were helpful, not humiliating, and they didn't require the people to undress—this alone brought immense relief. As the lines moved forward, the attendants first sprayed them—another delousing process—and then administered another injection. Rudolf heard that it was an inoculation against smallpox and tuberculosis, diseases that had become prevalent among those confined in unsanitary conditions for long periods. Here, the people were encouraged to wash themselves with soap and warm water, an unexpected pleasantry. In brief conversations, several of them learned that the humane treatment they were receiving was a direct result of the Potsdam Treaty, signed in 1945, in which Germany agreed to accept German citizens who crossed the border from the east. While few understood its meaning, it was clear that their situation here was far superior to being sent to unknown regions in Russia.

Finally, with their processing complete, the attendants issued each person a food ration ticket before ushering each one out of the building.

"What's this for?" Gerti asked her mother.

"God has answered our prayers," Elsa replied with a tender smile. "That is so we can get food."

"Food?" Rudi whispered with delight. "Real food?"

"That's what it says on the ticket."

"What will it be, Mama?" Willie asked.

"We'll soon find out," Elsa replied.

Rudolf joined the rest of the family outside the building and together, they walked back to the train station. There, they stood in a long line, waiting for their turns to use the food ration tickets. Each person received two slices of fresh bread with butter, a cup of fresh milk, and—much to everyone's surprise and delight—a full ladle of soup. After eating only limited quantities of stale bread and water for the past two weeks, this ration seemed like a feast, and the children's eyes lit up as if it were a Christmas dinner.

The platform outside the train station was filled with strangers boarding other trains. Rudolf, Elsa, and the children waited inside, extremely grateful for the food they'd received but also grateful that the gold coins that Rudolf had safely hidden in the false bottom of the wooden box had not been discovered. As Rudolf listened to the conversations of the people around them, he learned that the city of Bayreuth was known throughout the world for its famous playhouse, *Festspielhaus* (translated as Festival House) and was dedicated to the renowned operas written by Richard Wagner, such as *The Flying Dutchman, Die Walküre,* and *Siegfried.* Being a simple farmer from Hermannstadt, the names meant nothing to Rudolf, but the playhouse was said to be like a palace, and remarkably, although the city had been extensively damaged by Allied bombings, the *playhaus* had been spared.

The Langer family huddled together inside the station, Elsa never letting her eyes leave Fredi. They spent that night sleeping on the concrete floor of the station, their extra clothing and blankets providing all the warmth they needed. For each of them, it was an additional blessing to finally be able to sleep without the gnawing feeling of an empty stomach. In the morning, to everyone's delight, the Red Cross attendants distributed more soup, bread, and milk. After eating, people began to move outside, where another train waited. In a short time, the Langers entered another car that closely resembled the one they had left the previous morning. Sighing deeply at the thought of another long journey to an unknown destination, they settled in as best as possible. They were surprised, however, when the train stopped after just one full day of travel—they had gone barely one hundred kilometers when they were ordered off the train again. *Is this it?* Rudolf silently questioned. *Is this our final destination? Where will we go? What will we do? Where will we stay?* But these questions, though worrisome, seemed almost inconsequential when he stopped to consider the one that was uppermost in his heart: *Will we ever return to our own home and the life we once knew?*

* * *

The sign on the side of the train station read "Naila," a small city with a population of about six thousand. Even though it had considerably more commerce and businesses than in Hermannstadt, it reminded Rudolf of their beloved hometown, in that it was the largest city in the area and was surrounded by several, smaller farming communities. In addition to the usual businesses, stores, and restaurants, the city also boasted a hospital, a brewery, a Catholic church with a cemetery, and three schools: a high school with a gymnasium, a trade school, and a middle school.

As the Langer family and the other passengers exited the train, they were met by uniformed policemen, rather than the military officials of their earlier experience. But although the policemen were reasonably polite, they made it clear that they were very much in control of the people's lives. The mass of people was marched to a large building nearby that bore the faded name of Seifert-Klöbert—it was a factory that had once manufactured shoes but had been closed since the beginning of the war. The entire bottom floor of the three-story structure served as a holding area, and once everyone was inside, the Red Cross volunteers provided instructions in a calm and orderly manner. They explained that this particular facility would house all the adults and only some of the children. The balance would be sequestered nearby in a barracks beside the high school gymnasium. Initially, this news was not received well by the parents, who were reluctant to let their children out of their sight, but the volunteers further clarified that it was a matter of logistics and space. They also assured the adults that they could visit and spend as much time as they desired with their children. In addition, they had complete freedom to go anywhere and do anything they wished in the town—there would be no restrictions on their activities. Elsa and Rudolf looked at each other in shock and disbelief, shedding tears of joy at this remarkable news. Even though their freedom was still somewhat limited, this news was viewed as a blessing, and for that, Elsa offered prayers of thanks.

Because some of the children had to be moved to a different building, the parents were allowed to choose which two they would keep with them and which were to move to the barracks. After much difficulty, Rudolf and Elsa determined they would keep Gerti with them, because she was a girl, as well as Fredi, because he was the youngest. Rudi and Willie would go to the barracks.

"But we don't want to leave you," Willie cried when told the news.

"We're only going to be apart for a little while," Elsa said reassuringly, "and everything is going to be fine, certainly much better than it has been for the last two weeks." She smiled, offering comfort. "And you'll never leave us. You're only going to be down the street, and we'll see you every day."

"Besides," Rudolf added, "you'll be with other kids your own age and probably have lots of fun. It's been a long time since you had a chance to do that."

This argument made sense, and Rudi and Willie finally accepted that the experience would be more of an adventure than a form of punishment. Elsa handed the boys a blanket, and even though it was becoming warmer, she instructed them to keep all their clothes on—or at least with them—at all times. When it was time to say good-bye, the young boys felt a certain amount of apprehension again, but they smiled bravely and followed the Red Cross volunteers to the barracks. As soon as the children left the factory, there was much work to be done. The Red Cross people hung long, crisscrossed clothesline throughout the room, creating a pattern of squares. It was then suggested that the new residents hang blankets across the lines so that each family could achieve a degree of privacy. Rudolf helped the others hang blankets, but before leaving his and Elsa's area, he pointed to the wooden box on the floor and said, "Don't take your eyes off that." She nodded, and he went off to do what he could to assist.

Once that task was completed, large bags filled with straw were brought into the room and distributed—this provided their bedding for the duration of the stay. While not ideal, it did provide a degree of comfort that was greatly appreciated. Throughout these activities, Elsa kept a close eye on the wooden box, as well as on Fredi. While his getting lost at the Prague train station had not been his fault, it was normal for him to want to wander and explore.

At their home in Hermannstadt, while the other children were at school, it was common for Fredi to go off on his own, always with Fritzl at his side, to explore the nearby pastures and hills. He always had been the most inquisitive of the Langers' four children, always wondering why things were the way they were and seldom seeming afraid of anything. But at home, it was different. At home, there was no reason for concern or worry; he was always safe. Now, all that had changed, and Elsa was determined to keep him in tow, within her watchful and protective sight.

When Rudi and Willie entered the large, open barrack, the bags filled with straw were already in place, and they were allowed to select a spot where they wished to sleep. The majority of the other children were older and in order to prevent any potential altercations, the Red Cross workers were always present, acting as monitors and mentors and expressing care and concern for all. In a group meeting, the children were informed that they would be fed a healthy meal twice a day and that numerous activities had been planned for everyone. Rudi looked at Willie with a slight smile and said, "This isn't going to be so bad."

EIGHT

AFTER THEIR FIRST WEEK IN NAILA, A DEGREE OF NORMALCY set in. Every day, either Elsa or Rudolf would take Gerti and Fredi and go to the barracks to visit the other children. Whenever Elsa went there, she was careful to take the crucifix with her; the rosary beads, however, she left in the wooden box. As promised, everyone received healthy portions of food—milk and slices of fresh bread with butter in the morning; bread, milk, and a generous bowl of potato soup each evening. Gerti and Fredi rapidly discovered that Rudi and Willie were having more fun than they were. Their brothers had things to do, games to play, and others to play with. They almost wished they could be with their brothers, instead of in the factory with their parents.

While either Elsa or Rudolf was visiting the children, the other would stay within the confines of their small enclosure, keeping a vigilant eye on their precious wooden box—to lose it and its contents would be a complete disaster. On the occasions when they were together, it was common for Rudolf to take a coin or two from the hidden bottom of the box, go into town, and purchase necessary items, such as toiletries or additional food. Once, after returning from such a trip, he seemed deeply troubled. He pulled a Red Cross worker aside and asked seriously, "Why do the people in town treat us as if we're all outcasts? I know they're not happy to have us here, but are we not all Germans?"

The worker cleared his throat and calmly explained, "This place where you're staying is called a *Flüchtlingslager*—a refugee camp. And you people are referred to as the *Flüchtlinge*. Refugees. Displaced persons."

"I don't understand," Rudolf replied. "They know we'll be leaving eventually. Why do they look down on us, like we were dirt under their feet?"

"To be honest," the man said slowly, "and this may be painful and difficult to understand, they look down on you because you speak a different dialect from theirs. It's a dialect they call 'Low German.' And besides that, your clothing is torn and tattered and dirty."

"That's ridiculous," Rudolf insisted, his anger rising. "Don't they know we've been prisoners of the Russians and the Czechs and have had everything stolen from us?"

The Red Cross worker looked at Rudolf with sad yet understanding eyes as he nodded and explained, "They also think that anyone from the Sudetenland must have been poor and forced out of their homes because they were lazy and dishonest and not willing to work."

"That's not true!" Rudolf replied defiantly.

"I know that," the man said. "All of us here know that. But some of the people who live here in Naila do not. I'm afraid it will take a long time until they understand how wrong their opinions are."

Rudolf shook his head sadly and walked away. Like many of the other men, he took the opportunity whenever possible to go to town or to nearby farms to look for work. He would offer to perform any menial job—sweeping a store, cleaning houses, cutting kindling, cleaning animal stalls, even cutting grass with a scythe. He was willing to do whatever was needed to earn a little extra money to buy additional food for his family, yet it was extremely difficult to find work because the attitude of superiority from the local residents was so prevalent—as well as being heart-breaking and impossible to comprehend.

After the Langers had been at the holding facility for about three weeks, it was determined that the children who were staying with the adults in the factory building would be transferred to the barracks. It often was difficult for the adults to get a good night's sleep because the young children who stayed with their parents would cry at night. This situation caused much frustration and short tempers—exactly what the Red Cross people were doing their best to avoid. Additionally, most of the children had visited the barracks to see other brothers and sisters and felt much the same as Gerti and Fredi felt—they wanted to have fun as well, not be cooped up with the adults. It seemed a logical solution to move all the children to the barracks—they could play games and be with others their own age, and the adults would get much-needed restful sleep.

Just before the children were moved, Elsa took Gerti aside and softly said, "Please keep an eye on Fredi. You know how he's always curious about things and sometimes just wanders off."

Gerti nodded. "I will, Mama. I promise."

"And another thing," Elsa said. "Make sure your brothers say their prayers."

Gerti hugged her mother tightly and offered a bright smile. "Of course I will. You didn't even have to ask."

The children walked the two blocks to the barracks, carrying their blankets, a pillow, and all their clothing. It made quite an impression to the onlookers who watched from inside stores and on the street. While it was the beginning of an adventure for the children, it only served to solidify the opinion of the residents of Naila: *Look at the filthy children in their tattered clothes*, they thought. *Like their parents, they'll never amount to anything.* The Red Cross volunteers who walked with the children did their best to stifle the rude comments from onlookers, but the remarks meant little to the youngsters anyway—they didn't understand the local dialect.

Upon entering the barracks, Gerti and Fredi were relieved to find Rudi and Willie without any trouble. The Red Cross volunteers asked several of the children to move to other areas so that various families could be reunited, and it was done without complaint. Those who already were housed in the barracks were happy to see the newcomers—now there would be more new friends and new people to play with. On the first night that the Langer children were together, Gerti kept her promise to her mother and announced with authority, "Okay, everyone. We're going to say our prayers now, just like we always did at home. Fredi, since you're the youngest, you go first." Without hesitation, her brothers bowed their heads and followed her direction. In their own way, they each quietly offered prayers for their siblings and their parents, for the fact that they were still together, and for the hope that someday, somehow, they would be able to return to their home. Each night, after the others were still, Fredi also would say a silent prayer of his own for Fritzl, his loyal friend.

Next to the barracks and the high school gymnasium was a large sports field. After transferring to the barracks, Fredi and Gerti were delighted to find that they would now be able to take part in various organized activities led by volunteers, such as soccer games, calisthenics, or wheelbarrow races from one side of the field to the other. Sometimes, they would simply play tag or run and jump around, enjoying the freedom of movement and the ability to once again enjoy children's pursuits. On rainy days the children were led into the spacious gymnasium, where various volunteers provided entertainment to keep them occupied and out of mischief. Gerti loved to participate in group singing, which was always loud and enormously spirited. Fredi enjoyed hearing stories—classics such as *Hansel and Gretel* and *Rübezahl,* which told of an ancient and powerful German mountain gnome with power over the elements and who was able to make the crops grow. He also delighted in listening to *Junker Prahlhans,* the story of a character similar to Pinocchio, who exaggerates, twists the truth, and is forced to bear the consequences of his actions.

Back in the now adults-only factory, Elsa felt relief that her children were allowed to enjoy themselves in play, but she was experiencing a heart-rending problem. Although her heart encouraged her to attend services at the local church, she could not bring herself to do so. Her pain-filled decision was based on the fact that the family's clothing, which they had been wearing for the better part of six weeks, was not appropriate and would create even more snide comments from the residents of the town. She could not justify exposing the children to more taunting and being viewed as outcasts. Each night, however, before she put her head down on the bale of straw, she would touch the feet of Jesus on her crucifix, rub her hands gently over the rosary beads, and offer sincere prayers for their safety and redemption.

One afternoon while Elsa was visiting the children, Rudolf sat alone in their small enclosure. Usually, there was someone else around with whom he could engage in conversation, but on this day, the room was empty. Before Elsa returned, he felt a desperate need to go to the bathroom; waiting for his wife to come back was not an option. He pulled back the blanket-curtain and looked up and down the aisle. Hearing no other voices and satisfied that he was alone in the factory, he quickly made his way to the bathroom. When he returned moments later, he stopped cold in his tracks. His mouth opened wide but he was unable to scream; his heart was virtually broken. The precious wooden box that contained all they owned was gone. He ran up and down the aisles of the factory, looking inside each cubicle, searching frantically, but he found nothing. The wooden box seemed to have disappeared into thin air. His legs felt leaden as he trudged back to their own cubicle; he was completely devastated, distraught, and overwhelmed with grief. His sat on one of the bags filled with straw, his arms tightly hugging himself as he rocked back and forth. Never had he felt such a feeling of complete loss and despair, and he despised himself for being so careless.

And then he waited, alone and silent.

Later that afternoon when Elsa returned, she pulled back the blanket-curtain, eager to tell Rudolf about her pleasant visit with the children and how well they were getting along. She stopped short, however, when she saw Rudolf, doubled over and staring silently at the concrete floor. "Rudolf?" she said, trying to remain calm. "What is it?"

He pointed to the corner of their small space—a now-empty corner. Looking up into her eyes, he found himself unable to speak.

"The box?" she gasped.

"It's … been stolen," he moaned.

"But *how?*"

Rudolf shook his head sadly. "I went to the bathroom. I was gone for only three minutes. And when I returned …"

Elsa sat down beside him, feeling nauseated and short of breath. It was as if her very soul had been violated. It was a full sixty seconds before she could speak, and even then, her words seemed to be coming from someone else, someone standing outside herself. "Did you …" She was unable to say more.

Rudolf nodded. "I looked everywhere. It's gone. We're ruined."

Finally, Elsa took a deep breath, straightened her back, and slowly lifted her head. Clutching the crucifix to her chest, she took Rudolf's hand in hers and spoke with conviction and absolute belief. "My rosary is gone. All our money is gone. The last few things we treasured are gone. But we are not ruined."

Rudolf looked at her in astonishment. "How can you—?"

"We still have each other," she broke in. "We still have our family. We still have our dreams. We still have our faith in God. We are *not* ruined." He continued to stare at her, amazed, as she continued, "Everything we have lost can be replaced. We will work harder and longer and better than ever. But we are not ruined. It is *not* God's will that we are ruined."

Rudolf nodded slowly and drew her to him—this remarkable woman with such strength of character and faith in God's will. In his heart, however, he knew that there were some things that could not be replaced. Rudolf had also placed their valuable papers in the false bottom of the box—their birth and baptism certificates, marriage certificate, and the deeds and ownership papers to their house and land. These papers, tragically, would be close to impossible to replace.

* * *

The following day Rudolf reported the theft to the local police. A portly man wearing an ill-fitting uniform sat behind a desk. He wrote down

Rudolf's name, where he was staying, and a description of the box. In a flat tone and without meeting Rudolf's eyes, he said, "We'll do everything possible to find and return it." His manner told Rudolf that no such attempt would be made. In all probability, even if the box were miraculously discovered, everything in it would be gone. Deeply depressed, Rudolf was nonetheless determined that he would not let his family down. He spent his time in trying to find work and was gone from sunup until sundown every day. In response to his requests for work, door after door was slammed in his face, occasionally accompanied with harsh words, berating him and all the other *Flüchtlinge* who remained unwelcome and unwanted in Naila.

Still he persisted, never stopping or giving up his quest, willing to accept the unpleasant and unnecessary insults if it meant he could earn money for his family. Eventually, he found work on nearby farms, where local farmers took advantage of his proficiency with animals, their care, and farming in general—several days of hard labor generated meager wages, but at least it was something. Appreciation for his hard work—his habit of always doing more than expected—was never spoken, and in time, he grew to accept the unfair treatment, even if he could not understand it. Often, when he arrived back at their sparse cubicle, he was too spent to join the food line. On those evenings, Elsa would retrieve the food for him and, on occasion, even assist him with eating. Each time this occurred, she would offer a prayer before they ate, thanking God for their families and the blessings they had received. She would always end each prayer with, "It is not God's will that we are ruined."

With the small earnings Rudolf was able to accumulate, he would stop at a market for extra food to be shared with Elsa and the children. On many of the farms where he worked, he was able to pick vegetables, which he hid in his jacket. Over and over, as the sun burned down on him in the fields and sweat poured from his brow, he would remind himself of Elsa's powerful and encouraging words: "*It is not God's will that we are ruined.*"

Rudolf and Elsa agreed that they would not tell the children that the box had been stolen—no need to trouble them with that burden. Each time Elsa visited, the children asked why their father never came to see them. Elsa calmly replied that he had found work and was providing for the family. And each time she left them, the children always told Elsa to please tell Rudolf that they loved him. As Elsa walked back to their small enclosure, thinking about her children's sweet words, her eyes would become misty.

* * *

Over the next few weeks, the Red Cross volunteers periodically came to the factory building and recited a small list of names. Once their names were called, the people would gather their possessions, move to the outside of the building, board large trucks, and leave. No one had any idea where they went.

Unbeknownst to those left behind, the mayors of the smaller towns in the surrounding area had gathered on numerous occasions to discuss how many of the refugees their towns would take in. Their acceptance of the refugees also meant that those towns would be responsible for making sure the people had a reasonable place to live. The Red Cross was working in concert with the mayors by providing food and other necessary items until the newcomers got back on their feet. Some of the mayors strongly favored the plan—they fully expected to import cheap labor to their communities. Others adamantly vocalized their prejudice, insisting that they didn't want any *Flüchtlinge* in their areas at all.

One afternoon when the Red Cross worker read the list of names, the Langers' name was among them. Rudolf and Elsa were instructed to gather up all of their belongings and meet the worker outside; he was going to the barracks to collect the children. Rudolf and Elsa had little to take with them—a few blankets and a suitcase, which contained clothing for Elsa and Gerti. Other than the clothes on their backs, that was the sum total of their earthly possessions. They looked deeply into each other's eyes, glad to be leaving this place but concerned over where they would be taken. Once outside, they boarded a large, open army truck with five other families, who also were waiting for their children.

In the barracks, the children bade quick good-byes to the friends they were leaving behind, knowing they likely would never meet again. Grabbing their clothing, they scurried to board the rear of the truck, and with the grinding of gears and a lurch forward, they were once again on their way. A uniformed policeman drove the truck and another policeman sat by his side, and this caused apprehension in the passengers—were they under armed guard again? Seeing the policemen also reminded Rudolf of their lack of concern over finding his valuable wooden box. He hadn't believed they would make any attempt to find it on the day he reported the loss, and he felt no differently now.

* * *

Just as the sun was setting, the truck eased to a stop in the middle of a small town, which Rudolf and Elsa initially thought might be about the same size as Hermannstadt. It differed from Hermannstadt, however, in that it had several businesses in its downtown district. The policeman exited the cab of the truck and walked to rear, where he dispassionately instructed everyone to get off and bring their belongings with them.

"Where are we?" Rudolf asked.

"Selbitz," the policeman replied. "It's about three and a half kilometers from Naila."

"What will we do here?" another asked.

"You will each be picked up by families who have agreed to take you in and help get you settled."

Rudolf's brow furrowed. "But how will—"

"You will wait here until someone comes!" the policeman interrupted gruffly. He seemed irritated that he had to deal with the *Flüchtlinge.* "They know you're here. Don't wander around and get lost. Follow instructions, and don't cause any trouble." And with that, he got back in the truck and drove away.

Dumbstruck, the adults all looked at each other. They had been dropped off in an unknown town, waiting for complete strangers to come and get them. The sum total of their knowledge was that they were somewhere in West Germany, most likely in northern Bavaria, in front of a place called Schirner's Kiosk. And though the town seemed small, like Hermannstadt, it did not exude the friendly familiarity of their hometown. And this one had a preponderance of motorcars, trucks, and motorcycles. An occasional cart would pass by them, led by a horse or an ox, but this was rare. After ten minutes—which seemed much longer, due to their being unaware of what might happen next—a stranger approached and called out a family name. One of the families who had traveled with the

Langers from Naila joined the stranger and walked off with him into the distance. Then another came and called another name, and then another, then another. Within an hour, the Langer family found themselves in front of the kiosk—completely alone. Each time a car, truck, or person passed by, they wondered if it might be the family, come to collect them. But no one stopped for them—although a few offered unpleasant comments as they passed. When pedestrians walked toward them, they always moved to the other side of the street, whispering and pointing at the Langers as if they were space aliens—in addition to their general appearance, their short hair made them stand out.

Fredi looked up at Rudolf and asked, "Tata, why do they whisper about us like that? Have we done something wrong?"

Rudolf placed his hand gently on his young son's shoulder. "No, son. They're just not used to seeing strangers." But Rudolf knew differently; he knew the truth. He also knew their time ahead was going to be extremely difficult.

The sun set and still the family continued to wait. It appeared as if they had been forgotten as they stood in front of Schirner's Kiosk on this moonless night. Finally, thankfully, a city employee approached them, introduced himself, and asked, "Are you the Langer family?"

"We are," Rudolf replied, somewhat relieved.

His relief was short-lived when the man announced, "The family who agreed to take you changed their minds. They decided they didn't have enough room for six people."

Rudolf struggled to control the panic in his voice. "Then what are we to do?"

"Follow me. We found temporary lodging nearby—just until something permanent can be arranged."

They picked up their few belongings and followed the man about a block and a half until he stopped in front of a three-story building. Rudolf and Elsa stared at each other in disbelief—a sign on the building identified it as the Ludwig Shoe Factory. They'd just spent six weeks barely existing in an abandoned shoe factory. Now, here they were in another. Had the situation not been so disappointing, it might have been humorous.

The city employee opened the front door, led the family inside, and turned on the lights. Unlike the factory in Naila, vast pieces of complicated-looking machinery and equipment were still in place. He directed them to a small, windowless storage room at the back of the building; it obviously had been used for a similar purpose in the past, as it held now-familiar bags filled with straw that would again suffice as their bedding. "Bathrooms are on the far side of the building," the man said. "You must stay here until you are contacted by someone else—don't wander off." He left without further comment.

Rudolf looked, filled with despair, but Elsa brightened the mood considerably by offering her best smile and telling the children, "Well, we're already used to sleeping on bags of straw, so we know that at least we'll be comfortable."

Gerti set her blanket on top of one of the bags. "Mama's right," she said encouragingly. "This won't be so bad. At least it's warm."

That was an understatement. The enclosed room was stifling, and almost immediately, they all removed at least two layers of clothing.

"I have to go to the bathroom," Fredi said, shifting uncomfortably from one foot to the other.

"Rudi," Rudolf instructed, "go along with Fredi, and make sure both of you don't get lost or into any trouble." He added as an afterthought, "And don't touch anything."

As the two boys walked through the factory, Fredi peered at all the machinery. He was fascinated by these things, the likes of which he'd never seen before. His insatiable curiosity got the best of him, and he stopped to softly rub his small hand over the side of one of the large pieces of equipment.

"Tata said not to touch anything," Rudi warned.

"I won't hurt it," Fredi replied. He gazed at the machine and added wistfully, "I wish I knew how it worked and what it did."

"You're going to get into trouble," Rudi said.

"Not unless you tell," Fredi retorted with a sweet smile. He turned back toward the machine and said dreamily, "Perhaps someday I'll own a piece of machinery like this."

"And perhaps you'll get your hide tanned!" Rudi said, growing impatient. "Now let's go to the bathroom and get back before we both get into trouble."

Later, Elsa led them all in their evening prayers and then the family all settled for the night. But Fredi had two thoughts in his mind that kept him from sleep: first, as always, he thought of Fritzl; second, he thought of the remarkable piece of machinery he had touched with his very own hand.

* * *

The following morning they were awakened by strange sounds—whirls and twirls and thuds and clunks—as well as a cacophony of loud voices. Rudolf jerked open the door to the storage room, and to everyone's surprise, the factory was in full operation. Countless people were working feverishly and diligently at the various pieces of equipment, manufacturing shoes. Fredi stared in amazement, his eyes growing wide at the incredible sight before him. When Rudolf closed the door, Fredi pleaded, "Can't we leave the door open, Tata? I want to watch."

"It's too loud," Rudolf replied. "The noise will break your ears."

"I'll hold my hands over them," Fredi countered, wanting desperately to see everything that was going on.

Rudolf smiled, patted the youngster on the head, and explained, "I expect you'll probably have the opportunity to see more than you want." He then gathered the children together so that they could walk together to the bathroom. "Stay together," Rudolf warned. "Keep your eyes straight ahead. Don't look at any of the workers." His stern tone made it clear that any questions were unwarranted. As they all walked to the far end of the building, those working on the machines that so fascinated Fredi were not quite as polite or reserved. The workers frowned at the family as they passed, their faces clearly displaying barely suppressed anger. The Langer family walked swiftly, but they could hear the whispered complaints and insults that the workers shared with each other. Still, following Rudolf's advice, the family kept their heads held high and their eyes straight ahead.

Once back in the storage room, the children expressed their confusion over why they seemed so despised. Rudolf and Elsa could think of no logical answer—there wasn't one. Rudolf could only explain, "This is just the way it is, and it will probably continue until we prove to the local residents that we're honest and hard-working people."

Hungry and feeling uncertain, the family sat on their beds without speaking, listening to the increasingly loud sounds outside the confines of their room, feeling once again as if they were prisoners. But then, finally, there was a knock on their door. When Rudolf opened it and saw a Red Cross volunteer, he felt as if he was looking at an angel. She was holding a basket in her arms, and her glowing face expressed a warm and welcoming smile.

"Mr. and Mrs. Langer, my name is Maria," she said. "I can't tell you how sorry I am that acceptable housing has not yet been arranged, but that situation should be corrected within a day or so. I've brought you some food—it should be enough to feed all of you today."

Elsa touched the feet of the crucifix. Her prayers had been once again been answered. "Please allow us to share this food with you," Elsa offered.

"That's very considerate," Maria replied, "very kind. But this is all for you and your family. I'll be returning tomorrow with news of your new lodging." She turned to leave, then hesitated briefly as she added, "You're most welcome to leave your room and explore the city if you wish. But I must remind you that some of the people who live here may be less than polite. For this I apologize." Sadness came over her angelic face as she concluded, "In time, we hope this attitude will be reversed."

As soon as the door was closed behind Maria, the children eagerly gathered around their parents to look in the basket. Rudolf held up a warning hand, explaining that they would eat only what they needed and save the rest for tomorrow, a wise form of rationing to protect them for another day.

With reasonably full stomachs, the family followed the volunteer's advice and took a small walk around the city. Her warning had proven to be all too correct. When Rudolf or Elsa offered a smile and a friendly hello to those they passed on the street, the response from some of them was a frown or insults hurled at them. Elsa sighed heavily. *Our clothes may not be as fine as theirs*, she thought, *but are we not all the same? All Germans? All innocent victims of a lost and tragic war?* For his part, Rudolf suspected that being ostracized, treated as outcasts, and looked down upon was the treatment they would have to endure for a very long time.

They returned to the storage room in the shoe factory, determined to keep a positive outlook. That evening, following a tasty dinner and some lighthearted conversation, Elsa again led the children in their prayers. As

Rudolf turned off the solitary light bulb in their room and sleep finally came, none of them possibly could have imagined how their lives would be altered when they awoke in the morning.

NINE

WHIRLING, TWIRLING, THUDS, CLANKS, AND MYRIAD VOIC-
es—the Langers awoke to the same sounds as they had on the previous morning. Rubbing their sleep-filled eyes, each wondered what the
new day would bring. The walk through the factory on the way to the
bathroom that morning brought more of the same derisive looks and comments. Even though the children had been instructed again to keep their
eyes straight ahead, Fredi could not help but sneak a peek at the fascinating
machines. He remembered the words he'd said to Rudi: *"Perhaps someday
I'll own a piece of machinery like this."*

Later that morning, as they waited in their room, Maria once again
came to visit them with a basket filled with food. Before handing it to Rudolf, however, she said, "Gather your things and follow me. I have a surprise." They followed Maria up the stairs to the third floor of the building,
where they found a long hallway with six doors. Maria offered a gracious
smile, opened the third door, and indicated for them all to enter.

"This is your new home," she explained as they looked around. "It
isn't much right now, but we'll get whatever you need, and you'll be comfortable here—not forever, mind you, but at least for a little while."

Rudolf and Elsa were speechless. Their own home? Certainly not like
the one they had been forced to leave behind, but it was theirs alone. No
more trying to sleep on wooden benches. No more nonstop intrusions and

strange noises that made sleep impossible.

The apartment contained two small rooms, each with a window, concrete floors, and thin walls. There were three green cots, with a folded green blanket on top of each one. The second room contained a large straw mattress, roomy enough for three people and also covered with blankets. Maria explained, "These have been provided by the U.S. Army." Then she removed the covering from the basket she was carrying and added, "And so is this." The basket was filled with small cans, all a drab green color.

"What is that?" Elsa asked.

"It's food," Maria replied.

"But those are cans. And they're all green."

Maria smiled. "It's what they call C-rations. Look … I'll show you." She produced a can opener from the basket and opened one of the cans. To everyone's immense delight, the can was filled with an assortment of fruit—pineapple, apples, strawberries, melon. The smell permeated the room and caused everyone's mouth to water. Maria handed Elsa a spoon. "Try it. It's good. And it's also good for the children."

Tentatively, Elsa took a spoonful of fruit and cautiously tasted it. She chewed slowly, and after a moment, she broke into a wide smile. "It's delicious!" she proclaimed.

Maria pointed to other cans in the basket. "We have meat, breads, and vegetables," she said, and the she pointed at the can in Elsa's hand. "And fruit salad, as well as some other things."

A look of concern crossed Rudolf's face. "But we have no money to pay you."

Maria shook her head. "There's no need to worry about that," she said. "The army has agreed to help until you get back on your feet, and there also will be other things sent from the United States from time to time that will help you out as well."

He shook his head, perplexed. "I … don't understand."

Maria smiled gently. "The Americans are very generous people." She placed the basket down on one of the cots and then walked toward the door, adding, "The people of Selbitz also have been asked to help out with whatever they can spare. We're doing our best to find you a wood stove so you can cook your own food."

"I don't know what to say," Elsa quietly offered, tears of gratitude glistening in her eyes, "except thank you … from all of us."

"You're more than welcome. The war is behind us now, and we all want you to succeed." And with that, their "angel" was gone.

The children were eager to sample the food in the unusual cans. Elsa quickly mastered the can opener and gave each child a spoon and one can, each filled with a different food. They shared with each other, taking bites of the various foods, and expressing their pleasure with every bite. Rudolf moved to the window and looked down on the street below, which he'd learned was August Bauer Strasse.

"Come and eat something," Elsa said. "It's wonderful."

"I'll have some later," he replied, continuing to stare out the window. His face, still tanned from working in his fields, seemed lined with questions as he thought, *What strange people these Americans must be. They just defeated us in a war, and now they want to share their food with us. What strange people, indeed.*

* * *

During the war, the Ludwig Shoe Factory in Selbitz had been used to produce shoes for the German military. But as the war wound to its end, production ceased, and so the third floor stored only a few pieces of equipment. The day before the Langers were shown to their new home, while the electricians and carpenters constructed the walls and created the two-room apartment—along with five others—the machinery was moved to an unknown location. On each end of the third floor of the factory was a small room containing a toilet, which, strangely, held no water but did have a faucet on the outside of each wall and a bucket sitting beside it. This was an unusual arrangement—each time the toilet was used, it had to be filled with a bucket of water in order for it to flush. It was more of a "toilet room" than a bathroom, as there was no bathtub—nor even a sink—in the small room. Each of the six new apartments on the floor, however, had its own washbasin with running water.

Elsa later discovered that the nearby schoolhouse had basic shower facilities in its basement that were available to the public. Six showers were separated by concrete walls, with shower curtains for privacy. The room also had two separate changing areas—one for the men, and one for the women. A small fee was required each usage to cover the expenses for a worker to keep the boiler fired up and for a cleaning lady to keep the room sanitary. Rudolf was able to obtain menial jobs in town that paid enough for the family to bathe at least once a week.

Maria appeared every few days or so to check on the Langers and to bring the much-anticipated food. The American army also provided kitchen utensils and canteens from which they could drink. One day, Maria's regular visit brought with it an unexpected surprise—two assistants carried in a small wood-burning stove and set it near the window. A metal vent was installed so that the smoke from the fire could escape the room. Elsa felt as if she was in heaven; now she could prepare her own meals for the family. Getting the new stove also meant that the sleeping arrangements were altered. Initially, Elsa and Rudolf shared one of the rooms, and the children shared the other. With the new stove in place, it was decided that the children all would sleep in the same room with Rudolf—Gerti and Rudolf on the cots; the boys on the large mattress—and Elsa would sleep in the room that had the stove. This was decided because Elsa was the first to rise and start the fire so she could prepare a hot breakfast.

On Maria's visit that day, she also explained that the local people again had been asked to help in whatever way they could. She shook her head sadly. "I'm afraid most of them haven't changed their attitudes, although some have offered to share things they no longer need."

"What exactly does that mean?" Rudolf asked.

"Simply put, I would suggest that you check the sidewalk in front of the factory each morning. You may be able to find some things you can use."

Following her advice, Rudolf and the boys would go down the three flights of stairs to the front of the factory. On most days, they returned empty-handed, but on others, they found veritable treasures. They managed to obtain a table, some chairs, and real dishes, which meant they didn't have to eat from the tin cans anymore. The items were all well worn, but each piece helped to make their sparse apartment more livable and more like a real home. Elsa hung the crucifix on the wall, where it would always be looking down upon them and, she hoped, provide them with blessings, which they could most definitely use.

It was about this time that Elsa decided that the family should begin attending church. She decided that their clothing mattered little to God or Jesus. The important thing was what they felt in their hearts and what they believed in their souls. Elsa was quickly disappointed, however, when she discovered there was no Catholic church in the town. The vast majority of Selbitz was of the Protestant faith. An extremely large and ornate Evangelical church was the centerpiece of the town—it had a tall bell tower with a clock face on each of its sides. Church elders made sure that the clocks were always accurate and that the bells were rung every fifteen minutes, day and night.

Soon after the Langers settled in to their new home, they were ordered to report to the Selbitz City Hall, where they received a *Flüchtlings Ausweis*—much like a passport for refugees. This step of their journey initially was difficult because their important papers and documents had been stolen with the wooden box. After much discussion and explanation, however, the Langers were given their official identification papers, which they were instructed to carry with them at all times.

While the family appreciated their new living space, it was quite noisy during the day. From early in the morning until late in the afternoon, the machines kept up their constant clamor and clatter. The building also had a pervasive odor from the production of shoes—oil, leather, glue, acetone solvents, and numerous chemicals that were offensive to the senses.

The days soon became weeks, and Rudolf continued to seek employment. In his travels during the day, he learned that Selbitz, in the northern part of Bavaria, was guarded and protected by the American military. The Russians controlled the eastern part of Germany, and the two forces were divided by electrified fences and had watchtowers, with soldiers who stood guard behind machine guns. The American military patrolled day and night because, Rudolf learned, the Americans did not trust the Russians.

The American military kept a high profile in the area and always was on alert. The largest American military base in the area was in Hof, approximately twenty-five kilometers away. American radar installations were on the Döbra Berg, about twenty kilometers away, and on the Ochsenkopf, forty kilometers away. The U.S. Army even set up camouflaged outposts in the surrounding forests along the border, with tanks and cannons that were similar to the one used to destroy the beloved Maria Hilf Chapel back in Hermannstadt.

The locals welcomed the Americans with open arms, grateful that they had brought an end to a war that had caused such pain and hardship for so many people. The Americans were very generous—the Red Cross collected packages, known as "care packages," from the United States and delivered them to the refugees. Elsa and Rudolf soon discovered that these wondrous boxes contained canned food, blankets, toiletries, and clothing—and some of the boxes even had the thoughtful addition of toys, dolls, and other items for the children. Clothing that didn't fit or things that weren't needed by one family often were passed on to others. Sharing became commonplace, so much so that it reminded Rudolf of the old days in Hermannstadt—the way that friends and neighbors would help each other. These were fond memories, yet for Rudolf, they often brought with them the feeling of loss and a sense of depression. This depression might have deepened when door after door was shut in his face as he looked for work, but Rudolf always was reminded of the powerful words Elsa had proclaimed on that fateful and painful day not long ago: "*It is not God's will that we are ruined.*"

* * *

As the summer months drifted toward autumn, the food supply from the Red Cross and the occasional care packages began to dwindle. Rudolf persistently looked for day labor, doing anything he could to earn even small amounts of money, which was always used to buy food. But even that wasn't enough to provide adequate nourishment for his family. It was at this point that the Langer children decided they could help to solve the problem. They now were allowed to go outside on their own to explore the area, as long as they stayed together, and an idea occurred to them. Carrying their empty C-ration cans, they would go to a butcher shop and say politely, "Excuse me, sir. If it wouldn't be a problem, could we possibly have the leftover broth you use to prepare your meats and sausages?"

The butchers they visited were very willing to fill their empty cans with the broth—they had no further use for it. Elsa was thrilled to have the broth and used it to create a soup or stew. Because this venture was so successful, the children also visited the local bakery, a place that felt familiar to them because of the time spent with their grandfather. Again, they politely asked for any old bread that had grown hard and could no longer be sold.

And again, the bakers were willing to comply—they were just going to throw it out anyway. Elsa soon discovered that steaming the bread over a pot of boiling water would bring the bread back to relative freshness.

Between visits to the butchers and baker, the children also would find wild vegetables in the nearby fields—beets, potatoes, and spinach leaves— as well as a wide variety of berries and nuts. Another responsibility the children accepted was the accumulation of firewood for their stove. The Langer children were mature beyond their years, doing whatever they could to help out the family—they accepted a work ethic that would stay with them for the rest of their lives.

Late one afternoon, as Rudolf was returning to their apartment after working for a farmer, he was struck with unbridled curiosity when he noticed a large group of trees, the likes of which he'd never seen. He walked into the grove and closely examined them—they were scruffy, gathered close together, with thin branches and a preponderance of soft but prickly needles. His mind began to churn, considering the possibilities. Looking to his left, he noticed a good-sized and well-kept farmhouse set back a hundred feet or so from the road. Immediately, he walked up to the house and knocked on the door.

A middle-aged man with a large belly and rosy cheeks opened the door. He looked up and down at Rudolf, as if he were examining him. After a moment, he spoke: "Help you with something?" The voice was high-pitched and friendly, an indication that he might actually be willing to help with something.

Rudolf smiled and pointed to the area where he'd seen the strange-looking trees. "My name is Rudolf Langer, sir, and I was wondering if you owned that stand of trees over there."

"Wish I didn't," the man snorted. "Every year I try to kill the things— I think they are of the lodgepole pine variety and are worse than scrub brush—but they just keep coming back."

"Perhaps I can be of assistance."

The man raised his eyebrows and studied Rudolf. "In what way?"

"I'd be willing to trim all the branches and take them away. Then, when the branches are gone, it'll be much easier to dig up the trees by their roots and be done with them for good."

The man rubbed his chin and squinted his eyes. "How much would you charge?"

"If you'll let me keep the branches, I'd be glad to do it for no charge."

"For free?" the man asked, wondering if he'd misunderstood.

"No charge," Rudolf repeated. "And if you'll let me keep the tree trunks, I'll help you dig those up as well."

The man offered a slight smile, extended his hand, and said, "You have yourself a deal. I have no idea why anybody would want those scruffy old things, but if you want them, they're yours."

Rudolf shook the man's hand vigorously. "I'll be here in the morning."

When Rudolf returned to the factory, he approached Adolf Ludwig, the owner of the factory, a man he'd met on several occasions and who had treated him with civility.

"Yes, Mr. Langer?" Ludwig said, after Rudolf captured his attention. "Is there something I can do for you?"

Rudolf nodded. "I was wondering if you might have a saw that I could borrow. I promise I'll take good care of it. I'm very good with tools."

"I'm sure we can find one that would be acceptable."

Rudolf beamed. "That's wonderful! Oh, yes, one other thing. Would you happen to have any long, narrow strips of scrap leather?"

* * *

The following morning, bright and early, Rudolf was working in the stand of trees, busily cutting off the strange and somewhat ugly-looking branches. Each time he had four or five branches on the ground, he would bunch them up and bind them together with the strips of leather that Mr. Ludwig had provided. After working all morning, Rudolf stopped briefly for lunch, then made his way back into town, stopping at each farm along the way.

When he knocked on the door of the first farmhouse, a woman with a pleasant smile answered. "Can I help you?" she asked. Her face was weathered, making her appear considerably older than she probably was.

"Yes, ma'am," Rudolf replied with a friendly smile of his own. "My name is Rudolf Langer, and I live in town. I was wondering if you could possibly use one of these fine brushes in your home." He held up one of the bundles of tree branches. "They're handmade, and they'll make your cleaning chores much easier."

The woman was immediately intrigued but just as quickly she seemed unsure. "I'd like very much to have one of those brushes, but I'm afraid I have no money."

Rudolf handed her the brush, letting her feel for herself how helpful the brush would be. "That's not a problem at all," he said with another friendly smile. "I'll be glad to let you have this brush in exchange for some eggs or perhaps a few slices of bacon."

"Yes," she quickly responded. "We can certainly do that."

Rudolf smiled to himself as he carefully protected the two eggs in his jacket pocket. His idea had worked—he'd just started his own business. With additional hard work, he would now be able to provide much-needed food for the family. When he got back home, after having conducted successful transactions at nearly every farmhouse, he emptied his pockets to Elsa's great delight.

"I can't believe it," she said, as Rudolf set the items on the table—eggs, bacon slices, half a loaf of fresh homemade bread, even a small pail of milk. "Where on earth did you get all this?"

"I started my own business, selling brushes," he announced with pride. "From now on, we will have plenty of food."

Elsa's eyes filled with tears of joy. "Tonight I will prepare a feast for the Langer family—a feast such as we haven't experienced in a very long time."

Rudolf's brush business proved to be quite successful—and quite fortuitous, in that the food and other items of necessity provided by the U.S. Army and the Red Cross continued to diminish on a weekly basis. In addition, autumn was near, which meant the children would be attending school and needing various materials for their classes. Soon after that, the weather would turn cold and they would need even more wood for their stove and additional clothing for everyone. These things all required money.

By this time, Rudolf had cut all the branches from the scraggly trees and visited virtually every business and residence in the town and surrounding area. This meant two things: he now could help dig up the trunks that would provide firewood for the winter, but he had exhausted nearly every potential customer in the area. Then, during one of his last stops on the far side of town, he encountered a tall, thin man, wearing a wide-brimmed fedora with a feather stuck in its brim, not unlike the one Rudolf wore. Before he could offer the brushes for sale or trade, the stranger asked with authority, "Your name is Langer, isn't it?"

Rudolf nodded, taken aback. He wondered, *how does he know my name?*

The man pointed at the brushes. "You're the one who took those worthless, scrubby trees, made those brushes, and started your own business."

"Yes, sir," Rudolf replied tentatively, growing more apprehensive by the second.

"Very industrious," the man stated succinctly. "I like that in a man. Shows you're not afraid of hard work."

"No, sir. I've worked hard all my life—until …" His words trailed off as he stared down at the ground.

"I understand," the tall man said. "Show me your hands." Rudolf did as he was told and after a cursory examination of Rudolf's hands, the man continued, "You've worked the land; worked with livestock."

Rudolf brightened. "Oh, yes, sir. In Hermannstadt I owned a farm with crops and animals, and—"

"I could use a man with your background around here," the man said abruptly. "Would you be interested?"

For a moment, Rudolf was speechless. Were his ears deceiving him? He quickly found his voice and answered, "Yes, sir. I'd be very interested."

"I have livestock that needs tending, and crops that need harvesting, and even a small forest that needs trimming for firewood on occasion. The work will be hard, and the pay will be low," he said without apology.

"Your farm sounds like the one I used to own. I would be honored to work for you."

"When can you begin?"

"I'll be here at sunrise," Rudolf promised.

"Good. My wife will have a hearty breakfast waiting and when we finish eating, I'll show you around and explain what needs to be done."

Rudolf bowed slightly. "Thank you very much. I'll not disappoint you." As he backed off the porch, he stopped and turned around. "I forgot to ask you something."

"What's that?" the man said.

"What's your name?"

"Hartenstein."

"Very good, Herr Hartenstein. I'll see you in the morning." Rudolf's heart and hope soared to levels beyond his own comprehension: a real job, a steady job, and a job that would actually pay him money. As he walked down the road, he pinched himself, not actually believing his good luck— but luck had nothing to do with it. This job had come as a result of hard work, persistence, and refusing to ever give up; from believing that some-day, somehow, things would improve. Rudolf smiled to himself, fondly re-membering Elsa's prophetic words: *"It is not God's will that we are ruined."*

* * *

The news brought unbridled joy to the rest of the family and a great sense of personal satisfaction to Rudolf. After nearly three months of vir-tually begging for any kind of work and canvassing the entire town and surrounding area to sell brushes, his efforts had finally been rewarded. He was now not only gainfully employed but also doing what he loved best. As he gave the blessing for the evening meal, he offered a special thanks to Mr. Hartenstein for the opportunity he'd made available.

The following morning as he walked to his new place of employment, Rudolf noticed a small wood-framed building beside the main house. A light was burning from within the structure, and it appeared there was a man inside, doing some sort of paperwork. Outside the building, Rudolf saw several bundles of wood, stacked high—the perfect size for kindling used to fuel stoves.

Precisely at sunrise, Rudolf knocked on Herr Hartenstein's door. He met his wife, had a large breakfast, and then went to work. Across the dirt road from the house were the barn and the stable that held the horses, cattle, and pigs. Rudolf was in a familiar environment and felt very much at home. He gently petted the horses in their stalls, speaking softly to each one.

"You're good with animals," his new employer commented.

Rudolf nodded. "If you're good to them, they'll be good to you."

"Wish more people felt that way," Hartenstein said.

Rudolf looked at him and offered a slight smile. "It would be a better world."

Hartenstein nodded. "Indeed it would."

Rudolf then helped Mr. Hartenstein to hitch two horses to one of several wagons in the barn and watched as his new employer drove away into the field without explanation. On the edge of the forest, perhaps two hundred yards away, stood another wooden structure, this one fairly large. Rudolf thought he heard a sound from that direction but couldn't quite make out what it was.

Throughout the remainder of the day, Rudolf carried out the balance of his assignments, again feeling a sense of self-worth as he fed the animals, milked the cows, sent them out to their pasture to graze, and sharpened some tools that were in disrepair. When the cows returned later that afternoon, he milked them again and delivered a shiny pail of milk to the back porch of the house. Following that, he cleaned the stalls in the stable and in the entire barn. As was his habit, he always did more than was asked or expected.

When Mr. Hartenstein returned to the barn as the sun was setting, he was pleasantly surprised. "I didn't ask you to clean all this," he said.

"It needed cleaning," Rudolf replied.

Hartenstein was impressed. "You're a good worker. Here are your wages." He handed Rudolf two marks—just about two dollars. It was not very much, as had been clearly explained, but it was going to be regular and steady—exactly what the family needed.

As Rudolf walked home, he passed the stand of trees that had provided the brushes he made by hand, and he thought, *As soon as I have a day off, I'll come back here and help dig up the trunks so we can have some additional firewood for the winter.*

Elsa was pleasantly surprised as Rudolf handed her the money he'd earned. They soon would be able to purchase some second-hand winter jackets for the children and curtains for the windows. Curtains had been unnecessary thus far—living on the third floor meant they were high enough off the ground that no one could see inside their apartment—but when the weather turned cold, it would be prudent to find something to cover the window to help keep out the cold.

For the first few days, Rudolf worked in and around the farm, tending to the livestock, mending fences, and doing general chores. Each morning he would look across the road at the wooden building beside the house. Several times each day, people would stop, enter the structure, come back outside, and leave with several bundles of wood. He found this interesting, but he never asked about it. Each morning, Mr. Hartenstein would get on his wagon and drive to the other structure in the distance, the one by the forest. Rudolf never questioned this either, even though he wondered where his employer was going. But after about a week, Mr. Hartenstein asked Rudolf to ride along.

They rode in silence for a few moments until Hartenstein asked Rudolf about his home—the one they were forced to leave when the Czechs occupied their town. With great pride, Rudolf told Mr. Hartenstein about his family, his farm, the animals, the crops they planted and harvested, and the friendships they'd developed over the years. With sadness, he also related the invasion, the cruelty of the Czech soldiers, the fate of Maria Hilf Chapel, the horrible train rides, nearly losing Fredi, and the time that they were forced to spend in Prague, Bayreuth, and Naila. He spoke of the hopelessness and despair, and of their being near starvation.

"You've had a difficult life," Hartenstein commented.

Rudolf nodded. "Yes, but we've also been blessed. Having the opportunity to work here, for you, is going to make things much better."

"You want to know how I actually knew your name when you came to my door last week?"

"I would. I was a bit surprised."

"You were highly recommended as a hard worker. I was waiting for your visit."

Rudolf's eyebrows shot up in surprise. "Recommended? By whom?"

The tall man suppressed a smile. "You'll know soon enough."

About ten minutes later, they reached their destination. Herr Hartenstein had not told Rudolf the entire truth concerning what he referred to as a "small forest." In fact, the forest on his farmland—filled with tall pine and oak trees—was quite large, spreading as far as the eye could see. But the biggest surprise of all came when he pulled the wagon to a stop in front of the large building that was situated beside the Selbitz, a narrow but rapidly flowing river. A buzzing and whirling noise emanated from the bowels of the building, creating more curiosity. It was a sound Rudolf recognized.

"You told me about the forest you owned," Hartenstein began. "Perhaps you'll appreciate this."

They got down from the wagon, entered the building, and Rudolf's eyes widened in surprise. The building—an old sawmill—contained a large circular saw that cut logs of various thicknesses into planks. Underneath the gleaming, whirling, three-foot blade was a pit, which collected sawdust. The room also had a large piece of equipment that planed the wood planks until they were smooth to the touch. Two workers, covered from head to toe with sawdust, waved a greeting to their employer.

"This is a wonderful place," Rudolf said, slightly in awe.

"I had a feeling you'd like it. Come with me; I want to show you something."

Rudolf followed Mr. Hartenstein outside, where he saw a wooden bridge covering the river. On the other bank were great piles of logs, felled from Mr. Hartenstein's forest, waiting to be cut and processed into useable lumber. Mr. Hartenstein pointed about a hundred feet down the river. "Look at that," he said with a degree of pride in his voice.

Rudolf could see a vertical saw next to the river, but it appeared to be quite old—it was rusted by years of harsh and unforgiving weather. Beside the saw was an old waterwheel that continued to turn slowly, around and around.

"The waterwheel used to provide the energy to run the saw," Hartenstein said. "But the years have taken their toll, and it no longer works."

"It's wonderful," Rudolf said. "I wish I could have seen it in operation."

"It was a sight to behold." Without warning, a swirling wind cut through the trees and chilled them both; they pulled their collars tighter against the cold. "Let's go back inside," Hartenstein said, and Rudolf nodded agreement. As he followed his employer, he noticed an unusual device by the side of the building. It was made of steel, about two feet long, and looked like an upside-down U. Good-sized stacks of lumber and smaller logs, about fifteen inches long, were piled beside the machine. As they entered the building, Hartenstein commented, "Perhaps when the harvesting is finished and the livestock has been cared for, you'd be interested in working here as well."

Rudolf stood straight and tall, just as he had taught his children. "Oh, yes, Herr Hartenstein. I'd like that very much."

One of the other workers joined them, wiping the sawdust from his face as he held out his hand. "Hello, Rudolf," he said. "It's good to see you again."

Initially, Rudolf was taken aback, wondering how this man knew his name. Then he recognized him—it was Adolf Gross, a neighbor from Hermannstadt who used to help Rudolf on his own farm. "Adolf!" Rudolf exclaimed. "How did you get here? Where are you living? Is your whole family with you?"

Adolf and Herr Hartenstein broke into laughter at Rudolf's barrage of questions. "All in good time," their employer said. "Working together, you'll have plenty of opportunity to catch up on the old days."

Rudolf shook his old friend's hand vigorously. "It was you who recommended me?" he asked, his face still filled with astonishment and disbelief.

"I said you were a good worker and an honest man."

"I can't begin to thank you enough."

"You can show your thanks by working hard for me," Mr. Hartenstein said, not unkindly.

Rudolf smiled broadly. "I surely will," he promised. Then, feeling more confident in his new role as employee, he asked, "What was that strange machine outside? The steel one that looked like an upside-down U?"

"A bundling machine," Herr Hartenstein replied. "I sell wood to people so they can cook and heat their houses and businesses."

"That's why people are always stopping at the building beside your house," Rudolf surmised.

"Very observant," Hartenstein said with a smile. "I believe Mr. Gross has recommended a very good employee."

As Rudolf walked home that evening he couldn't stop smiling. Now he knew he would have employment through the fall harvest, then through the winter—and had been reunited with an old friend from home. He appreciated the remarkably good news as if it were a miracle. Little did he know, as he continued his brisk walk home, that another small miracle was taking place at exactly the same time.

TEN

THE LUDWIG SHOE FACTORY WORKERS HAD ALL RETURNED to their homes for the evening, so the incessant sounds of the great machines were silenced. Elsa was taking her turn cleaning the communal washing trough on the first floor—something she and her neighbors on the third floor ensured was done on a daily basis, as well as cleaning their own hallway and the stairs that led to their floor.

"Mrs. Langer?" said a voice from behind her.

She turned quickly, startled. No one, other than her fellow tenants on the third floor, was supposed to be in the building. "Yes?" she answered tentatively.

When the man stepped from the shadows, she could see it was Mr. Ludwig, the man who owned the factory. He heard the concern in her voice. "I didn't mean to startle you," he said.

"No ... it's just that ... well, I didn't think anyone else was here."

"I offer my apologies."

"Completely unnecessary," she replied, wiping her hands on a dry towel. "Is there something I can do for you?"

Mr. Ludwig cleared his throat, a habit he had before speaking. "I've noticed how well you and the other tenants take care of the hallway and the stairs. That's very thoughtful, and I wanted you to know I appreciate it. It's a good example for my other workers."

"Thank you," Elsa replied demurely.

"And I've also noticed how you're always thoughtful enough to clean the wash basin each night after everyone else has gone home."

Elsa was slightly confused. "We're glad to help. It's a small way of thanking you for your generosity. But … I am curious about something."

"What's that?"

"How did you know my name?"

Again, he cleared his throat. "I've noticed you more than the others. You seem to be very conscientious and thorough with the work you do, even though it's without pay."

Elsa began to relax a little. "I used to run a large household and stayed very busy. I enjoy working. It gives me a sense of worth."

"That's a trait that is difficult to find these days."

Elsa nodded, and she said with a hint of sadness, "But soon my children will all be entering school, and I'll have too much time on my hands. It's a troubling thought."

"That's why I wanted to talk with you," Mr. Ludwig said.

Elsa eyes widened. "You wanted to speak with me?"

Mr. Ludwig smiled. "Would you consider working for me? Here, in my factory?"

Elsa was taken aback. "But what would I do? I have no skills. I'm a simple housewife and mother. Do you need a cleaning woman?"

"I will teach you how to operate one of my machines."

"Oh!" Elsa said, ducking her head in embarrassment. "I could never learn to do such a thing."

Mr. Ludwig shook his head. "I've watched you work. I have no doubt that you could learn. And as you said, when your children start to school, you'll have plenty of time on your hands." He offered a kind smile. "And just think … you'll certainly be close to home."

Elsa already knew she would accept, but she asked, "Would it be all right if I spoke with my husband about it and gave you my answer in the morning?"

Mr. Ludwig's smile broadened. "That would be perfectly acceptable." And with that, he offered a slight bow and walked back into the shadows, returning to his office.

* * *

"But you've never worked anywhere in your life," Rudolf said. "Certainly not with anything like those machines." It was clear he wasn't comfortable with Elsa's working outside their home.

"Mr. Ludwig is convinced I can learn. He handpicked me over anyone else he could have chosen. We can certainly use the money, and I'll be here every afternoon when the children get home from school." Her argument was as convincing as it was practical.

Rudolf sighed resignedly. "Is it something you really want to do?"

"From a realistic standpoint," Elsa argued, "I think it's something I *need* to do. And we know he's a fair man—providing us with a place to live, loaning you his tools."

Still, Rudolf's protectiveness overshadowed the reality of their circumstances, and he argued again, "Do you really think you can learn how to operate one of those machines?"

Elsa smiled. "I learned how to take care of you and our children. How hard can a simple machine be?"

He returned the smile; her logic had won him over. "All right, then. Give it a try, and we'll see how it works."

Fredi had been listening attentively to their conversation, and now he excitedly questioned, "Can I help you, Mama? I'll be good, and I can learn too."

"You'll be busy with your schoolwork," Elsa explained.

"But at least you'll let me watch," he added hopefully, pleading for the opportunity to be close to the magnificent pieces of equipment as they functioned.

She patted the youngster on the head. "We'll see. All in good time." Then she turned toward Rudolf, smiling broadly. "I can't believe you found Mr. Gross. It'll be so good to see someone from home."

"It's a miracle," Rudolf said.

Elsa looked at the crucifix on the wall, but this time, her small but knowing smile was for herself. *A miracle indeed*, she thought. *Thy will be done.*

* * *

That autumn, the Langer family adopted a new routine. Early each morning Rudolf would go to the Hartenstein farm and assist several other workers with the harvesting, cutting the tall grass by hand with scythes and sickles and then turning it into long rolls that would become hay to feed the livestock during the winter months.

Not surprisingly, Elsa mastered her new job quickly and became proficient at operating the clicker press, a machine that had a bed plate made of hard wood, placed over a piece of thick steel. Its operator would place leather sheets on the plate and then the clicker die—similar to a cookie cutter but made of heavy steel with a razor-sharp edge and bent to a specific shape—would slam down on the bottom and stamp out the leather patterns. It was an exacting, if monotonous, position, one that called for extreme concentration in order to avoid serious injury. It also provided the opportunity to meet some new people and, Elsa hoped, by her actions and work ethic, change their attitudes toward those considered to be *Flüchtlinge*—the results of which would be widespread and beneficial.

The largest change occurred when the children began school. Gerti, Rudi, and Willie had hoped to make new friends, but initially, this proved difficult—they were looked down on as refugees, a result of the clothing they wore and the fact they spoke Sudeten German, a different dialect from the High German most of the students used. Fredi was the most apprehensive because he was entering the first grade, his introduction to the educational system. He was both nervous and excited as Elsa prepared meager lunches and reminded her children to pay attention to their teachers and mind their manners. "You're already registered at the school," she told them, "so you should report to the main office as soon as you get there." Before the children left, she gave each of them one mark. Fredi stuffed it into his pocket, even though he had no idea why he would need it.

The four Langer children walked to the nearby school building together, the older ones teasing Fredi about how difficult school would be and that he would probably get into trouble. Noticing his growing concern, Gerti scolded her other brothers and took Fredi under her wing, reassuring him that everything was going to be fine.

The school, formally known as the *Volksschule*, had eight grades, and the school building, next to the City Hall, was nearly as large as the factory where they lived. It had a red-tiled roof and three floors with several classrooms—and it was all very confusing to the children. As they entered the structure, they were greeted by obvious stares from the other students. Gerti wore a scarf over her head, but because the boys' heads had been shaved not that long ago, barely a stubble of hair was showing. Whispers, giggles, and hurtful comments filled their ears.

They reported to the main office and gave their names; Gerti, Rudi, and Willie were each assigned different classrooms. The secretary looked through a batch of papers and finally looked down at the youngest of the four. "I'm sorry," she said, "but I don't have registration papers for anyone named Fredi Langer." Fredi stared at the floor, confused, a little frightened, and close to tears. The secretary kept shuffling through her papers, and then said, "Would your name happen to be Alfred?"

"Yes, ma'am," he replied in a soft voice.

The woman offered a comforting smile. "Well, that explains everything. You're registered as Alfred." She whispered, as if she was sharing a secret with the youngster. "It's all very official, you know. We have to use legal names, not nicknames."

"Oh," Fredi responded, not understanding what she had tried to explain.

Gerti walked Fredi to his classroom and gave him a warm hug. "Just remember what Mama said, and you'll be fine."

"But why are they all laughing at us?" he asked innocently.

"Because our hair is so short," she answered. "But don't let it bother you. It'll grow back."

Fredi was greeted by his teacher, Frau Wölfel, an attractive young woman with dark hair and a friendly face. "What's your name?" she asked, offering him a welcoming smile.

"Fredi," he replied.

Frau Wölfel looked at a chart she was carrying, frowned, shook her head, and said, "I don't have anyone named Fredi listed here."

Fredi bowed his head and said meekly, "I'm sorry. I guess my new name is Alfred."

Frau Wölfel smiled again. "Ah, yes, here it is. Welcome to my class, Alfred." And with that, she led him to his assigned seat.

Fredi was the only *Flüchtling* in the class and as such, he received strange looks from his classmates, especially due to his lack of hair. In looking around the room he noticed three distinct things that set him apart from the others: his clothing was nowhere near as fine as his classmates' clothing. While his lunch consisted of an apple and two slices of bread in his jacket pocket, all the other students had paper bags or lunch pails underneath their chairs. And—strangest of all—on each of the other desks sat a cone-shaped container, nearly a foot tall. This, more than anything, made him feel out of place because he didn't have one.

The teacher read the children's names from her chart, introducing them to each other and asking them to say hello and greet their neighbors. Fredi said hello to a boy named Herrman Lautenschläger. Herrman seemed a nice enough fellow, not taunting, like most of the others. Once the introductions were completed, the teacher picked up pieces of slate, which she referred to as a *Schiefertafel*—Fredi had no idea what the strange object was or for what purpose he would use it, but he soon learned that the children would write on it with chalk. He also learned why his mother had given him money that morning—as Frau Wölfel gave each child the slate, the student would hand the teacher one mark.

A man entered the room, carrying a camera. Fredi had seen such things before but had no real knowledge of how they worked or what they actually did. One by one, Frau Wölfel asked the children to come to the front of the room, where, as each held the strange, cone-shaped object, the man took the student's picture. When Fredi—now Alfred—was called he walked to the front of the room, empty-handed and embarrassed. Several of the children began to giggle. "Please be quiet," Frau Wölfel said sternly, and the laughter subsided. "You're being impolite, and I will not tolerate that in my classroom."

At lunchtime, the children went outside to eat. Fredi held back, wanting to be the last to leave so he could speak with the teacher. "Frau Wölfel?" he said timidly.

"Yes, Alfred."

"May I ask you a question?"

"Of course, dear. What is it?"

"What are those cone-shaped things that everyone has?"

Frau Wölfel sat down in a chair so she could look at Fredi at eye level. "I forgot; you're new here," she said softly. "The cones are called *Zuck-*

ertüten."

He cocked his head to one side, confused. "What's that?" he asked.

Frau Wölfel thought for a moment, wanting to make her explanation as easy as possible to understand. "Mostly, it's just a tradition. Do you know what that means?"

"I think so."

"That's good. The cones are filled with sweets. Candies. The grandparents or parents give them to their children for the first day of school, and they have their pictures taken with them."

"Do they eat the candy in school?" Fredi asked.

"No. They have to take the *Zuckertüten* home after school. Then they can open them."

Fredi nodded, somewhat sadly. Frau Wölfel clasped her hands together and rested her chin on them. Looking deeply into Fredi's eyes, she said, "You don't have any money to pay for your schoolbooks, do you?"

Fredi shook his head, embarrassed. "I didn't know I needed to have money."

She patted him gently on the head, the same way his mother and father did. "Well, don't worry. I'll make sure you have the books you need."

"Thank you, ma'am."

Frau Wölfel smiled again and suggested, "Why don't you go join the other children and have your lunch?"

The other students were seated at a small grouping of tables, and everyone seemed to be talking at once. When Fredi appeared, they all stopped talking and stared at him. He wasn't quite sure what to do. Finally, Herrman Lautenschläger, the boy he'd met in class, motioned for him to come over and sit beside him. All the others had their sacks or lunch pails before them and were eating a variety of fine-looking food—thick sandwiches, puddings, cakes covered with icing.

Fredi bowed his head and offered a silent blessing. Then he slowly removed a piece of bread from his jacket and nibbled on it, as the other children continued to stare. Under their glaring eyes, he took out his apple and took a small bite. No one said anything, but he could feel their eyes boring into him.

Herrman took a bite of his own sandwich and asked, "Why does your head look all funny?" His tone was conversational; he wasn't taunting or making a judgment. "What happened to your hair?"

Fredi took a deep breath and bravely lifted his chin. He stared straight ahead as he replied, "The Czech soldiers stole our home and our farm. They took everything we had, even my little dog. They made us ride in a train car where many people died. We had no food to eat for a long time. Then, when we finally stopped, they shaved all of our heads."

The table remained silent, but now it was for a different reason—now the other children were embarrassed and ashamed of the way they had treated their new classmate. After finishing their lunch without further comment, everyone returned to the classroom, where Frau Wölfel announced, "Children, for our first day in class, we're going to learn about sharing. Does anybody know what that means?"

Fredi knew—he had lots of experience with sharing—but chose to not raise his hand.

Frau Wölfel smiled as she explained, "Sharing means you let others use some of the things you don't need. That way, you can all feel good about yourselves, because you've helped someone else. Does everyone understand that?" Most of the children nodded their heads. "That's good. Today we're going to practice sharing so you can see how good it makes you feel. Okay?" They nodded again, and Frau Wölfel continued, "Alfred is a brand new student. He just moved to our town from a place far away. So, all of you who have extra paper or coloring pencils to write with that you don't need can share them with him."

At first, no one was sure what to do. Finally, Herrman reached over and handed Fredi two different colored pencils. Then, others began to do the same—nothing big, just a few pencils and a few pieces of paper. Frau Wölfel was pleased. "Alfred?" she prompted him.

Fredi stood up, looked around the room, and quietly said, "Thank you. Thank you, everyone." And then to their surprise, he offered, "Your parents should all be very proud of you." The rest of the children and the teacher were speechless.

Frau Wölfel distributed several books to the children, excluding Fredi, and told them to be very careful with them. "Books are valuable, as well as important," she reminded them. At the end of the day, Fredi stopped at his teacher's desk, as she had requested. She smiled at him. "Alfred, what you said today to the other children was very nice." She handed him three used books. "These will get you started. I'll have more for you later."

"Thank you very much, ma'am. I'll take good care of them."

"I know you will … and another thing. Tomorrow, the other children will have some sort of a bag to carry their books and their slates. I'm sorry, but I don't have one of those to give you."

"That's all right," Fredi assured her. "I can carry them just fine." Walking home with his sister and brothers, Fredi clutched the books and slate as if they were priceless treasures. During dinner, as everyone talked about what all they'd done that day, Fredi casually mentioned the book bag his teacher had mentioned. "Frau Wölfel says the bag will keep our books and slate dry and safe. But … I guess I don't really need one." He understood that his family could not afford to provide one for him, and he accepted this.

Later that evening, Rudolf used a piece of canvas from a discarded army cot, some pieces of unused wood from the sawmill, and some leftover leather straps from the shoe factory, and he constructed a book bag for Fredi to take to school. The next day, Fredi's bag was the envy of all the other children, and his teacher was enormously pleased. Although some of the children continued to tease him, the book bag was the first step in his beginning to feel like he fit in.

Almost every day, Fredi would eat his lunch with Herrman, his new friend. And every day, as Herrman ate a thick sandwich filled with several slices of different cold cuts—Herrman's father owned one of the butcher shops in town. His sandwich was so big that he could never finish the whole thing and always threw away at least half of it.

After several days of watching Herrman toss away half his lunch, Fredi asked quietly, "Do remember what teacher said about sharing?"

Herrman nodded. "Yes, why?"

Fredi scratched his chin. "I was just wondering. Since you throw away half your sandwich every day, would you share that half with me, so that good food will not go to waste?"

"Sure" was his simple reply.

With that, Fredi was able to eat a healthy lunch every day—and Herrman could tell his parents that his entire sandwich had been eaten.

* * *

Acceptance of the refugees did not come easily. Some of the Selbitz residents would not acknowledge or allow the *Flüchtlinge* into their social strata or circle of friends. For a while the children were referred to as *Igels*—porcupines—because of their stubble of hair as it slowly grew back in. Several times, Rudi and Willie got involved in fistfights because of a demeaning and taunting comment. When this occurred, Rudolf would acknowledge their right to stand up and defend themselves, but and each time Elsa also would firmly explain that fighting was never a solution to anything.

Rudi and Willie felt conflicted—they respected their mother's words, but they also talked between themselves, wondering what might have happened if the people of Hermannstadt had stood up and fought for their rights and their property. They knew the concept by itself was unrealistic, but they couldn't rid themselves of the feeling that surrendering to a bully should never be an option.

The first winter in Selbitz brought additional challenges but the Langer family was prepared. After school and on weekends, the children stopped at the butcher shops and the bakery, collecting broth and stale bread. They also cleverly discovered another means of income: gathering the foil from discarded cigarette packs. The foil had a paper backing, but it would separate from the foil when soaked in water. After discarding the paper, the children would create a ball of foil, and when it reached three or four inches in diameter, they could sell it to a scrap dealer for a few marks. Sometimes they would also venture into nearby fields after the harvest, especially those that had been planted with potatoes. After the harvesting and picking, there was always an abundance left in the ground. Digging in the cold, hard dirt was difficult and tiring, but each time they did, they returned home with an ample supply of vegetables.

In addition to Elsa's expertise in the kitchen, she soon became proficient at working the clicker press. so much so that Mr. Ludwig offered her the opportunity to work some overtime hours whenever she was able. In exchange, he offered to provide fine leather boots for the children and Rudolf at a greatly reduced price. Without hesitation or consultation, she accepted his generous offer.

Other than the chilling walk on those winter mornings to Herr Hartenstein's farm, Rudolf thoroughly enjoyed his new position. Following a hearty breakfast with Herr Hartenstein and his wife, Rudolf would perform his chores in the barn and then join his employer for a ride to the sawmill. He usually worked alongside his old friend, Adolf, and he treasured the conversations they had with each other. Rudolf particularly liked working in the sawmill in the winter; two large stoves kept the building at such a warm temperature that the men could work in their shirt sleeves.

Such was not the case in their apartment. The only thing to provide warmth in their two rooms was the stove in the room where Elsa slept. The second room was never warm enough for comfort. It was difficult, however, to maintain regular warmth from the kitchen stove because wood had to be added on a regular basis or the fire would burn out. Elsa and Rudolf would take turns getting up during the night to feed the fire, but as a result, they weren't able to get a decent night's sleep, which made the following day's work more difficult.

Another problem with using the wood stove was the effort necessary to provide enough wood on a daily basis. One day Rudolf noticed a wagon in the corner of the sawmill. It was rusty and appeared that it hadn't been used for a very long time. It gave him an idea. "Mr. Hartenstein?" Rudolf began.

"Yes, Rudolf."

Rudolf pointed toward the wagon. "Is anyone using that?"

"Nope," Mr. Hartenstein replied. "Just taking up space. Been here for years."

"Would it be all right if I used it?" Rudolf asked.

"With my compliments. We could use the space."

Adolf helped Rudolf to grease the wheels and shine up the wagon, and within a few hours, it looked as good as new. Rudolf's plan was to use the wagon to collect firewood on his way home that evening. The amount of wood he found, together with the few pieces the children always carried home, kept them reasonably warm for the next two days.

From then on, the children used the wagon on Saturdays and on two days each week after school to collect enough firewood to keep the stove burning for a week. Still, the small stove simply couldn't warm the entire apartment on frigid winter evenings. Finally, Rudolf created a solution. He knew a man who owned a combination scrap metal/junk lot establishment on the edge of town. The man had numerous empty, fifty-five-gallon oil drums in his scrap yard, and when he heard Rudolf's idea, he was so intrigued that he agreed to help. First, the man used a blowtorch to cut off the top of the oil drum, making a replaceable lid. At the bottom of the drum he cut a small rectangular opening and installed a hinged door. He also cut a circular hole in the drum to install an oven pipe that would lead out the window for the smoke to escape, once the contraption was mounted in the second room of the apartment.

To use this makeshift heater, Rudolf would lift the hinged door and insert sawdust—which was readily available without charge from the sawmill—and pack it down tight. Then he would strike a match to a piece of paper, place it in the drum with the sawdust, and close the hinged door. This would cause the sawdust to smolder, and as it slowly burned, this strange creation would effectively generate heat for as long as eight hours. Each Saturday morning, the boys would go to the sawmill, crawl into the pit underneath the large circular saw, fill several burlap bags with sawdust, and then haul them back home. Carrying them up to the third floor proved to be remarkably messy, but Elsa always made sure the sawdust was cleaned up afterward, so as to not damage their reputation for cleanliness.

The family also used the wagon for excursions into the woods, where trees had been cut down and stumps were left. Using shovels, saws, axes, mallets, and crowbars—all tools borrowed from the sawmill—they would dig the stumps from the ground and cut them into usable sizes of wood for their kitchen stove and the makeshift heater in the bedroom. Elsa proved to be an integral part of the team effort. She wielded an ax; dug with her hands, if necessary, to unearth stubborn stumps; and assisted in hauling the much-needed fuel back to their home.

One winter's day, Rudolf took Fredi to the sawmill. The child was mesmerized, wanting to know how everything worked and exactly what it did. Mr. Hartenstein noticed Fredi's enthusiasm with the equipment and, taking a liking to the youngster, he offered Fredi the opportunity to earn some additional money. He took Fredi outside and showed him the strange piece of equipment Rudolf had noticed the first day he visited the sawmill—the upside-down U-shaped thing. "This is a bundling machine," Mr. Hartenstein explained as he demonstrated how it worked. "You load pieces of wood into the machine, wrap a string of baling wire around them, and then pull really hard on the handle—that tightens the wire. Once it's tight, you cut the wire with these scissors, and you're done." He looked down at Fredi, whose face was beaming in a huge smile. "I know you're only seven years old. Do you think you can handle the bundling machine?"

Fredi nodded vigorously. "Yes, sir! I sure do."

"Each bundle has to be about twenty inches thick—just this size." He smiled and winked at Rudolf. "You really think you can handle that?"

"Oh, I know I can!" Fredi assured him. Then he added, "If it's all right with my father."

When Rudolf nodded his approval, Mr. Hartenstein said, "Tell you what I'll do ... you can work on Saturdays. Bundle as many as you want, and I'll tell you where to deliver them—you can use your wagon for that—and I'll pay you a nickel for each bundle. How's that sound?"

"That sounds fine to me," Fredi enthusiastically replied. "I'll be a good worker."

"I believe you will." Mr. Hartenstein said. He smiled and extended his hand, which Fredi shook with vigor.

Each Saturday, Fredi would go to the sawmill, prepare several bundles of wood, and deliver them, as promised. His second delivery produced a pleasant surprise. The man at the door, noticing how small Fredi was and how hard he was working, gave him a tip of one mark. With this as motivation, Fredi worked harder and longer, usually coming home at the end of a long day with three and sometimes four marks, all of which went into the family fund. Fredi never asked for anything for himself; he knew that he was contributing to the family, and that alone gave him great satisfaction, as did the fact that his parents were noticeably proud of him, as well as the rest of their children.

Disaster fell for Fredi in the form of the first snowfall. The wagon was useless in the deep snow, as it was impossible to navigate. It seemed that Fredi's firewood-delivering days were effectively over until spring. He became despondent over the uncontrollable situation and felt bad that he was letting everyone down. Rudolf took him to the sawmill, as usual, although Fredi didn't understand why—there was nothing for him to do if he couldn't bundle and deliver the firewood. Upon entering the building, however, his mouth dropped open in complete surprise, as his father and Mr. Hartenstein stood with broad smiles on their faces. In front of Fredi was a small sleigh, just his size, with slats on each side enabling it to carry firewood.

"That sleigh hasn't been used for years," Mr. Hartenstein explained, "but now, Fredi, if you wish, you can use it to deliver wood to our regular customers."

Fredi beamed; he was thrilled to be back in business.

Work for the Langer family never seemed to stop, but their collective efforts proved to be worthwhile. They had a warm place to live, a decent and healthy amount of food to eat, and relatively new clothing. Perhaps most important of all, though, was the knowledge that, as Elsa had once proclaimed, "It is not God's will that we are ruined."

ELEVEN

FREDI WOKE UP EARLY ON THIS CHRISTMAS EVE MORNING, stretching his arms and legs. The makeshift stove had kept the room warm all night, and he'd slept soundly. It was still dark outside, but morning light came later in the winter. Even so, he was surprised to discover that Rudolf was already gone. *Probably in the other room*, he thought. He entered the room, where his mother was stoking their other stove, but his father was nowhere in sight. "Where's Tata?" he asked.

"I don't know," Elsa replied, chewing on the corners of her mouth to suppress her smile. "When I woke up, he was already gone."

Fredi shrugged. "I guess I'll walk to the sawmill by myself, then."

"Before you do, sit and have some fresh bread with marmalade," his mother urged. "It'll warm you up. You can't always be in such a hurry."

"But I have deliveries to make," the boy protested.

"Another fifteen minutes won't ruin anyone's day."

Fredi sat down and laced up his new leather boots, telling his mother, just as he did each time he laced them, "Thank you for the boots, Mama. They're very warm."

"You're welcome, dear. But you don't have to thank me every day."

Just then, the other children entered the room, also stretching, also asking where their father was. And again, Elsa replied that she didn't know.

The children all moved toward the door at once to use the toilet down the hall.

"It's my turn to go first," Willie said.

"You went first yesterday," Rudi reminded him.

"I'm the girl," Gerti announced. "Girls go first. You should all know that." She filled the bucket with water and was out the door before anyone could protest—though none of them would have.

Rudi looked out the door and called after her, "Don't be too long." With six of them using the same bathroom—as well as the other families on the floor—there occasionally were uncomfortable moments.

Fredi's brothers laced up their boots as Elsa prepared the bread and marmalade, humming a soft tune to herself. The boys all looked at each other, their eyes wide with surprise.

"Mama hasn't sung since we left our house," Rudi whispered. "What's going on?"

When Gerti returned she handed the bucket to Rudi, who filled it up and left. As Gerti washed her hands, Fredi whispered, "Mama was singing." She turned to look at her youngest brother, understanding the significance of Elsa's humming a tune. *Something* was going on, but no one quite knew what it was. The day seemed to begin as normally as any other Saturday. The boys had their miscellaneous chores to do, and Gerti, as she did each Saturday, would assist Elsa with the washing of clothing and bedding. Still, something seemed out of sorts.

After all trips were made to the bathroom, everyone finally sat down for breakfast. They had just closed their eyes for a prayer when the door opened and Rudolf entered.

"Where have you been, Tata?" Gerti asked.

"Just doing some errands," he replied casually.

"What sort of errands?" Rudi said.

"Questions, questions, questions," Rudolf said. "That's all you children ever have."

Fredi scratched his head, puzzled. "But, Tata, you told us it was good to ask questions. That's how we learn things."

"You're right, son. Just eat your breakfast and dress warmly, and all your questions will be answered soon."

To their parents' amusement, the children ate their food as quickly as possible and then grabbed jackets and scarves. "We're ready!" they announced in unison, excitement clear on their faces.

"You, too, Elsa," Rudolf said with a wink. "And don't forget to bring some blankets along."

Now the children were truly intrigued. It had been a long time since they'd had a surprise, and their anticipation and excitement grew with every step as they made their way to the first floor. Rudolf opened the front door of the shoe factory, and the children gasped in delight when they saw a horse-drawn sleigh. They looked at their father, wondering what they should do next.

"Well," Rudolf said, trying to suppress his own excitement, "it's not going to be there forever. Everybody in. And wrap yourselves in the blankets."

No further encouragement was necessary. The children piled into the back seat, and Rudolf assisted Elsa into the front. Before he could crack the whip, the questions began anew: "Where are we going?" "What about our chores?" "Where'd you get the sleigh?" "Can I ride the horse?"

"In good time," Rudolf replied. "Just sit back and enjoy the ride." He smiled warmly at Elsa. It had been a very long time since the family had the opportunity to do anything together. Today would be a special day. Driving through the center of town in the sleigh, which Mr. Hartenstein had loaned them, the Langer children felt like royalty, as if they were as rich as some of the other children in their school. They laughed and poked at each other and sang songs that had been learned in a place now far away, but songs that would remain in their memories forever—the joyous songs of Christmas.

The sleigh turned off the road, passing Mr. Hartenstein's house and heading toward the forest. Ahead, they saw a picture-perfect scene: tall, dark-green trees covered magnificently with pure white snow. Memories of home filled their minds, memories of better times, memories of Christmases past. *Could it be?* they all wondered. They nearly held their breath in anticipation as the sleigh entered the great forest and came to a stop. Rudolf turned in his seat and calmly said, "Well, come on, everyone. We have to pick out the perfect Christmas tree."

The children gave a loud whoop and jumped off the sleigh. As they romped in the snow, any thoughts of chores or other work that day was forgotten. The family was together, enjoying a perfect holiday. Their merriment was all the greater for the fact that the children had been certain that there would be no Christmas for them that year. While others at their school talked of great feasts, and parties with friends and family, and services at the massive church on Christmas Eve and Christmas Day, the Langer children had expected the day would pass like any other—delivering wood, collecting sawdust, and gathering frozen potatoes from nearby fields. Now, those unhappy thoughts couldn't have been farther from their minds. Rudi laughed as he packed a snowball and fired it at Willie, missing him by a mile. Willie fired back but hit Fredi instead. Fredi joined in the snowball fight and within seconds, even Gerti was a participant. Rudolf and Elsa watched their children with a glow of satisfaction. They held hands, thankful for the opportunity to see their children laughing and playing. Since their long ordeal first began, their lives had been nothing but hardship and work and hunger. Today, at this very moment, all that was forgotten.

Rudolf grabbed an ax from the rear of the sleigh and began to hike toward the trees, with Elsa by his side. The children scrambled after them, still laughing and throwing snow at one another. "Over there!" Rudi shouted. "That's the one!"

"Too small," Rudolf replied. "We're going to have a tree that reaches our ceiling." The children squealed with glee.

"There it is," Gerti said, pointing.

"Too skinny," Rudolf pronounced. "We want a fat one, big and round."

After about ten minutes of searching, the entire family suddenly came to a complete halt as they found themselves standing in front of what was most certainly the perfect tree. No words needed to be spoken; they all knew this was the one. They walked around it, checking every branch, making absolutely sure it was perfect. Everyone smiled and then nodded. Rudolf gave it a firm shake, removing most of the snow. Then, with great ceremony, he picked up the ax and gave a mighty swing at the base of the tree. He stood straight up, seeming to consider something, then handed the ax to Elsa. "You take a swing," he told her. "This is going to be a real family tree."

Initially, Elsa was surprised by his suggestion but then recognized the significance of the gesture. She took her own swing, and then handed the ax to Gerti. In order, by age, the children all took a turn, and Rudolf made the final swing, knocking the tree to its side, which was greeted with a large cheer from everyone.

They dragged the tree back to the sleigh, tied it on the rear, and made the return trip home. Bundled under the blankets, their cheeks rosy and their eyes sparkling, the children sang songs and laughed with excitement and happiness. The Langer Christmas, while not as grand or glamorous as many of the others in Selbitz, would be a wonderful celebration after all.

Planning ahead, Rudolf had prepared a base for the tree—two narrow boards nailed to the bottom of the tree. Dragging the large tree up three flights of stairs proved to be a challenge, but unlike lugging the bags of sawdust or bundles of kindling, this task was met with more laughter. When they stood the tree up on its trunk again—in among the stove, sink, table with six chairs, a cabinet for dishes and utensils, and Elsa's cot—it filled the room.

"Do you boys still have a ball of the tin foil?'" Rudolf asked.

"Yes, Tata," Rudi replied, wondering why his father had asked.

"Well, I think that instead of selling it as you usually do, you should unwrap it, tie the pieces together, and use it to decorate our new tree." It was a brilliant idea, which was enthusiastically accepted. Then, as an additional surprise, Rudolf reached inside his jacket pocket and produced a handful of small candles. Smiling as he held them out to the children, he added, "Perhaps you can use these as well."

Everyone was speechless. They would have a tree—their very own family tree—that was exactly like the one they'd always had at home. The children were ecstatic, their eyes bright with joy. Elsa turned away, as her own eyes filled with tears.

When Rudolf returned the sleigh to Mr. Hartenstein's barn, the boys created a great length of tinsel out of the tin foil and carefully wrapped it around the tree. They also cautiously attached the candles to various branches, making sure they were spread far enough apart so as to prevent a fire. While they busied themselves with this, Elsa and Gerti washed potatoes and beets for the main portion of their meal. They even created a very special treat for dessert—*Mohnschlitschken*, a layered cake. They began by buttering a slice of white bread, then soaking it in milk. After that, they covered the top of the bread with a generous layer of poppy seeds and then topped it off with sugar. Five layers of this was placed in a circular pan and baked until it was crispy brown. It provided an incredible delight for anyone's palate.

When Rudolf returned home, he was carrying a burlap sack. The children gathered around him again to see what this surprise might be and saw that the sack contained a whole chicken, already plucked of its feathers and ready to cook. Elsa clasped her hands over her heart, barely able to believe her eyes. Rudolf reached into the sack again, and this time, he pulled out six apples—one apple for each of the children, which would be placed underneath the tree—they would be able to follow their time-honored tradition!—and two more apples that would be placed inside the chicken to add to its flavor. The children and Elsa gathered even closer to Rudolf and embraced each other in a group hug.

"The tree looks wonderful," Rudolf said, as the boys beamed with pride. "And our home is filled with delicious aromas."

"Not nearly as delicious as it soon will be," Elsa said, her smile lighting up her face. As she and Gerti prepared the great feast, Rudolf and his sons talked about the excitement of the sleigh ride, playing together in the snow, the adventure of choosing the perfect tree, the decorating, and even about the work each of them was fortunate enough to have. Rudolf carefully led the discussion, interjecting the importance of principles, honesty, and integrity. He explained the consequences of exercising proper morals and ethics—values he hoped would take seed in their young minds and have a lasting effect.

Although Elsa was happily busy in the kitchen and thankful for their blessings that Christmas, she missed the joy the family experienced while attending church services at Maria Hilf. She also missed their friends and neighbors and wondered where they all were and how they were getting along. And she missed the comfort of their former home, even though she was immensely grateful that the family was still together.

As the sun dipped below the horizon, the table was set and the Christmas feast began. The blessing Rudolf offered was longer than usual and much more from his heart than he usually offered. When he'd finished, Elsa quietly recited the true meaning of the day, the birth of their Lord Jesus Christ. With a face filled with love, she glanced at the crucifix on the wall and thanked God for the blessings they had received. This would be a Christmas that would last in their hearts and memories forever and ever.

* * *

Christmas Day provided another unexpected event. The Langers stayed at home, relaxing and nibbling on leftovers from last night's wonderful meal. In truth, Elsa and Rudolf—and the children, too—felt a twinge of guilt because they were not working somewhere. After dinner, the children went outside to play in the snow—for them, this frolicking was a rare treat.

As Rudolf sat at the table, reading the newspaper, Elsa watched her children through the kitchen window. Seeing them at play caused her to miss their home in Hermannstadt. Rudolf sensed her melancholy. This had been too good of a day to have it spoiled by sad reminiscences. He stood up, put on his jacket, and handed Elsa's jacket to her. "Put this on. We're going for a walk."

"It's nearly dark," she protested.

"The perfect time for a walk."

She shrugged as he helped her into her jacket and then followed him down the stairs and out into the brisk air. "Children!" he called out. "We're going for a walk." They were delighted. It didn't matter to them where they were going; the fact that they were together was motivation enough.

A light snow was falling as they walked the two blocks to the town square. As they got closer, they could hear music. The square was decorated with bright lights, hanging in front of the stores and twinkling in the moonlight. The entire scene looked magical, unlike anything the children had ever seen. A large contingency of townspeople were in a bright and festive mood as they stood in front of a group of musicians and sang songs of the season: "*Stille Nacht, Heilige Nacht*," "*O, Tannenbaum*," and several other well-known tunes. The Langer family joined in, feeling for a fleeting moment as if they actually belonged here.

Across the square was a *Wirtshaus*—a pub—filled with happy and boisterous revelers, who also sang loudly. Rudolf grabbed Elsa by the arm and gave her a wink. "We've worked enough. Tonight, we will celebrate." And with that, they entered the pub, the children in tow and their faces filled with anticipation and wonder.

Herr Tunger, the rotund owner of the *Wirtshaus*, greeted them as they entered the establishment. He smiled, his lips barely visible under a large handlebar mustache, and thrust a tray at Rudolf and Elsa that held shot glasses containing Jägermeister. Rudolf and Elsa each took a glass and quickly downed it. "Take another. Take another," Herr Tunger insisted. They smiled in return as they accepted his generosity.

The large room, constructed from dark oak, was packed with happy people—men, women, and children. Rudolf and Elsa made their way through the crowd to the bar, where they were offered another shot glass. The belly-warming liquor created a sense of kinship. This evening, there were no *Flüchtlinge* and locals. They were all simply pleasant and congenial residents of Selbitz, all having a wonderful time. The children enjoyed sweet-tasting soft drinks, and everyone sang their hearts out.

Later, as they walked home, the children threw snowballs at each other until their hands could no longer stand the cold. They looked back at their parents and saw that Rudolf and Elsa were holding on to each other, slipping and sliding in the snow, and still singing.

That night, after everyone was fast asleep, Fredi lay awake in the bed that he shared with his brothers. He had said his prayers as usual, offering a blessing and a hope that Fritzl had found a new home and was happy, but his mind would not rest. He walked to the window, appreciating the warmth of the sawdust stove, and he looked up at the brilliant stars above as he thought about all that he and his brothers and father had spoken about the day before. While he truly didn't comprehend everything that had been said, it was still meaningful. He also thought about what his mother said just before they ate their fine meal—the true meaning of this special day. He was thankful for his parents, his brothers, and his sister; for all they had worked so hard to accomplish; and even for the small apple that had been placed underneath the Christmas tree for him.

* * *

There was no school on the days between Christmas and New Year's, and the majority of people in Selbitz took the time off to relax or to vacation in other places. This was not the case for the Langer family; they all went to work—Rudolf at the sawmill, Elsa in the shoe factory, and the children performing their various chores. On New Year's Eve day, however, they had time to relax again. Gerti had heard about an unusual tradition that took place in Selbitz and the surrounding area, and she suggested they all give it a try. On New Year's Eve day, youngsters would go from house to house, knocking on doors, and wishing the homeowners a happy New Year. It was the custom that each time a "Happy New Year" was offered, it was rewarded with a small gift of money, usually a few pennies. By the time the Langer children had visited well over fifty houses, they collected nearly twenty marks—for them, a small fortune.

The first day back at school after New Year's was filled with excitement. Most of the children were wearing new clothing and bragging about the gifts they'd received for Christmas, the relatives who visited, or the places they'd visited. The Langer children didn't participate in any of these animated conversations. New clothing was nice, but they had plenty of clothes. A relative's visit might be enjoyable, but they didn't have room for anyone anyway. And although vacations sounded interesting, they were happy to stay at home and spend time with their own family.

Frau Wölfel asked each of her students to tell something about their favorite Christmas present. One by one, the children stood and described the gift that was the best or most pleasing. It seemed to Fredi that the children were trying to outdo each other; that they somehow felt superior if they'd received better or more expensive gifts than their classmates.

When Fredi's name was called, he smiled broadly and proudly stated, "I got an apple."

The room went silent, including Frau Wölfel, who seemed to not know what to say. Then his classmates taunted him:

"That's all?"

"You just got an apple?"

"Were you bad?"

Fredi's head snapped from side to side, looking at each of the voices, not understanding why the other students seemed to be mocking him.

"That's enough, class," Frau Wölfel said firmly. "You're being impolite, and if it continues, I'll tell your parents." The room grew instantly silent, and Frau Wölfel spoke with compassion. "Alfred, I think it's very nice that you received an apple. There are many children who receive nothing at all for Christmas. All of you are very fortunate." She smiled at Fredi as she continued, "Alfred, can you tell us why the apple you received was so special?"

Fredi thought for a moment, then said, "Every year, after we put up our tree, our parents put an apple underneath it for my sister and brothers and me. It's what you call a ..." He hesitated, unable to think of the word he wanted. He looked hopefully at his teacher. "Do you remember on the first day in school, when all the other kids got those cone things, and I asked you what they were?"

"Yes."

"I asked you why they did that, and you said it was a ... it was a ..."

"Tradition?" she asked.

"Yes. That's it! Tradition. Our parents give us apples because it's a tradition. It's something we've always done. Our family has all we need."

Frau Wölfel was emotionally touched by the little boy's words and had to look away.

At lunchtime, the cold and snowy weather prevented the students from eating outdoors, so they ate their lunches inside, seated at their own small desks. Herrman leaned closer to Fredi's desk and asked, "An apple was *all* you got?"

"Yep."

"No clothes?"

"Got plenty."

"No toys?"

"Don't have time for toys."

"Well what did you do on Christmas Day?" Herrman asked.

Fredi explained in great detail the most wonderful day of his life—the sleigh ride, exploring the magnificent forest, the snow-covered tree, the decorating, the fabulous meal, the joy of being with his family. As he spoke, the other children left their desks and gathered around Fredi, listening to his every word. By the time he finished his description, although he couldn't be certain, it seemed to Fredi that many of them were wishing that they, too, had received a small apple at the end of such a perfect day.

* * *

The relentless winter finally gave way to spring, and with the melting of the snow came the replacement of the sleigh with the wagon. Pulling the heavy sleigh loaded down with firewood during the bitter winter months had provided Fredi with a strong and sound body, more so than anyone else in his age group. He didn't pay much attention to his new physique, but his classmates noticed—and because of it, he was no longer picked on as he had been when school first began.

The coming of spring and decent weather brought another change in their lives. Elsa decided it was finally time for them to begin attending church. After working as hard as they had, they finally had saved enough money to purchase some new clothing. On the first Sunday they attended church, they all dressed in their fine new attire, and Elsa led the family procession as they walked to Naila, about three and a half kilometers away. Seeing the town again brought back many memories, most of them unpleasant, especially the time their precious wooden box had been stolen. Still, Naila had the closest Catholic church. Elsa was initially apprehensive, but the family was welcomed into the church with open arms. The kindly priest made them feel at home and comfortable, not at all like they were generally treated in Selbitz. Even though Fredi attended church when he was younger, this was the first time he was old enough to truly appreciate it. He found the pomp and circumstance of the Catholic Mass fascinating. He listened closely and paid attention, just as he did in school, even though he was totally confused, as the Mass was said in Latin. Elsa spent the time on the walk back home to try to explain what it all meant.

On most Sundays, Rudolf would accompany the family to church, but occasionally, work prevailed and he was unable to attend. On those occasions, their next-door neighbor, Herr Ulrich, would walk along with Elsa and the children to Naila. The Langer children especially appreciated those days because Herr Ulrich was always kind enough to secretly hand them a ten-penny coin after the service was completed—just the right amount for them each to purchase an ice cream cone.

Summer arrived and provided a respite from the long days spent in the classroom, but those hours were replaced by outside work in various activities. Fredi was now working five and a half days a week. Mr. Hartenstein had increased Fredi's customer route, now that he was out of school for the summer, so that he could stay busy and earn additional income. Each of the Langer children worked diligently through the summer. Rudi assisted a tile setter, mixing grout, and Willie helped out on construction sites. They continued to work part-time as school began again.

Fredi considered learning an exciting challenge. With each year he became more fascinated with all things mechanical and how they worked. It was not surprising that he developed an affinity for mathematics because the two subjects were connected, each one contributing to a clearer understanding of the other. That year, a new gymnasium and several classrooms were being added to the school, and at every available opportunity, Fredi would disappear to the construction site and watch the workers. He was curious about the functions of the tools they used and often asked the workers about them.

His curiosity carried over to the following summer, when he figured out how to use the wood-bundling machine more efficiently than it had been used in the past. With a few simple yet creative moves, he was able to generate nearly a hundred bundles of wood on each Saturday. Delivering them throughout the week earned Fredi an income of about ten marks, plus tips—a huge amount of money for someone his age.

While delivering wood one afternoon, Fredi became determined to earn even more money and devised a plan to do so. Fredi convinced Herr Hartenstein to enlarge his delivery route, and he obtained another serviceable wagon. Then Fredi hired the son of one of Herr Hartenstein's employees to become his assistant. Fredi paid the youngster three cents per delivery and let him keep all the tips he received—Fredi also received two cents for each bundle delivered by his assistant. In this way, like his father before him, Fredi created his own successful business.

With their collective incomes, the Langer family finally reached a point of not having to scrimp or deny themselves small luxuries. All the money they earned was placed into a family fund, and the children were each given a small allowance, which they could spend on anything they wished; they also were allowed to use a portion of the money they earned for special things—such as the used ice skates that the boys all chose to buy that winter. They enjoyed going to the Selbitz River, tightening their ice skates to their boots, and joining several others in gliding across the smooth ice. Chilling wind swept across their faces as they raced each other up and down the river and underneath the stone bridge, with City Hall and the schoolhouse in the background. They could even see Schirner's Kiosk underneath a large tree, now devoid of leaves, where they painfully had waited that first evening in Selbitz for someone to take them into their home. That was a sad day indeed, but now all that had changed—thankfully—for the better.

* * *

News of the world outside of their small town was now easier for the Langers to obtain. Rudolf learned that during the five long years of the war, millions of German soldiers had been killed or were missing in action. Virtually every family in the country had felt the effects of Germany's losing the war—many lost loved ones, most lost a once comfortable standard of living.

Because of the decimation of the male population, beginning in 1949, the German government strongly encouraged families to have children by providing a subsidy—a monthly support payment for each child born, until that child was eighteen years of age. This program, known as "Das Deutsche Wirtschaftswunder," became an enormous success, assuring a new generation of Germans to rebuild the country.

One family, in particular, was beneficially affected by this financial subsidy.

TWELVE

KARL HEINZ LANGER WAS BORN ON JUNE 27, 1948. AS THE other children were hustled outside to play, he was delivered in the Langers' small, two-room apartment, with the assistance of a midwife. He entered the world, screaming at the top of his lungs. Rudolf decided he would be called Heinz.

Outside, the other children excitedly discussed the new baby. "I wonder if it's a boy or a girl," Rudi said.

"I hope it's a girl," Gerti replied. "We could use another girl around here."

"Where will the new baby sleep?" Willie asked.

"With Mama, silly," Gerti said, "until he gets bigger. Then he'll have his own bed."

The boys looked at each other with wide eyes. Their two small rooms were already crowded, especially now that they were acquiring belongings of their own. Where would they put the new baby's bed?

After the children had been outside for about an hour, they were called back into the apartment. Gerti raced past her brothers to ensure she got there first. "It's a girl, isn't it?" she asked optimistically.

Elsa held the small bundle to her breast, smiled, and answered, with a voice weakened from the ordeal, "You have a fine, strong little brother."

"Oh," Gerti said, somewhat disappointed.

"Can I see him?" Fredi asked, entering the apartment behind Gerti.

"Of course you can," Elsa answered.

Rudolf smiled to himself, fondly remembering the time, not that many years ago, when Gerti had asked the very same question about Fredi. Elsa pulled back the tiny, warm blanket, revealing the infant.

"He's so little and so red," Fredi observed. "Can I touch him?"

Rudolf smiled again.

"Gently," Elsa quietly replied. Fredi placed his forefinger on the infant's arm, and it was the softest thing he'd ever felt in his life—and he was in awe of the miracle that had taken place.

Three days later, Elsa was back at work at the shoe factory, although navigating the three flights of stairs proved to be a challenge for the first week or so, until her strength returned. There were other challenges as well. As Gerti predicted, Heinz slept with his mother until Rudolf built a small crib at the sawmill. Materials were readily available, and Rudolf constructed a quality piece of furniture. It was placed in the kitchen, where Elsa could attend to him when he cried in the night, doing her best not to interrupt the sleep of the others in the next room. But the biggest challenge for the family was childcare. Rudolf and Elsa both had to work—it was a necessity. The only realistic solution was to give the daytime responsibility of Heinz' care to his siblings.

Gerti loved the responsibility and fawned over their baby brother. This arrangement worked well for the remainder of the summer, but with the coming of autumn, the family was faced with another challenge—who would care for the baby when the older children returned to school? After much discussion, it was determined the children would take turns staying home from school one day each week to care for their baby brother. Initially, the idea was well received—they all liked the idea of having a day off from their studies and boring lectures—but they quickly discovered that caring for an infant was not a vacation. The idea that they would enjoy missing school also proved to be incorrect, as there was homework to do on the days they each stay home, and it had to be done while trying to feed, change, and care for Heinz. As a result, they often fell behind in their studies.

Still, life for the Langers seemed to be changing for the better. In addition to the new member of their family, another welcome change was that the family was able to purchase a large bed for the three boys—the first time they'd slept in a real bed in more than two years. While comfortable, however, the bed only added to their space problems. All the children had clothing, school books, bags, ice skates and boots, and even skis, all of which took up space. Their cozy apartment was beginning to feel very crowded.

* * *

One day each week, Elsa washed the bed sheets in a washtub before leaving for work. Whoever had the responsibility of caring for Heinz on that particular day would finish the job by taking the wash to the riverbank to bleach the sheets. On Fredi's day that week, he pushed Heinz in his stroller, while pulling the wagon loaded down with the wash behind him. Once they reached the River Selbitz, Fredi spread the sheets out on the grass, filled a watering can from the river, and then drenched the sheets with water. With the help of the blazing sun, the linen was soon bleached a snowy white. While waiting for the sun to do its work, Fredi rolled the stroller into the shallow water by the edge of the river, as he often did, and let the cool water gently rush over the baby's feet. Heinz always enjoyed this—it seemed to soothe him and provided Fredi with a little relief, as the baby amused himself by paddling his feet in the water.

Once they returned home, Fredi decided to take Heinz for a ride in his wagon. He often pulled Heinz around the town, smiling and waving to people on the street; it was satisfying entertainment for the toddler. On this day, Fredi decided that he would like to ride along with Heinz—all he needed was a little incline to get them going and a wooden pole to use as a brake. Nordstrasse was the perfect street—built on a high hill that led to a flat bottom. Fredi walked about halfway up the street, climbed behind Heinz in the wagon, and together, they rolled down the hill. Fredi held the wooden pole in front of the wagon and pushed down on it to slow them down. After the first few runs down the street—to the vast amusement and entertainment of both boys—Fredi wanted to make the ride even more exciting. This time, he pulled the wagon farther up the hill, farther than they had ever been before.

"Hold on tight!" he instructed his little brother. And the great ride began. The wagon rolled fast, and then faster, then even faster! Heinz squealed with glee, his blond hair tousled by the wind. Fredi, however, was not enjoying this ride. He quickly discovered that control of wagon was escaping him. He pressed the wooden pole against the pavement, again and again, in a desperate attempt to slow them down, but it was no help; they were already going too fast. The wagon continued to pick up speed, fairly flying down the hill, as Fredi pushed down harder and harder on the pole, grinding it into the street without results. And then …

The pole caught in a pothole in the street, causing the little wagon to cartwheel into the air. Heinz went flying over Fredi's head, and Fredi bounced on the street and rolled over several times, as the wagon crashed into a nearby bush. Heinz was screaming, as Fredi, ignoring his own scrapes and bruises, rushed to his brother's side. Heinz' blond hair was covered in blood, a sight that caused Fredi great alarm. He quickly retrieved the wagon, placed the still-screaming Heinz into it, and made his way home as fast as his bruised legs would allow. Once back at the factory, he was relieved to see that Heinz' wound had stopped bleeding and actually was only superficial, not the massive wound he'd thought it to be. Fredi cautiously eased up the stairs without being noticed and then did his best to clean up Heinz and calm him down, knowing there was only an hour before their mother would return to their apartment.

When Elsa arrived, she was not pleased with what she discovered. Following a stern glance at Fredi, who tried to explain what happened, she carefully examined Heinz, who began to cry again upon seeing his mother. She cleaned his bruises and applied bandages; then she attended to Fredi. The leather strap made him learn his lesson the painful way—no more long rides down the sloping hill would be in his future.

A few days later, Fredi joined some other boys along the Selbitz River for a favorite pastime—pole-vaulting the narrow part of the river. Taking turns, each boy grab a long, sturdy pole, run toward the water, insert the pole into the center of the river, and catapult himself to the other side. Each successful attempt was met with loud cheering from the others. When it was Fredi's turn, he clenched the pole tightly, dashed toward the river, and jammed the pole into the middle of the river. Unfortunately, he hadn't been running fast enough to propel him to the other side, and he got stuck, hanging on to the pole, suspended, in the middle of the river.

The other boys waiting on the riverbank convulsed with laughter as Fredi wondered what he should do next. He didn't have long to think about it, though. Within a few seconds, his weight on the pole caused it to slowly bend over, depositing Fredi into the River Selbitz. He just stood there, in water up to his waist, feeling completely humiliated.

He could hear the laughter of the other boys as they rode off on their bicycles, leaving him, alone and soaked to the skin, sitting on the riverbank. Fredi didn't know if he was more dejected that the others had laughed at his predicament or that he was the only one in the group who did not have his own bike. While waiting to dry off, however, he decided that somehow, he was going to have his own bike.

The next day, after completing his deliveries, he walked two blocks from their apartment to a small shop that sold bicycles, which was owned by Ernst Seidel, a trim and fit young man with a shock of blond hair. "Mr. Seidel," Fredi said, "I'd really like to have a bike, but I don't have very much money. Do you have any used bikes for sale?"

Ernst Seidel was sympathetic to Fredi's dilemma and appreciated his sincerity. "Tell you what," he said. "I have a lot of discarded parts behind the shop. Let's go take a look and see what we can find."

Behind the shop was a veritable junkyard, filled with various parts that were rusted, bent, broken, and in general disrepair. Fredi's heart sank, but Mr. Seidel optimistically told him, "You're more than welcome to look through all this stuff and see if you can find anything that might be use-able."

Fredi scrounged through the abundance of parts—bent wheels, flat tires, broken chains—searching for nearly an hour, until he found a frame, some slightly bent handlebars, pedals, a chain, and even some inflated tires that still had useable tread. When he walked back inside and presented them to Mr. Seidel, Fredi asked, "How much would all this cost?"

"Tell you what," Mr. Seidel said again. "You've picked out some pretty good stuff. I'm impressed. You come back tomorrow, and we'll see if we can put something together."

The next day—and for two afternoons after that—the two of them worked side by side until the bike was finally assembled. If a tire rim was bent, Mr. Seidel straightened it. If a bearing was rusted, he polished and greased it until it worked as good as new. If the chain was missing a link, he replaced it. Fredi watched intently as each procedure was accomplished, always asking questions, fascinated to learn how and why things worked. When the bike finally was completed, they both looked at their work with a smile of satisfaction.

But Mr. Seidel still had not mentioned a price, so Fredi cautiously asked, "How much do I owe you?"

Mr. Seidel smiled broadly. "I've really enjoyed working with you. You've been a good helper and a fine student."

"Thank you, Mr. Seidel," Fredi replied. "But how much do I owe you?"

Ernst Seidel patted Fredi on the shoulder. "You did most of the work yourself, but because I've enjoyed working with you so much, I've decided there will be no charge."

"No charge?" Fredi repeated, not sure he'd heard the man correctly.

"No charge."

Fredi's face was wreathed in smiles. "I really appreciate that … but it doesn't seem fair."

Mr. Seidel waved away Fredi's concern. "I know you have older brothers. Perhaps when they want to purchase a bike, and when you're ready for a new one, you'll think of me."

Fredi nodded vigorously, unable to believe his good fortune. "I'll repay your generosity," Fredi said. "I promise I will. And I promise I'll tell my brothers and all my friends about you."

"Enjoy your bike," Mr. Seidel said, smiling as Fredi pushed his bicycle out the front door. The youngster waved as he rode down the street on his very own, nearly brand new bicycle.

* * *

Elsa frowned thoughtfully. She seemed to be against the idea that Fredi had just presented to her. "I really think you should be saving your money for school," she said. "It's a noble gesture, but it's just too much."

"But you also said if something was really important, we could use our money for that," Fredi argued logically.

Elsa smiled; she could see that her nine-year-old was not to be dissuaded. "This is really important to you, isn't it?"

"It's important to him as well," Fredi insisted. "I think it's important for all of us."

"How will you explain it to him?" she asked.

"I'll keep it a secret and won't tell him until we're there," Fredi explained. "Besides, if it hadn't been for him, I wouldn't be able to do it."

"How much will you need?" she asked, and Fredi could tell his mother was softening.

"I've already checked. About a hundred marks."

She shook her head worriedly. "I don't know, Fredi. That's a great deal of money." Then, looking into his face, she was taken by his sincerity. Finally, she nodded. "All right. I'll keep it a secret as well. When are you going to do it?"

Fredi beamed. "Next week."

The following Saturday, Fredi and his father were standing on the railroad platform, the son looking pleased but the father seeming annoyed. "We should both be working," Rudolf said gruffly.

"Herr Hartenstein agreed to let us both have the day off," Fredi reminded him.

"You know I don't like secrets," Rudolf responded, "especially when those secrets cost us money." Rudolf always had been a frugal man, and he was unable to comprehend not working when work was available. He also was uncomfortable with not knowing what was going on and conceding to the wishes of a nine-year-old, even though he knew that Fredi would never do anything without thinking it through. He sighed, wondering what it was that his son had planned.

The train ride to Hof took about thirty minutes. Hof was nearly ten times the size of Selbitz and was a major shopping center for all the communities in the surrounding area. There were theaters, several restaurants, and specialty stores. The town, surprisingly, had been relatively untouched by the war.

As father and son walked down the sidewalk past finely dressed people, Rudolf muttered, "This is a waste of time. We should both be at work."

Fredi suppressed his smile as he led his father into the Anders Department Store, the largest establishment in town.

"What are we doing here?" Rudolf asked.

"You'll see," Fredi replied. They walked to the men's clothing department, which was filled with a wide assortment of new clothing and accessories.

A salesperson approached them, offering a broad and welcoming smile. "Good afternoon, gentlemen," he said. "How may I be of service?"

Fredi pointed to his father. "We want a brand new suit for him," he said.

Rudolf looked from Fredi to the clerk and back to Fredi, his confusion clearly written on his face. "I'm afraid there's been some sort of a mistake," he told the clerk.

"No mistake at all," Fredi replied. "That's exactly what we want."

The clerk smiled. "Right this way," he said, moving toward the area where countless suits were displayed on wooden hangers.

"What's this all about?" Rudolf asked in a stern tone.

"I'm going to buy you a suit," Fredi said.

"You most certainly are not!" Rudolf replied firmly.

Fredi placed his hand gently on his father's arm. The youngster spoke softly, clearly, and from his heart. "Tata, you've done everything a father could possibly do for his family. You take care of us, and you got me a fine job. I want to do something nice for you. It's my way of saying thanks."

Rudolf turned away, fighting to control the emotion that swelled inside. He patted Fredi on the head, a gesture of appreciation and love.

The clerk held up a fine suit. "How about something like this?" he asked.

"It's beautiful," Rudolf said softly.

"Pick out whatever you like best," Fredi encouraged him. "I want you to have whatever you want."

Rudolf looked at several styles, each time looking toward Fredi for approval. And each time Fredi would reply, "Get the one you want."

Finally, after much deliberation, Rudolf chose a suit that was light tan in color, nearly like sand. It was a modern-looking suit with a matching vest and was made of thick, quality wool that would last for many years. Fredi also insisted that his father get a crisp white shirt and a matching tie. It was a fine ensemble.

On the train ride back to Selbitz, as Rudolf clutched the box that held his brand new suit, he put his other arm around Fredi's shoulders and pulled him closer to his side in an unspoken gesture of appreciation.

The following Sunday, Rudolf wore his new ensemble in public for the first time. On the walk to Naila and at church, people stopped to compliment him on his fine suit. Each time, he pointed to Fredi and proudly announced, "My son bought it for me."

THIRTEEN

SUMMER SEGUED GENTLY INTO FALL, AND FALL INTO WINTER. That New Year's, the children carried on with their newly acquired tradition of going door to door in the blustery weather, wishing people a happy New Year and receiving a small compensation for their efforts. The best treat of all that New Year's, though, was the addition to the family of Harald Langer, born January 2, 1950.

The family routine remained the same as ever, with Rudolf working at the sawmill, Elsa at the shoe factory, and the children with their own jobs and chores. The children continued to each attend school four days a week and stay home one day to take care of Heinz—and the new baby, Harald.

Rudolf built a larger bed for Heinz so that Harald could sleep in the crib; they both remained in the kitchen with Elsa. Whenever time permitted, Rudolf would look for a larger space, but none was available in the price range they could afford. The saving grace was that the only time that the entire family was home together was at dinnertime, when they were sleeping, and for breakfast in the morning.

Winter soon gave way to the new season, and one fine spring day, Fredi was engaged with several other children in a rousing and boisterous soccer match on the street in front of the shoe factory. The score was tied, and the excitement was at a fever pitch. Everyone was running full speed, back and forth, yelling at the tops of their voices. Suddenly, one of the boys looked at a pocket watch and screamed, "It's time to go!" The game came to an abrupt halt.

Fredi stood in the middle of the street, confused, as the entire group stopped the game, picked up the ball, and walked away. Curious, he followed behind them as they walked briskly into a nearby forest. Trying to keep up with their pace, he called out to them, "Why did we stop playing? And where are we going?"

The others looked at him and replied matter-of-factly, "We're going to the cabin. It's time for Brother Matheus' *Jugendstunde*." Fredi was still confused, but one of the boys explained to him that the Jugendstunde was an hour each week that was specifically designed and devoted to the youth of the town. Brother Matheus was the director of the town's Evangelical youth groups. He had been responsible for building a log cabin where the children, aged five through fifteen, would gather for games, singing, and spiritual instruction. Fredi remembered seeing Brother Matheus many times—a gentle young man who had a way of reaching out, touching, and making a positive impact on the children.

When the group reached the rustic-looking log cabin, Fredi optimistically asked with great innocence, "Can I come in with you?"

The others stopped in their tracks and stared at him disdainfully. "No, you're a *Flüchtling*," one responded, as if it was some sort of a communicable disease.

"And a Catholic," another one chimed in.

"The cabin is only for Evangelicals," a third one said. "You're not allowed."

Fredi felt tears well up in his eyes as he watched the other boys enter the cabin. He felt as alone just then as he had when he was five years old and lost at the railroad station. He sat down dejectedly on a nearby log, wondering why his family was so different from the others, as he valiantly fought back tears.

Brother Matheus came walking up the path and noticed Fredi and his obvious dismay. He looked down at the youngster and quietly asked, "Why aren't you inside with the others?"

Fredi swiped at his eyes as he answered, "They said I wasn't allowed because I'm a *Flüchtling*. I'm a Catholic."

Brother Matheus sat down beside him and put a comforting hand on his shoulder. His voice was calm and reassuring, "You must be excited about your new church being built."

"Yes, sir," Fredi replied, although the new Catholic church's construction in Selbitz had been the last thing on his mind.

"What's your name?" Brother Matheus asked.

"Fredi."

The man offered a sincere smile. "You know, Fredi, even though people are different and sometimes believe different things, God loves us all. Do you know that?"

"Yes, sir, I do."

"Do you understand that?"

"Oh, yes, sir. My parents taught me."

"You must have very nice parents." He thought for a moment and then said, "Do you ever feel like you're alone, Fredi? All alone?"

Fredi looked up into the man's compassionate eyes. "Yes, sir. I feel that way right now."

Brother Matheus nodded wisely. "I have something very important to tell you. You're never alone because God is always with you. He's always in your heart."

Fredi smiled again. "That makes me feel better."

Brother Matheus stood up and extended his hand. "Would you like to come inside and join the others?"

"I'd like that very much," he replied. "But they don't want me."

"Come with me, son, and we'll see."

Fredi took Brother Matheus' hand, and side by side, they walked into the cabin, where the other children were running and jumping and having great fun. Brother Matheus raised his hand and the pandemonium ceased. "Boys," he said in a calm and clear voice, "This is Fredi, a friend to most of you. I want you to know and understand that all children are welcome at the Jugendstunde."

With that simple explanation, Fredi became a part of the group.

Brother Matheus began the meeting with a prayer, and then everyone sang songs and played games. Brother Matheus gathered them in a semicircle and told fascinating stories from the Bible—told in a way that Fredi had never heard before. Brother Matheus' explanations were expressed in a way that could be understood by all the children in the room. At the close of the meeting, they said another prayer and then went their separate ways.

As Fredi walked home, the warm feeling he had when he was part of the group stayed with him. For one hour, he'd felt as if he had been given the opportunity to finally fit in. For one brief hour, he actually felt accepted. When he entered the apartment, he looked at the crucifix hanging on the wall with a completely new and different perspective.

* * *

By the time Fredi—or Alfred, as he was now known—was eleven, he had formed friendships with several other boys his own age—Peter John, Gerhard Plessgot, Erich Weinczik, and Klaus Wiesel. They referred to themselves as a "band of brothers" and would do everything together whenever they were able. They rode their bikes on great excursions, especially in the summertime, when they would go to Naila to frolic in the public swimming pool. Sometimes they would walk to the Königsee, an abandoned stone quarry that had filled with water, creating a small lake surrounded by high, imposing cliffs. They normally went there after dark and swam in the nude. Even though there were shallow areas in the quarry, it still remained a remarkably dangerous pastime—and that was part of the fun for the mischievous boys. The boys were just as impish in the classroom, always whispering to each other, passing notes, annoying other students, and poking at each other.

Herr Eckhardt was their teacher in the sixth grade, and after issuing several stern warnings to the boys, he finally decided he'd had all he could take. He abruptly stopped the lesson he was teaching and shouted out their names. "Peter, Gerhard, Erich, Klaus, and Alfred! Step to the front of the room!"

Their classmates giggled as the five boys reluctantly moved to the front of the room and stood in front of the podium where Herr Eckhardt usually delivered his lectures. The teacher faced the boys with a stern glare. "You have disrupted this class for the last time!" he barked at them, enraged. "Your parents will be notified of your childish actions, and you will be severely punished!" Out of the corner of his eye, Herr Eckhardt noticed that Alfred had placed his hand in his pocket. While unintentional, it was seen as a sign of disrespect. Herr Eckhardt became even more furious. He drew back his hand and, with an enormous swing, slapped Alfred across the face. The blow carried such force that it knocked Alfred backwards and off balance. He fell over the podium, knocking it over, and tumbled against a tripod that held the blackboard. Alfred landed on the floor as the podium, blackboard, sponges, chalk, books, and assorted papers fell on top of him. The entire class jumped to its feet in total disbelief; many of the girls shrieked in horror. Then, everything seemed to freeze in time, and the room was immersed in total silence.

Through the pile of rubble, Alfred slowly raised his hand, which was holding a handkerchief. He'd not been showing any disrespect toward his teacher; he merely had been reaching for his handkerchief, trying to blow his nose. Herr Eckhardt realized his mistake but was not about to acknowledge it or offer any apologies. "Pick up the mess you've all made and return to your seats," he barked.

The class continued as if nothing had happened, and no words concerning the incident were ever spoken. The following day, however, as the class was about to have their lunch break, Herr Eckhardt called Alfred to his desk. The youngster was worried, concerned that additional punishment was coming. He was surprised when his teacher asked, without expression or emotion, "You know where I live?"

"Yes, sir," he answered softly, still confused.

"I want you to go to my house and bring me back my lunch."

At first, Alfred stared blankly at his teacher, but wishing to avoid any further confrontation, he nodded. "Yes, sir," he said and quickly left the room.

His teacher's house was less than two blocks away. Mrs. Eckhardt was a kindly woman with white hair and a warm smile; she obviously was expecting him. She handed Alfred a sack. "This is for my husband," she said. And then she handed him another sack. "And this one is for you."

Alfred stared at her for a second, wondering, questioning, and finally replied, "Thank you." On his way back to school, he couldn't resist looking in both sacks, and he discovered that the lunches were virtually the same, the highlight being a thick sandwich filled with several slices of meat. After much thought, he concluded that even though Herr Eckhardt could not bring himself to apologize, this was his way of saying he was sorry for the incident, and it was his attempt to make amends. As Alfred devoured the delicious sandwich, he decided it was a reasonable exchange—a slap on the cheek for a fine lunch, free of charge. He was pleasantly surprised when his teacher continued to send him on trips to get his lunch—and one for Alfred as well—throughout the rest of the school year.

* * *

The Langers' living conditions had become intolerable. Eight people in the two small rooms severely tested their tolerance and patience. The previous year, on September 21, the Catholic church in town was officially christened, and while their regular attendance provided the family a degree of strength, their fragile emotions were constantly strained.

After two years of searching, Rudolf finally learned that a larger apartment was available, and he quickly went to see it. As he stood on the sidewalk in front of the building, his mouth dropped open in amazement. It was a large house that had been divided into two separate apartments, each consisting of three rooms. The house itself was in good repair, and a wooden fence surrounded the front yard and backyard, which had four mature laurel trees. The apartments were set up to accommodate two families in their own spaces, although they would have to share the one bathroom. Even that fact, however, was a great improvement from the arrangements they'd had over the years.

One slight disadvantage was that the house, located on Friedhof Strasse, or Cemetery Street, was between two railroad tracks. The constant passage of freight and passenger trains at all hours of the day and night made living there a remarkable challenge. Rudolf, however, quickly accepted the opportunity—they desperately needing the additional living space—and over dinner that night, he shared the news with the family.

"When can we see it?" Rudi asked, filled with excitement.

"We'll move this weekend," Rudolf answered.

"Will we all have our own rooms?" Gerti asked, hoping for more privacy.

"No, but we'll have a lot more space."

"Where is it?" Willie chimed in.

Rudolf cleared his throat. "On Friedhof Strasse," he replied.

Rudi, now fifteen, leaned forward in his chair with a slight look of disbelief on his face. "Are you talking about the house between the railroad tracks?"

Rudolf nodded. "That's the one. It's a very nice house with a yard and trees."

"And with *trains!*" Willie sniped. "How will we sleep with all that noise?"

"We'll get used to it," Rudolf assured him.

"What about the babies?" Elsa worried.

"They'll get used to it as well," Rudolf assured her. "And the little ones can play in the yard without supervision." When no one responded, Rudolf continued, "We'll all get used to it. It's a fine house." His words seemed to be falling on deaf ears, and he sighed heavily. He had thought they'd all be pleased. "We've been through much worse. You all know that. We definitely need the space, and this will be a vast improvement." Still, no one responded to his comments. "You'll all see this weekend." And with that, he returned to his dinner.

Rudolf borrowed a horse-drawn wagon from Herr Hartenstein to make the move. It took four trips up and down the three flights of stairs to remove their table and chairs, a used couch, all the beds, and their personal belongings. Rudolf explained that they would leave their stove behind because the new house had no provision to connect an oven pipe to a window or chimney.

Elsa looked aghast. "But what am I supposed to use to cook our food?"

Rudolf smiled, knowing she would be delighted with his surprise. "I've arranged to have a new electric stove installed. No more kindling. No more getting up in the middle of the night to stoke the fire."

After everyone piled in the wagon, the short trip was made without conversation or further comments. Even though the children still seemed opposed to the idea of their new home, Rudolf knew without question that he had made the correct decision.

Just as the new house came into sight, it was temporarily blocked from their view as a train passed by. The horses were unaffected by the noise and the trembling of the ground; the passengers in the wagon were not.

Once the train was gone, the horses crossed over the tracks without hesitation and were directed to the side of the house. Rudolf and Elsa, who was carrying Harald, entered the house, as the children grabbed a handful of things and followed.

Once inside the apartment, their earlier opinions were considerably altered. The floors were made of a fine, polished wood. The walls were clean and sturdy. Each room had electricity and an abundance of windows. A fence surrounded the entire yard and was covered with lush green grass. The kitchen not only had the electric oven that Rudolf had mentioned but also a large sink.

It was decided that Elsa would continue to sleep in the kitchen area beside Harald in his crib. The larger of the two bedrooms would be for Rudolf, in his own bed; Willie, Alfred, and Heinz in the large bed; and Rudi in a bed of his own. Gerti held her breath, wondering where she was to sleep.

Rudolf smiled. "Gerti, because you're a girl and need more privacy than the boys, your mother and I have decided that you should have the small bedroom for yourself."

Gerti squealed with delight as she ran to her parents and hugged them both. "Oh, thank you, Tata! Thank you, Mama!"

Their bathroom, which they would share with the family in the other apartment, had a tub and another sink. Although no one spoke the words, everyone was most appreciative that they would no longer have to carry a bucket of water each time they used the bathroom.

And then, the next train passed by. The windows shook. The house vibrated. The noise sounded as if the train was traveling through their new living quarters. They all stared at Rudolf, who offered a weak smile. "We'll get used to it," he insisted. Elsa slowly shook her head as she carefully affixed the crucifix to the kitchen wall.

The first evening in the house, the only Langer who got any sleep was baby Harald. They were awakened when the trains passed and stayed awake in anticipation of the next. The second night proved to be a little better, and by the third night, sleep came in bursts, but lasted no longer than an hour each time. The family was beginning to go through their day in a zombie-like state. By the fourth night, however, they were only awakened one time. And by the end of their first week in their new home—just as Rudolf had predicted—they slept through the night as if there were no trains at all.

As in their previous apartment, the kitchen functioned as a dining room, living room, family room, and gathering place. There was a small nook in the kitchen beside the window, which became Rudolf's favorite place to sit in relative peace and calm while reading his newspaper. The family also appreciated the four trees in their backyard—laurel trees, a variety that Alfred had seen while on nature hikes. Elsa would make her favorite tea from the laurel blossoms.

* * *

By this time, the older children were all teenagers—Gerti was seventeen; Rudi was sixteen; Willie was fifteen; and Alfred, thirteen. The older three had graduated from *Volksschule*, the high school, where it was anticipated that most graduates would go on to *Mittelschule*, the equivalent of a junior college, and—if finances were available—on to *Oberschule* in the city of Hof, for a higher and more specific education.

But if higher education was too expensive, graduates of Volksschule were expected to find a job, initially becoming an apprentice. Rudi and Willie were fortunate enough to find skilled work in the construction industry, and they attended a *Berufschule*, a trade school, at least one day a week for three years.

Gerti, a bright student and quick study, was offered a job at the Bodenschatz textile factory. It was about two blocks from their new house, and she rapidly mastered a machine that spun yarn into fine thread before it was passed on to other machines for processing.

With three of the children now gainfully employed and contributing to the family's living expenses, they no longer needed to visit the local butchers and baker, asking for scraps. One minor issue, however, was that once the family moved to their new home, Mr. Ludwig's shoe factory was too far away for Elsa to walk to work on a daily basis. Sadly, she was forced to resign her position, one that she had grown to enjoy.

"Mr. Ludwig," she said, just before leaving the factory for the final time, "I can't begin to thank you for all you've done for me and my family."

He smiled warmly. "Elsa, I'm deeply touched with your sincerity and thoughtfulness. And I'm going to greatly miss your talents and upbeat personality."

Elsa stayed at home for a few weeks but discovered she missed the companionship of other adults. She also wanted to continue to contribute to the family finances. Work, in general, was difficult to find, but Gerti recommended her to her manager at the textile factory, and shortly afterward, Elsa began to work at the Bodenschatz factory, performing general cleaning duties. Elsa was pleased: it was light work, easy to accomplish, and gave her the opportunity to interact with several other women her own age.

* * *

The first day of May was a celebrated holiday, as it officially marked the end of winter and the beginning of spring. If the weather was amenable, nearly everyone in the area could be found hiking the trails through the surrounding woods, walking from town. Most of the pubs in the Frankenwald, a densely forested area surrounding Selbitz, were filled to capacity, jammed with hikers who were celebrating the weather change by downing great volumes of bratwurst and Hefeweizen beer.

Bavaria, the state where the Langers now lived, was renowned as beer country—even children drank beer at an early age. Workers in most of the factories and farms drank beer with their lunch. On Sunday mornings, those who did not attend church services often could be found in local pubs, drinking beer and playing cards, before going home for their noon meal. Nearby, small Naila, where the Langers first were placed, even had its own brewery.

During the May celebration, the children and adults competed with one another in gymnastics, track and field, ping-pong, and even beer drinking. Alfred and his "band of brothers" participated in all the activities but were careful to never drink beyond the point of moderation. They were all in the eighth grade now, their last year in school, and were expected to conduct themselves as adults. While there was still time for hiking, riding bikes, and other activities, Alfred realized that his childhood would soon come to an end. He knew it was important to plan ahead, to earn as much money as possible before the harsh reality of adulthood stared him squarely in the face. And so, he put in even more hours at the sawmill, bundling and delivering wood.

Following graduation three of his friends were going on to *Mittelschule*, and the other had already obtained a spot in an apprenticeship program. Alfred knew life held much more for him than bundling and delivering wood, so the day after school was completed, he began his quest. Dressed in his finest clothes, he went to both shoe factories, the textile factory, the local carpenter, and even the construction sites, where Rudi and Willie worked, looking for a job. While most of the potential employers were aware of his industriousness, no jobs were available.

During dinner that evening, Elsa noticed his long face. "What's wrong, dear?" she asked with concern.

"Nothing," he replied softly, toying with his food.

Everyone stopped eating and looked at him. After a moment of silence, Rudolf cautiously asked, "How was your day?"

"Not very good," he admitted, still staring at his plate.

"Tomorrow will be better," Rudolf assured him, hoping to raise his son's spirits.

Alfred looked into his father's eyes. "There are no jobs," he finally explained. "I've talked to everyone, and there are no openings."

"You already have a job," Rudi offered.

Alfred sighed heavily. "Delivering wood allowed me to earn some good money as a child. But now I'm old enough to have a real job, one that has a future."

"As I said," Rudolf interjected, "tomorrow will be better."

But it wasn't. Alfred had run out of places in Selbitz to apply for a job. He was despondent and morose. He considered moving to another town to seek employment, but he found that option distasteful. Although he occasionally felt as if he were an adult, at age fourteen; he knew in his heart that he was not yet prepared to leave the safety and security of his family.

That evening, as a remorseful Alfred once again looked as if a black cloud was hanging over his head, Gerti gently spoke up. "Alfred?"

"Yes?"

"I spoke to the general manager of the factory today."

Alfred pushed food around on his plate, not interested in hearing any more discouraging news. "So?"

"He told me there was a position open that already has had several applicants—"

"That doesn't help me very much," Alfred interrupted. "Yesterday, when I tried to apply, I was told they already have all the people they need."

"I told him you just graduated from *Volksschule*, were a hard worker, and were looking for employment."

Alfred looked up with continued disinterest. "So?"

"So, he wouldn't make any promises, but did say if you wanted to apply, he'd see you in the morning."

Alfred's eyes widened. "Really?"

Gerti smiled. "Really. If you're interested, be there at eight o'clock. His name is Mr. Ewald Thieroff."

That night Alfred was once again unable to sleep, but this night, it had nothing to do with the trains passing back and forth on either side of their house.

FOURTEEN

T HE TEXTILE MILL OF HEINRICH BODENSCHATZ HAD BECOME
the largest business in Selbitz. It consisted of four different manufacturing plants, as well as a general office. One building was where raw cotton was transformed into yarn, referred to as *Spinnerei*. Another building,
where Gerti worked, was where yarn was spun into thread, called *Zwirnerei*.
This building also contained the machine shop. In a third building spools
of thread were dyed different colors, a process called *Färberei*. In a building called the *Gaserei*, the thread was run through an open flame to burn
off unwanted cotton fibers. Another facility, with a two-hundred-foot-high
smokestack, housed the boiler system and the steam engine. A smaller
structure had a lunchroom, showers, and separate immaculate dressing
rooms for the three hundred men and women employees. Each dressing
room contained a large, circular washbasin with several hot and cold water
faucets.

Alfred arrived at the main gate of the mill at 7:30, announced himself,
and said he was there to see Mr. Thieroff. He was admitted and waited
nervously in an outer office until 8:00. The manager of the plant, Mr.
Thieroff, a tall man with perfect posture and a stern face, finally appeared,
shook hands with Alfred, and told him there were six other applicants for
the job of machinist. This did not seem like positive news. Alfred felt his
chances for the position were slim, at best.

"If you're interested," Mr. Thieroff informed him, "you can return in the morning and take a written test to determine your aptitude and knowledge."

At dinner that night, Alfred repeatedly told the story of his visit to the factory. Each time the family listened politely to his understandable excitement. In truth, he was petrified. *I don't know anything about their equipment*, he thought. *I have no mechanical background. I don't have a chance.*

Elsa felt differently and during her nightly prayers, she asked God for his approval and acceptance.

After another sleepless night, Alfred arrived at the appointed hour and was directed into a room with the six other applicants, where he was instructed to sit behind a grouping of tables. Each applicant was given pencils and the aptitude test. The others the room began immediately to answer the questions—a fact that caused Alfred even greater concern. He took a deep breath ... and began.

Some of the questions were relatively easy for him, due to his background and experience with watching workers at the sawmill, asking questions of tradesmen, and even assisting in the assembly of his own bicycle.

Other questions, however, proved to be rather difficult. One, in particular, asked: "How would you combine two different pieces of metal, such as steel, brass, tin, and/or copper?" Alfred was stumped. In desperation he wrote: "With a rope, chain, or wire." At the conclusion of the two-hour test, the seven applicants walked toward the front gate, discussing the test and some of the answers they gave.

"What did you put down as the answer to combining two pieces of different metals?" one of them asked.

Another applicant answered with a chuckle, "Obviously, either welding or soldering."

Upon hearing this, Alfred's face turned a bright shade of crimson, and he felt as if he was a complete idiot. He walked home in a state of complete frustration and felt certain that he'd lost what would have been a wonderful opportunity.

After two days of abject depression, during which time no one in the family could manage to cheer him up, he finally received a note from Mr. Thieroff, asking him to come to his office in the morning. Alfred shook his head slowly, imagining that he was being called in for the express purpose of being told what a moron he was and that he would never amount to anything.

But to his surprise and amazement, when he arrived at the office, Mr. Thieroff was quick to shake his hand and welcome him aboard. Alfred was speechless—certain he'd misunderstood the words he'd just heard.

Mr. Thieroff waited for a response from him, but when Alfred didn't speak, Mr. Thieroff prompted him. "Alfred?"

"Yes, sir," Alfred replied tentatively.

"You *do* still want the job, don't you?"

The job! He *had* been offered the job! "Oh, yes, sir!" Alfred said enthusiastically.

"Fine, very fine. We'll see you on Monday morning," Mr. Thieroff said, clapping him on the back as they walked toward the door.

Alfred hesitated momentarily, unsure whether he should ask the question for which he desperately wanted to know the answer. He decided he had to find out. "Mr. Thieroff?"

"Yes?"

"Do you remember the question about how you would combine two different pieces of metal?"

Mr. Thieroff smiled, nearly chuckling, and replied, "I certainly do. You didn't do very well on that one, did you?"

"That being the fact," Alfred said with caution, "why did you still choose to hire me, rather than any of the others?"

The kindly gentleman placed his hand on Alfred's shoulder and replied, "I gave it considerable thought and finally decided it would be a great deal easier to teach someone like you—someone who's eager and anxious to learn—than to hire some smart-aleck wise guy who thinks he already knows it all."

That evening, dinner at the Langer household was filled with joyfulness and jubilation. Gerti, ever the big sister, had her own words of wisdom for her brother. Just as she had done when she walked Alfred to school on his first day, Gerti took him under her wing. "It's important that you make a good impression from the beginning," she instructed. "If you look like you're a grease monkey, they'll treat you like a grease monkey." Alfred nodded in agreement as she continued, "You saw how the workers dressed? Just remember, you will not only be judged by your skill but also by your appearance."

"Yes." He'd observed the workers on the day he'd taken his test.

"Then that's the way you should dress."

Alfred smiled at his older sister. "How did you get to be so smart?"

She smiled back and nodded at their parents. "I suppose they had something to do with it."

* * *

Early the following morning, before sunrise, Alfred rode his bike to Naila. He waited impatiently until the store opened; then he quickly entered and selected two sets of work uniforms: navy blue pants with matching jackets—exactly the same as those the other six machinists wore. Riding back home with the summer breeze whistling through his hair, he beamed with excitement. He was going to be a machinist, an occupation in which he'd had a lifelong interest. Alfred was thankful now that he'd been rejected by both of the shoe factories, by the carpenter, and even by the construction company. He was also thankful that he had a sister who was kind, thoughtful, and loyal.

He dashed through the door of the kitchen and proudly showed his mother his new uniforms. Elsa nodded her approval and added, "Perhaps I can be of assistance." When he showed up for work on Monday morning, his brand new uniform had been ironed to perfection. Elsa had done a magnificent job—it was almost as if one could shave with the crease in his navy blue pants. Gerti's suggestion concerning making a good first impression was not lost on Mr. Thieroff. As he introduced Alfred to the other machinists, he made a point of mentioning how professional Alfred looked.

After the introductions, Mr. Thieroff showed Alfred his locker. "All the workers have a locker," he explained. "They leave their uniforms here at the mill and change into them when they arrive at work; then they change back into their street clothes at the end of the day." Alfred nodded; he was becoming more excited about getting started. Mr. Thieroff went on, "You have been enrolled at the *Berufschule*, the trade school in Naila. You'll attend classes one day each week."

Alfred was thrilled with the news. He was going to be an apprentice for three years and when he graduated from the *Berufschule*, he would become a full-fledged journeyman machinist. His future seemed secure.

Mr. Bodenschatz, the owner of the mill, never spoke to any of his workers. He spent the majority of his time in another building, which contained the executive offices. The same building also had an apartment, which was where Mr. Thieroff lived. Mr. Thieroff also had a glass-enclosed corner office in the machine shop, where he would stand for hours in his spotless, snow-white lab coat, observing his workers.

Alfred was eager to begin his new duties. Mr. Thieroff led him to a nearby workbench, which had a vice attached to one end. "It is critically important," he said firmly, "that you learn the basics first." He handed Alfred a twelve-inch-long file and a piece of junk steel. "File the steel flat until it meets my approval." Alfred nodded and began to work, as Mr. Thieroff walked off to another part of the building.

Alfred worked day after day, filing the piece of steel, reducing it to half its original size. Each day, Mr. Thieroff would stop at the workbench, look at the piece of steel, and reply, "Not yet." At the end of three weeks of filing, and after Mr. Thieroff examined the piece of steel from every possible angle, he finally said, "Very good." The compliment helped Alfred to ignore the blisters on his hands. But before he could bask in any glory of accomplishment, Mr. Thieroff assigned him the task of sawing another piece of steel in half with a hacksaw.

By the end of the first day, the blade became dull; its notches were completely gone. Alfred never considered asking for a new blade. Instead, he kept on sawing, back and forth, over and over. Two weeks later, he completed his assignment. He didn't notice Mr. Thieroff standing behind him, looking over his shoulder, as he emitted a heavy sigh of relief and made the last and final cut.

"Very good," his employer commented again.

By this time, Alfred seemed to have blisters on his blisters! More pain-filled assignments followed, including drilling holes through hard steel with a hand drill and tapping holes in other pieces of metals by hand. It was uncommon for the machinists to speak with one another as they worked. They simply went about their jobs with precision and concentration. But one day, while Alfred was busily engaged, one of the others stopped at Alfred's workbench. His name was Hans Schrepfer. Hans tapped Alfred on the shoulder and quietly said, "Mr. Thieroff is a taskmaster, but he's the best in the business. Listen to what he says, and you'll learn a great deal."

Alfred nodded thanks as Hans returned to his own workstation. He appreciated Hans' words of advice, conceding that someday, perhaps, the mindless tasks he was performing would be important to his growth and knowledge as a machinist.

Alfred was now earning eighty marks a week, a fine wage for an apprentice. He contributed half his salary to the family fund to pay expenses, such as food, rent, and other needed items. One of those items was a new couch to replace the one they'd had at their old apartment. and another was a front-loading washing machine that made it considerably easier for Elsa to do the laundry. But the purchase that most excited Alfred was a Grundig radio. It had a shiny lacquered-wood housing and was about the size of a large breadbox.

Music became an integral part of their household after that, something that had not occurred since the celebrations following the harvesting in Hermannstadt. Their favorite program was the Sunday noon hour of the *Bayerischen Landmusik*, which featured the regional country music of the Alps, complete with an abundance of yodeling, accordions, and brass. Sometimes, Rudolf and Elsa danced around the kitchen to the music, as if they were once again a young couple on their first date, falling in love for the first time.

* * *

Berufschule, the trade school, proved to be more difficult than Alfred initially envisioned. This was partially due to the result of his missing one-fifth of his earlier education while caring for his younger brothers. But in the Langer family, every disadvantage was turned into an opportunity. As his mother had said on countless occasions, "Whenever God closes a door, he always opens a window."

The class for machinists had thirty students who came from different towns surrounding Naila. They were not in competition with one another; they were in competition with themselves. No grades were given for the classes; the only grade that mattered was the one that came at the end of the three-year course—the test that determined whether or not the student would become a journeyman machinist. Any free time that Alfred had was spent studying the textbooks from the class.

On one day each week, he would ride his bicycle to Naila, spend the day in the classroom, and then ride back home. During one such trip, the front wheel on his old bicycle began to wobble—just a little at first but then more violently. He decided it was finally time for a change.

After his class that day, he went straight to Ernst Seidel's bicycle shop. Walking in the front door of the shop, he smiled and asked the owner, "Remember me?"

Ernst Seidel smiled his acknowledgment. "I remember a much shorter young man, who spent three days helping me build him a bicycle. Still got it?"

"Right outside."

As they warmly shook hands, Mr. Seidel said, "We must have done a pretty good job. Are you ready for a new one?"

Alfred nodded. "I promised you I'd be back when I was."

"You also promised you'd tell your friends and brothers about me."

"And I did."

"And they came. I'd estimate that I sold new bikes to about half the kids in town because of you. You probably also know that your older brother bought a new moped."

"Yes, sir. I've ridden on the back of it many times."

Mr. Seidel smiled again. "You've grown into a fine young man, and I want you to know I appreciate all the business you've sent my way."

"After all you did for me, it was the least I could do," Alfred insisted.

"And now you're finally ready for the new one we talked about all those years ago. Let's see what we can find for you."

Shortly afterward, Alfred left the shop with a brand new Italian racing bicycle that could be shifted into three different gears. To show his appreciation for all the customers Alfred had sent his way, Mr. Seidel insisted that Alfred pay only the wholesale cost for the new bike, without any profit for the owner himself. Alfred started to protest, but Mr. Seidel was adamant. He waved good-bye to Alfred, who rode down the street with another smile of satisfaction and happiness covering his face.

* * *

Mr. Thieroff was impressed with Alfred's attitude, quest for knowledge, and enthusiasm. Soon, he became Alfred's mentor, tutoring him in his studies, making sure his lessons were completed successfully and that his work at the mill was accomplished with precision. He not only taught Alfred his trade but helped shape his character as well. Any time that Mr. Thieroff spoke to Alfred, he expected Alfred's undivided attention. He would stand squarely in front of his protégé, with his finger pointed directly at Alfred's belly button whenever he wanted to make a specific point. He never asked Alfred if he understood; Mr. Thieroff correctly assumed that if Alfred did not understand, he would make the effort to figure it out by himself.

That year there were more changes for the Langer family. Gerti, now a young woman with a good job, moved into her own apartment nearby. Although it was beneficial to have the extra room in their house, they all missed her regular presence, her positive outlook on life, and her overwhelming generosity. Still, she saw her mother each day at the mill. She was also a regular at church each Sunday and joined the family for Sunday dinner. The "baby," Harald, was now six years old and had started first grade. The bittersweet reality of her children growing up was a fact of life that touched Elsa deeply. They were no longer babies, and soon more would be off on their own, but she knew in her heart that they would be with her forever.

Alfred, though already a young man in training for a professional career, was still a teenager and of the age when it was customary to enroll in a dance course to learn—in addition to dance—the proper manners and how to interact appropriately with the opposite sex. The classes were held in Naila in the high school gymnasium. While the gym seemed considerably smaller than it had when he'd seen it ten years ago, it still retained the same aroma—and that did not bring back pleasant memories. The lessons were conducted once a week on Friday evenings, between 7:00 and 10:30.

At the first lesson the boys sat on one side of the room and the girls on the other, staring across the floor, wondering what they were supposed to do. Alfred had never been on a date in his life—he hadn't even been alone with a girl—so he was understandably nervous. Finally, the instructors encouraged the girls to cross the floor and select the partners with whom they felt they could be comfortable for the remainder of the course. *Will anyone pick me?* Alfred wondered, as he fidgeted nervously on the wooden bench.

The girls were hesitant, especially at the prospect of choosing a complete stranger with whom they'd spend the next eight weeks. The boys were equally concerned, hoping they'd be selected but wondering what they'd do if they weren't. The class, however, was divided equally, boys and girls, so everyone would have a partner.

Alfred's heart began to beat faster as the girls approached, cautiously examining the boys as if they were pieces of poultry in a butcher's window. Even though he was a handsome young man with a fine physique, at that moment Alfred felt awkward and unattractive. One attractive young lady, however, did not seem to share his concerns. Her deep blue eyes focused on him as she moved closer. Soft blonde hair with just a hint of curls fell gently to her shoulders. Alfred squirmed, thinking, *She can't possibly be looking at me*. But she was. With a controlled sense of confidence, she stood in front of him and somewhat meekly asked, "Would you like to be my partner?"

Alfred jumped to his feet, convinced he just heard the voice of an angel. She was beautiful—soft, gleaming skin and a smile that could melt the very heart of darkness. "Oh, yes," he replied nervously. "I certainly would."

She extended her hand gently. "My name is Inge Schrepfer."

"And mine is Alfred Langer." He politely shook her hand and added, "I'm very pleased to meet you."

She bowed her head slightly. "And I as well."

"Students," one of the female instructors announced in a booming voice. "Form a circle in the middle of the floor with your partners." She smiled. "We're all going to dance."

Alfred and Inge walked side by side to their assigned position. Suddenly, something occurred to Alfred, and he asked, "Your last name is Schrepfer?"

"Yes," Inge replied.

"Are you by any chance related to Hans Schrepfer?"

She smiled politely. "Yes, I am. He's my brother. Do you know him?"

"We work together at the Bodenschatz mill."

"My, what a coincidence," she said with a slight smile, and he wondered if she was teasing him. Had Hans told his sister about Alfred and what he looked like? *But how could she possibly know?* As he was deep in thought, the instructor stepped into the middle of the circle and said, "We're going to begin with a dance you probably already know—the waltz. My partner and I will first show you, and then I want you all to join in. We'll be moving among you to personally instruct. Are there any questions?" There were none. "Then let the music begin."

The record on the Victrola played "The Blue Danube," a perfect selection. The students watched intently as the instructors glided with ease and precision across the wooden floor. After the first stanza, they encouraged the students to join in. Everyone tried to mimic the instructors, who made it look so easy. Alfred held Inge at arm's length, studying the instructors while staying separated enough from Inge so as to not show any sign of disrespect or impropriety.

One of the instructors carefully showed Alfred and Inge the proper steps and exactly how they should be executed. But then, to Alfred's surprise, she pushed the two young people together so their bodies were touching. "You have to feel each other move, to always sense what your partner is doing," she said. "You have to dance as if you were one." At first, Alfred was hesitant, but when Inge didn't pull away, they began to master the basics of the dance. It was the very first time that Alfred had ever held a girl tightly in his arms—he found it to be highly pleasurable.

The three hours of class passed much more quickly than Alfred expected it would—he didn't want the evening to end. He politely shook Inge's hand and said with sincerity, "I've had a very nice time and look forward to next week." Then he nervously added, "Sorry I stepped on your toes."

She smiled. "No more than I did yours."

"We'll get better."

"I'm sure we will."

The last train for Selbitz had left at ten o'clock—half an hour ago—so about a dozen boys and girls walked back home as a group, discussing the evening and how much they enjoyed it. Alfred was in a world of his own, thinking only of the girl with soft skin and shoulder-length blonde hair.

At work the next day, Alfred thought about Inge and wondered if she might be thinking of him. He could have asked Hans if she had mentioned anything about the lesson or about him, but he would never be so bold.

The following Friday, the class practiced the waltz and then learned the basics of the polka, a happy dance with free-flowing movement. The lesson sometimes called for leaping across the floor, which created great laughter from many of the participants. Alfred's nervousness with Inge had abated, and he noticed a hint of lilac when he stood close to her. He complimented her on the fragrance and secretly hoped she had worn it just for him.

Over the next six weeks, they learned how to dance the fox-trot, the rumba, and even the basics of the enormously difficult tango. Although Alfred thoroughly enjoyed his work at the mill and his instruction from Mr. Thieroff, it was on Fridays, between 7:00 and 10:30, that he felt as if he was in heaven, held in the arms of an angel.

Traditionally, on the Saturday following the last class, there was a graduation ball. Family, friends, and dance enthusiasts would fill the brightly decorated gymnasium to watch the students exhibit what they learned and even join in themselves. It was one of the major social events of the year. Alfred and Inge had developed into one of the best couples in the class; they danced gracefully as one and enjoyed every minute of being together. Alfred logically assumed that he and Inge would attend the ball as the couple they had been for the past eight weeks. He even purchased a new suit for the festive occasion.

"Where would you like me to pick you up next Saturday," he asked at the end of the last class.

Inge hesitated a moment, a slight blush creeping onto her attractive face. She avoided eye contact as she explained, "Another boy has asked me to be his partner, and I've accepted."

Alfred looked at her for a long time without speaking. He was devastated, feeling as if he had been betrayed. He slowly turned around, left the gymnasium, and walked home by himself.

Elsa compassionately felt her son's pain and tried to comfort him. But Alfred was sixteen and dealing with his first heartache, and so her efforts were unsuccessful. She suggested that he attend the ball by himself. Surely, she said, there would be other girls with whom he could dance. Alfred knew that this alternative had merit, but also knew there was no way he could face Inge.

On Saturday night, instead of attending the dance, he walked to the riverbank where he had taken his younger brothers so many times over the years. He sat down on the soft grass, watching the flowing water as it gently passed over pebbles, glistening in the moonlight. He knew Inge had accepted the invitation from a boy who attended a college, whose parents owned a photography studio, and who was highly respected in Naila. He also knew Inge's parents owned a fine house in Marlesreuth, a small town near Naila, and were well known and respected. His sad but logical conclusion was that in Inge's parents' eyes, it would have been improper for someone like him to be seen in such a public arena with someone like Inge. And this thought plunged him into a pit of despair.

It wasn't so much the thought that he'd lost a potential relationship with Inge, someone of whom he'd grown fond. Rather, it was the reality that, as when he was younger—and as it probably always would be—he was looked down on and treated as a second-class citizen, a person without dignity or proper upbringing. A single word echoed through his head, hammering itself into his brain with the same power as the hammer he used on pieces of steel. The word both haunted and defined him: *Flüchtlinge.*

FIFTEEN

ALFRED TRIED TO DISGUISE HIS GROWING DEPRESSION BY immersing himself into work at the mill and his studies. Elsa, compassionate as always, did her utmost to alleviate his broken heart by offering words of encouragement, even Scriptures. He listened politely to her wisdom and advice, but in his state of mind, they resounded like echoes in an empty cathedral and did little to lighten his burden.

Eventually, realizing that his melancholy was affecting the rest of the family, he concluded that he needed to divert his attention to other matters. He reflected on the perseverance of Sir Edmund Hillary, the first man to reach the summit of Mount Everest, and the fact he never gave up, no matter what. Using that unprecedented example as motivation and following a hasty yet superficial investigation, he discovered an outlet that would, he hoped, redirect his mind-set. It was an exercise class, held once a week in the new gymnasium in the Volksschule.

The class instructor was a man named Willie Beyer, an elderly gentleman, who had lost an arm in an explosion during the war. As a result, he encountered a variety of difficulties in his day-to-day life. His background as a soldier suited him well as an instructor but his physical limitations prevented him from doing the exercises himself. Instead, he would boisterously call out the moves, which the students would follow. This restriction, however, created the need for an able assistant. Mr. Beyer took an instant liking to Alfred because of his attitude, work ethic, and enthusiasm. At the end of one of the classes he called Alfred aside and, in a voice resembling that of a drill sergeant, said, "Young man! Would you have a moment to help me out?"

"Yes, of course, Mr. Beyer," Alfred responded.

"I can untie my gym shoes," Mr. Beyer explained, "but I can't tie the street ones. I was wondering if you'd—"

"I'd be more than happy to help," Alfred assured him.

As Alfred tied his instructor's shoes, the retired soldier looked down and said, "You seem to be enjoying the class."

"Yes, sir," Alfred replied enthusiastically. "Very much."

"Would you have any interest in becoming my assistant in the class we teach for youngsters?"

Alfred was taken aback by his offer. "I'm not sure I'm capable of such a responsible position."

"I've watched you carefully for the last few weeks. You possess a passion and a desire to learn. I can teach you everything you need to know, and I'm quite confident you could not only handle it but handle it well."

Alfred smiled, then shrugged. "If you really think I can do it, I'd be honored."

The Langer family emitted a collective sigh as Alfred opened the front door. They expected that he would return in the same morose state he'd been in when he'd left—bringing with him a black cloud of depression each time he entered the room. They were pleased beyond words when a beaming Alfred greeted them with an exuberant, "Mr. Beyer has asked me to be his assistant. I'm going to help teach kids with their exercises."

In a matter of seconds, it seemed, Alfred had done a complete turnaround. His outlook on life and his attitude in general had altered so dramatically, it was virtually incomprehensible to his family. This new attitude carried over to his work at the mill, where he spent many extra hours, learning as much as he could from Mr. Thieroff, an exercise that was not unnoticed by his employer. At Berufschule, his trade school, he put forth more effort than ever, greatly pleasing his instructors. But the person most pleased was his mother; she was pleased that he finally had gotten over his tragic first case of puppy love. She was not aware—nor did Alfred ever explain to anyone— that his depression and despondency had little to do with Inge; it was a result of not being accepted, of feeling he was not as good as the others.

* * *

Alfred also discovered other ways to divert his time and attention—he went to a theater and saw his very first motion picture, *The Glenn Miller Story*. Even though the English-speaking movie used subtitles, Alfred greatly enjoyed the music. Long after the end of the movie, the music would not leave his mind. He had heard similar music on occasion—the American military maintained a large contingent in the area, and it was inevitable that the local population would become affected by various portions of American culture. Alfred would often hear radios playing American music from such popular artists as Perry Como, Louis Armstrong, Bing Crosby, and the teenage heartthrob Frank Sinatra. Big bands including Tommy Dorsey, Count Basie, Woody Herman, and Glenn Miller filled the airwaves.

Even though Alfred couldn't understand the lyrics, he felt the emotions behind them and upon hearing various tunes, he would often think of Inge, especially on the days he went to Naila to attend his machinist class. Although he'd initially hoped to see her when he made those excursions, now he was thankful that he had not. After all, he was older now; he had more important things on his mind.

Gradually, the music on the American stations changed. Glenn Miller and Frank Sinatra were replaced by a group called Bill Haley and the Comets and their song, "Rock Around the Clock." Rock 'n' roll had arrived, and with it came Little Richard, Fats Domino, Chuck Berry, Jerry Lee Lewis, and Elvis Presley. Because of the effect the music had on the young people—and to the consternation of the older residents—the youth of Germany would never be the same.

One Sunday afternoon, following church services, Gerti brought a friend home with her for dinner. Erwin Weiss was an attractive young man who had a good job as a shoemaker at the Rührschneck Shoe Factory. He was also a talented soccer player, a fact that caught Alfred's undivided attention. The well-spoken young man with good manners made a fine impression on Rudolf and Elsa. While the men sat around the table discussing soccer, current events, and their occupations, Elsa and Gerti prepared what would be a special and delicious meal. Elsa leaned toward her daughter and whispered, "Is he the one?"

Gerti smiled, slightly embarrassed, and softly replied, "I hope so."

* * *

In order to become an efficient instructor, it was necessary for Alfred to be an excellent student. Mr. Beyer taught him well, explaining how the various exercises should be conducted and then critiquing him until he had attained perfection. An unexpected bonus to teaching the exercise class was that Alfred got in exceptional shape himself.

His students progressed, pleasing their parents and causing them to send others to the class. He worked the students hard, getting them in tiptop shape. His exercise regimen was strict, but he also made it fun, so much so that his students brought others with them to subsequent classes. Many times, the parents would observe Alfred putting the kids through their paces and were impressed with his enthusiasm and competence. After about a year of watching his instruction, a group of parents approached Mr. Beyer at the end of his class and asked if Alfred could be their instructor as well. They meant no disrespect toward Mr. Beyer, and Mr. Beyer was not offended in the least; he agreed with their suggestion.

Following another successful fitness class, while Alfred was tying Mr. Beyer's street shoes, the older man looked down at the youngster and said. "Several adults have asked for you to teach their class. How would you feel about that?"

"I'd feel uncomfortable," Alfred replied without hesitation.

Mr. Beyer looked at Alfred quizzically. "Why would that be?"

Alfred shrugged. "The men are older than me. Many of them are stronger and can run faster, jump higher, and do more push-ups. I'm not sure I could gain their respect, and if that's the case, some of them might take their children out of the classes as well."

Mr. Beyer shook his head. "Your concerns are unfounded. Enough of them have watched you work to know you could do an excellent job. They want to see how the exercises should be done; not just hear about them as I teach. And I'll be by your side the whole time." Alfred still hesitated, so Mr. Beyer continued, "The goal is to get everybody in the best possible shape. That's the reason they attend. And that's the reason they want you to be their instructor." Alfred finally conceded to the request, and with

Mr. Beyer's guidance, Alfred was a great success with the adults—so much so that each week, the classes for the youngsters and for the adults both increased in number.

* * *

Having a few days off from work, Alfred decided to ride his Italian racing bike to Bamberg, about ninety kilometers from Selbitz, to visit his uncle Hermann and his aunt Emmie. It was a Thursday, just two days before Gerti's wedding to Erwin, and the excitement was at a fever pitch. The trip would be an easy ride—he'd be there by midafternoon, spend a pleasant evening, and come back the following day to participate in the festivities prior to the wedding.

He left early in the morning under heavy and ominous-looking clouds. He didn't consider this necessarily a bad sign. The clouds would protect him from the unrelenting sun and humidity normally found on a day at the end of August. All was going well until midway through the trip. At first, the rain started as sprinkles, which were refreshing and lowered the temperature. But the sprinkles turned to rain—and then a cloudburst. Alfred was soaked and chilled to the bone within a matter of minutes. Realizing it was dangerous to continue, he stopped in the small town of Lichtenfels and found the nearest pub to escape the weather. He sat in front of a roaring fire, desperately trying to dry himself and waiting for the rain to cease. Once he was relatively dry, he determined that going forward was not a viable or wise course of action; he decided it would be best to return home.

Arriving late that evening, he went straight to bed. When he got up in the morning, however, he felt worse than he had on the previous night. Elsa immediately noticed that he looked pale. "You're going back to bed, young man," she ordered. "You need to rest." His temperature slowly increased, and he felt as if he was falling into a bottomless pit. His stomach began to ache, with a churning, gripping feeling. Elsa tried to feed him soup, but it refused to stay down.

Elsa did her best to lower his temperature by applying mudpacks and towels soaked with cold water. But her efforts were of no avail, and her concerns continued to grow—and Alfred felt worse for taking up so much of his mother's time. That evening, there was to be a celebration preceding the wedding, and he insisted that his mother attend, assuring her that he only needed rest and would soon feel better.

The event was a tradition referred to as a *Polterabend*, during which, friends and family members gather in front of the bride's house with bags and sacks filled with rejected porcelain plates and saucers. One by one, they smashed the dishes on the sidewalk, and the bride and groom then cleaned up the mess, while the crowd watched and cajoled them. Once the cleanup is completed, tradition states that everyone is treated to glasses filled with Champagne, schnapps, and Jägermeister. With each sip, a toast for a blessed and long life together is offered to the happy couple.

When Alfred awoke the following morning, the events of the Polter-abend were described to him, and he was deeply sorry that he'd missed the celebration. His condition, however, had not improved. Elsa felt great remorse for leaving him when he'd needed her, and she insisted that she was going to stay by his side for the remainder of the day. It was only following strong persuasion from Rudolf, Alfred, and his brothers that she finally agreed to attend her only daughter's wedding. Alfred watched the family dress and then leave for the church, and was deeply regretful that he would miss the most important day of his sister's life.

The wedding was a fine event, held at the recently constructed Catholic church. The ceremony was conducted in Latin and attended by at least forty-five guests, many of them soccer players. The reception followed at Erwin's parents' house, where he and Gerti would live until construction of their new condominium was completed. Alfred listened attentively as the story of the nuptials and reception were recited in great detail. His physical discomfort was exacerbated by the sadness in his heart, by his feeling that he had somehow let Gerti down. This feeling remained with him for many years to come.

* * *

Later that fall, Alfred was excited to learn that his machinist class was going to take an educational and inspirational field trip. Mr. Thieroff shared Alfred's enthusiasm and offered various tips—things to which Alfred should pay particular attention in order to advance his knowledge and career.

The class gathered in Naila and boarded a train for the three-and-a-half-hour trip to Frankfurt. Once there, they got on a bus, which transported them to Rüsselsheim, the home of the factory that produced Opel automobiles. The factory itself was huge, so large that it was only possible for them to see a small portion of it. Alfred was completely fascinated by the countless lathes and milling machines that produced various parts. Equally fascinating were the machinists, who professionally and effectively operated the precision equipment with skill and apparent relative ease. One of the highlights of the visit came at the end of the tour, when the class got to see the finished automobiles as they rolled off the assembly line.

On the way back to Frankfurt, the bus was filled with nonstop conversation concerning the remarkable things they had seen. But instead of taking the group to their lodging for the night, the bus turned into the sprawling Rhine Main Airport. Once inside the immense terminal, they received another treat: a look at the Super Constellation airplane, a four-engine turbo-prop plane that everyone was talking about and, at the time, the largest airplane in existence. It was the biggest thing any of them had ever seen. Later that night, sleep at a local school dormitory was replaced by animated dialogues and in-depth discussions that lasted until the first morning light.

* * *

Alfred realized that he had no personal life. In addition to his full-time job, his classes at the trade school, and his instructing the youngsters and adults in their exercise classes, he'd also become a member of the LAV (*Leicht Athletischer Verein*) Track Club in Naila. As a well-trained athlete, Alfred excelled in the hundred-yard dash and the long jump. Track and field had become a hugely popular spectator sport throughout the American sector of Germany. Alfred and his club would travel to surrounding towns and compete with other local clubs. They were so successful that they qualified for participation in the area championships held in Hof. Alfred was a proud member of the relay team, and in this competition, the race was remarkably close. Alfred took the baton for the final leg, and exercising all his strength and will, he made an incredible charge to the finish line to win the race. A photograph of the smiling victors appeared in virtually every newspaper for miles around. Although people often stopped Alfred to congratulate him for winning the race, he would always politely insist that it was the team who'd won. This concept—being just one part of a team—had a positive and lasting impact on his thinking process for the rest of his life.

* * *

Alfred's apprenticeship class was nearing its end and as a result, it was critically important that he pass both the practical and theoretical test, the combination of which would last for four full days. Failure was not an option; to do so would, in all probability, mean beginning anew in another profession. After all the time and effort he put forth, the idea of starting over in a different apprenticeship was unfathomable.

Hans Schrepfer, Alfred's coworker, had been remarkably correct in defining Mr. Thieroff as a taskmaster. The man's insistence on perfection was legendary. He held many advanced degrees, among them a master's degree in tool and die making. Because he was Alfred's mentor, he was not about to let Alfred fail on his practical test. He drilled the youngster constantly, covering miniscule details over and over, putting him through every exercise he could possibly think of.

* * *

The assignments that Alfred was asked to perform came with relative ease; the challenge was the surroundings. His practical test, which lasted three days, was in a large metal-fabricating factory in Hof. Workers were everywhere, flame-cutting and welding. Blinding lights flashed and sparks flew all around Alfred as he tried to concentrate on the tasks at hand. Huge punch presses, screw machines, lathes, and milling machines surrounded the area where he was taking his test. The practical portion was difficult and exhausting, but Alfred passed with flying colors. His training and mentoring from Mr. Thieroff had proven successful. The theoretical test lasted a full day and was administered by one of the instructors with whom Alfred had studied for the previous three years. Again, study and hard work resulted in reward. Unlike many others who took the grueling test, Alfred passed both sections.

In 1957, Alfred became a full-fledged journeyman machinist. He was given a small raise and promoted out of the machinist area to the boiler room, a position that called for a great deal more responsibility—the boiler room provided all the power for the entire factory. Because the first shift began work at 5:30 a.m., Alfred would get up at 4:00 a.m. to arrive at his new assignment by 4:30. Once there, he assisted the technician who was in charge of the boiler room and the steam engine, a giant of a machine nearly thirty feet long, both of which were necessary components for providing the power for the plant. The first step was to get a huge, twenty-foot-diameter flywheel in motion. The flywheel had a five-foot-long steel handle that had to be pushed back and forth, engaging a ratchet. Each push and pull made the wheel turn a short distance. As they pushed the flywheel and got it turning, one of them would open a valve to allow the steam to push a ten-inch-diameter piston rod to the other side, where another valve opened while this one closed. This action sent the piston back and forth, making the flywheel turn faster and faster. The flywheel, powered by the steam, was connected to a generator that produced the electricity to run the entire factory.

While seemingly simple, it was a critically important function. Alfred was proud that he had been chosen for this vital position, for the boiler room was, without question, the very heart of the entire factory. Each component of the vast, complicated, and precision equipment had to be kept in perfect working order. If the generator was not working by 5:30 each morning, the entire plant would be shut down, leaving three hundred workers without pay—and Mr. Bodenschatz extremely unhappy.

Shortly after passing his journeyman's test, Alfred took a course in welding, also held in Hof. After passing that examination and becoming a certified welder, he was called on with regularity to repair high-pressure pipes, which needed to be welded from behind, calling for the use of a mirror. His confidence grew as he felt more and more like a valuable addition to the company.

* * *

While Hans Schrepfer and Alfred were never close friends, they occasionally talked about their jobs and their futures. One thing that was never part of their conversations, however, was Hans' sister Inge.

On the job, Alfred watched closely as Hans took apart, cleaned, and reassembled the equipment on the assembly line, which consisted of precision Swiss machines that spun thread. The workers who were assigned to these machines usually operated about twenty at the same time, so they needed their machines to be in perfect working order at all times. These workers were friendly with Hans because they knew that his ability to fix broken machines kept them from losing income. They were equally friendly with Alfred, because they knew he was responsible for providing the electricity that powered all the machines.

Hans would occasionally let Alfred assist him, which Alfred appreciated—he felt this additional knowledge would be invaluable to his future with the company. Eventually, whenever there was a malfunction with any of the machines in the factory, the workers would ask that Alfred do the repairs.

One day, completely out of the blue, Hans calmly told Alfred, "I'm leaving the company."

Alfred couldn't hide his shock. "But why?"

"I'm going to America," Hans announced. "I have relatives who live in a place called Queens. It's somewhere near New York City."

"But what will you do there?" Alfred asked.

"My relatives will sponsor me. I can stay with them, and they'll help me find a good job."

Alfred shook his head in disbelief. "When are you leaving?"

"Next week."

Alfred was curious to learn about Hans' new life in America, so he asked Hans to write to him and tell him what America was like. As Alfred rode his bike home that evening, he felt excitement for Hans and the great adventure that Hans was about to undertake, but he was also concerned—Hans was going so far from his home and the people who cared for him.

After Hans left, Alfred was promoted and took over Hans' old position; he also kept the one he already held. He also received another raise—he was certain now that his job and future were secure.

Over the next year, Hans wrote to Alfred several times and always commented that America was indeed the "land of milk and honey." Hans' older sister, Helene, who had emigrated several years earlier, worked in Manhattan as a nanny for a wealthy family. She took Hans sightseeing, and he reported witnessing things that Alfred could not even begin to conceive. He wrote about the Atlantic Ocean, a building called the Empire State Building, the fast-paced living there, and the friendly Americans he met. Hans' first job was with a coffee-grinding company as a maintenance mechanic. The pay was acceptable but Hans was not really happy there; he wrote that he was looking for another job. But in 1959, good jobs were extremely difficult to find.

* * *

The Langer family continued to undergo dramatic changes. After Gerti's marriage, Rudi moved into his own apartment, and Willie was drafted into the German Luftwaffe for a mandatory eighteen months of service. The household was now reduced to Rudolf, Elsa, Alfred, Heinz, and Harald. But Alfred, because of his heavy work schedule, was seldom at home, other than to sleep.

In 1960 Willie married a lovely young woman named Brigitte, and this time Alfred was able to attend both the wedding and the reception.

Then another event of vast importance occurred.

The upper management of the Bodenschatz mill decided they would send one of their employees to a two-year, fully paid program to become a *Meister*—a master machinist. When Alfred heard this news he was remarkably excited. *I've been here four years,* he thought. *I've received two promotions, two raises in pay, and two positions of great responsibility.* In his mind, he was by far the best and the most qualified prospect for the position. He eagerly waited to hear the news, no doubt from Mr. Thieroff himself. His confidence and anticipation soared; he was completely convinced that he would receive the assignment.

When the company announced that they had chosen Manfred Böhm, a machinist considerably younger and with much less experience than Alfred, to attend the Meister Program, Alfred deduced—to his dismay and despair—that all hope for advancement within the company had disappeared. It seemed it was not so much a matter of qualification as it was the status one's family enjoyed or with whom one was closely associated. And although there was no way to know for certain, Alfred also felt that his being passed over for this assignment had something to do with his being a *Flüchtling*. Even after all his achievements, all his devotion, all the hours and expertise he provided to the company, he was still a second-class citizen, still looked down on … still not as good as the rest of them.

He kept his disappointment to himself and went about his duties with the same professionalism that he had displayed since his first day on the job. But now his tasks were performed by rote, without his usual optimism and enthusiasm. Many of his coworkers sympathized with Alfred that he had been passed over, but no one spoke openly of it—they weren't about to jeopardize their own positions by voicing their opinions.

Soon afterward, Alfred received another letter from Hans. He'd found a job he greatly enjoyed with a tool and die shop in New York City called the Manhattan Die Company. Further, one of the three owners of the company was moving to California to open a shop in Los Angeles, and Hans was going to be a part of this relocation. Although he could read Hans' excitement in his letters, Alfred had no idea where these places were located. His only real contact with Americans was standing along the curbside as a child, as the American soldiers passed through town, throwing candy and gum to the children, and from the American music he had grown to appreciate.

Alfred had never given the slightest thought to ever living anywhere but Germany. Still, as he reflected on the letters from Hans and the amazing things he was seeing and doing, he couldn't help but feel just a little envious. Alfred realized that he had a decent job that paid reasonably well and had a certain security. On the other hand, even though the job was tolerable, there didn't seem to be any prospects for ever rising higher than the position he now held. In his own mind he had reached the pinnacle of his occupation—a quagmire from which there was no escape. Then, one day, Alfred received another letter—and this one changed his life.

SIXTEEN

HANS DESCRIBED LOS ANGELES AND THE SURROUNDING area as if it were a slice of heaven. The weather was perfect, the people were friendly, and mountains and ocean were beyond description. The brief letter read:

Dear Alfred,

The new firm I work for in Los Angeles, the Manhattan Die Company, is doing well and is achieving great success. However, we're short-handed, and finding a good machinist has been extremely difficult. I mentioned your name and qualifications to my employer, Mr. Gannon, and he said if you wanted to come to America, he would give you a job. I would sponsor you, and we could share an apartment until you get settled. If you have any interest in this proposal, please let me know, and I'll tell you exactly what you need to do. Hopefully, all is well there, and I'm looking forward to hearing from you soon. Your friend,
Hans

Alfred read the letter several times, thinking the words would somehow change or mysteriously disappear. But they didn't. They were there, and the proposal from Hans was sincere. The idea, the possibility of moving to America, while remarkably exciting, was equally terrifying. Thoughts of not being with his parents were as difficult as they were complex and complicated. He mulled over the proposal, filled with great angst, and kept his dilemma to himself, weighing the opportunity against the safety and security of his job and his home. When he was alone, he would look lovingly and respectfully at the crucifix on the wall and pray, asking for guidance, begging for the correct answer, searching for the solution to the biggest decision he'd ever faced in his entire life.

While contemplating this quandary, his mind drifted to thoughts of his hero, Sir Edmund Hillary. He thought about how difficult that climb to the top of the world must have been; how each step in the bitter cold must have nearly frozen Sir Edmund's feet; how frighteningly alone he must have felt to conquer the summit, accomplishing something that had never been accomplished. He never accepted complacency or second best as he successfully overcame all adversity. These dramatic thoughts, along with his heartfelt prayers, gave him the strength and courage to write to Hans to inquire which steps were necessary for him to take.

Hans immediately replied with the address of the U.S. Embassy in Munich where Alfred should make contact and begin the procedure. Within days after contacting them, they wrote back, sending instructions as to where he should go and what he should bring with him. Alfred collected the indicated items and, only then, told his parents of his plans. To ease their pain, he tempered his announcement by explaining that he was only looking into it and had not yet made a final decision. Even as he made plans to go to Munich, it was, he insisted, just to look into the possibility.

In February 1961, with his heart pounding like a large bass drum, Alfred boarded the train to Munich, a two-hundred-fifty-kilometer trip. He checked his pockets for the hundredth time, confirming that he had his passport and an official letter confirming that he had tried unsuccessfully to obtain a copy of his birth certificate from the Czech government. His mind flashed back to nights of sleeping on the straw mattresses, separated from his parents, having no concept of what life ahead held in store.

When he arrived in Munich, he walked through a sea of strangers to the American Embassy. Once inside, he felt as if he was in a foreign country. The entire building was filled with military policemen and officers dressed in spotless uniforms. Everyone he came in contact with in this building was an American citizen who spoke German with a heavy accent. At the appointed hour, he was directed into an inner office, where he presented his papers, applied for a visa to go to America, and was taken to another part of the building, where he was given a mandatory physical examination, which he passed with flying colors.

Then came the long train ride home again, as well as the anticipation, increasing anxiety, and fretful waiting. Alfred still kept his plans, hopes, and dreams to himself, not wishing to cause his parents unnecessary concern until he was absolutely certain that his decision was final; that he actually would actually make the dramatic leap of faith and journey halfway around the world.

Alfred turned twenty-one years old that July 11. The Langers, like most others in that part of the country, did not celebrate birthdays. But three days later, he received his visa in the mail, and in an instant, his entire world turned upside down. When he announced to his family that his immigration papers had arrived, the response from his siblings was much the same as if he had just told them he was going for a bike ride. They simply could not believe he would actually carry out such a foolish plan.

But Rudolf and Elsa believed he would do it. They were extremely concerned, asking a plethora of nonstop questions: "Where will you live? Where will you work? How will you exist in a country where you can't even speak the language?" But the most heartbreaking question of all, the one that brought tears to Elsa's loving face, was "When will we see you again?"

With patience, Alfred explained, "Hans is going to pick me up at the airport. I'll be staying with him until I can afford my own place. He's already arranged a good job. I'll learn the language." He also told them his feelings toward the Bodenschatz mill and the fact he might be stuck there for the rest of his life without any chance for advancement, without any opportunity to better himself or his position. As for his mother's last question, though—"When will we see you again?"—he had no answer.

He'd had five months to prepare for the monumental moment when his visa arrived, and now that it was here, Alfred began immediate action. He sold everything he could: his Italian racing bike, his skis and poles, skates, even books he'd collected as a member of a book club. Those items that he could not sell, he gave away. With the money he raised, he purchased the one-way ticket from Frankfurt to Los Angeles for 1,320 deutschmarks. In addition to that, he had a total of two hundred deutschmarks (the equivalent of fifty dollars) in his pocket for the trip. Both Rudolf and Elsa offered to give him a little more, but he politely refused, convincing them he had all that he needed, and they shouldn't be concerned. He was going to be just fine and would write them as soon as he arrived.

In the midst of this ongoing yet organized confusion, Alfred received another unexpected piece of mail—an official notice from the German government, informing him to report for his physical examination prior to his being drafted into the *Bundeswehr*, a branch of the restricted but rebuilding army. Even though his plans called for leaving the country within two weeks, he had no choice in the matter. If he failed to report for the physical, they would most certainly come and get him. The unknown ramifications of this possibility were far too dangerous to even contemplate. So, with understandable concern hanging heavily over his head, he reported, as directed, at the local movie theater in Selbitz, where the examinations were being held. Chairs were moved out of the way making room for a military doctor and his staff to administer the physical to several young men from the surrounding area. Alfred easily passed all the requirements and was informed that his official draft notification, with reference to where he should report for duty, would be delivered to him shortly.

Anxiety mounted as he waited for the draft notice, hoping beyond hope that he would leave the country before it arrived. If the draft notice came first, he would be forced to serve the required eighteen months of active duty, a situation that would ruin his opportunity to go to the United States, where his new job and future were waiting.

And so it was that five weeks after receiving his visa, Alfred found himself in the kitchen with his mother on that August morning, picking unenthusiastically at his breakfast.

"I helped you pack," she said softly.

"I know, Mama. Thank you very much."

She stared at the son she loved so very deeply and, with a trembling voice, asked, "Are you really sure this is what you want to do?"

Alfred nodded. "I've prayed very hard, asking for guidance, just as you've taught us. And I honestly feel in my heart that God has something truly wonderful in store for me."

"You should always trust God to do what's best," she replied. Then, with her voice trembling slightly, she offered, "You should eat. You'll need your strength."

Even with her encouragement he barely touched his food. When it was time to leave for the train station, she insisted on carrying his suitcase. Upon reaching the boarding area of the Selbitz train station, Elsa finally set the suitcase on the ground, as Alfred checked once more that he had all the necessary tickets and documentation. Within moments the conductor shouted the words that mother and son both had been dreading: "All aboard!" Their collective tears became uncontrollable, though the train's insistent whistle drowned out their sobbing. Alfred stroked his mother's hair and whispered in her ear, "I love you, Mama."

With great difficulty, she softly replied, "God speed," as she wiped away her tears with the white handkerchief he'd given her as a Christmas gift.

Alfred boarded the train at the last possible second, just as it began to pull away from the station. He watched from the doorway of the railcar as his mother—along with the family and life he had known—slowly disappeared into the distance.

Now, his old life was behind him, and the new one lay ahead—virtually halfway around the world. Alfred wiped away his own tears with the sleeve of his jacket and when he looked up, the station was no longer in sight.

* * *

Alfred entered the railcar, placed his suitcase behind a row of seats, and sat down beside a middle-aged woman named Frau Herpich. She was also a resident of Selbitz, and while Alfred knew of her and had seen her numerous times in the past, they had never actually spoken. She looked into his reddened, tear-filled eyes and, with concern and compassion, softly offered, "I saw you on the platform. Did someone close to you pass away?"

The question seemed well-intentioned, if slightly odd. "No, ma'am. I'm going to America."

She appeared to be offended, as she stiffened in her seat. "It's not polite to joke about something that serious." She turned away and looked out the window.

"I'm serious. I'm going to a place called Los Angeles. A friend of mine has lined up a job for me, and I'm going there to work."

She turned back toward him and asked, "Aren't you one of the Langer boys?"

"Yes, ma'am. My name is Alfred."

Suddenly, her demeanor altered significantly, and she smiled warmly. "I've heard a great deal about you."

"Really?" he asked, taken slightly aback.

"My son was a student in one of your exercise classes, and he thinks the world of you. You made quite an impression on him, quite a positive impression."

Alfred flushed with embarrassment. "I'm very pleased to hear that. I did my best to help all the youngsters."

"Well, you certainly helped my son. And for that I want to thank you very much."

"Believe me, Frau Herpich, from the bottom of my heart, the pleasure was all mine."

They continued to converse until the train reached Hof, her destination. As she left the train, she wished him good luck and God speed. He spent the remainder of his journey in silence, reflecting on the final words from both Frau Herpich and his mother: *God speed*. Other thoughts concerning family, friends, and experiences were embroidered in his mind like a vintage tapestry during the duration of his trip.

After arriving in Frankfurt that evening, Alfred boarded a bus that traveled through the heavy traffic to the Rhine Main Airport. As he reached the boarding area listed on his ticket, he nearly dropped to the floor, so stunned was he by the vision outside the window on the tarmac. He'd expected that he would be traveling on something akin to the Super Constellation, the giant airplane he had once seen. Instead, the waiting plane was much larger—so large that it seemed inconceivable it would be able to lift off the ground. He soon discovered that the huge plane was a Pan American Boeing 707, a truly unbelievable and remarkable airliner.

With mild concern over the aerodynamics, he entered the cavernous machine and was directed to a window seat. After everyone was settled, announcements in both English and German instructed the passengers to fasten their seatbelts, and the plane slowly moved away from the terminal. The giant engines began to whine as the plane pulled toward the runway. The 707 began to move forward, faster, then faster, then even faster. Alfred was pushed back into his seat, feeling as if his chest would explode. By now the engines were screaming and the body of the plane shook violently, yet all of the other the passengers seemed to be calm. Alfred gripped the armrests tightly with both hands until his knuckles turned white, and within seconds, the plane was airborne. His journey had begun.

* * *

A small pouch in the back of the seat in front of him held magazines printed in both English and German, but Alfred paid them little attention. His face was pressed against the window, watching the twinkling lights of Frankfurt slowly disappear beneath him. The plane climbed through a light cloud covering and into a crystal-clear sky filled with millions of brilliant stars, some seemingly near enough to touch. The sight provided a religious epiphany, and he immediately thought about the crucifix hanging on the wall in their home. For some strange reason, he could not recall having seen it before he left earlier that morning.

The plane had been in the air for about a half-hour when an attractive young woman in a finely tailored uniform gently tapped him on the shoulder. When Alfred turned toward her, she smiled and cheerfully asked in English, "Would you care for the steak or the chicken?"

Alfred didn't understand her words, but he didn't want to appear unsophisticated, so he simply returned the smile and shook his head. Moments later, the same young woman pushed a metal cart up the aisle and delivered trays of food to fellow passengers; Alfred did not receive one. At that moment, as his stomach began to gurgle, he realized the importance of learning to speak English as rapidly as possible.

The countless stars were the backdrop for a gleaming full moon. Out the window, Alfred could see the endless, magnificent ocean as the moonlight glistened on the water. No one in the Langer family had ever been on an airplane; most had never even seen one up close. And here he was, miles above the earth, somewhere between its splendor and that of heaven. Even with his mixed emotions of growing anticipation, slight anxiety, restless energy, and concerns for his family, he felt that he was a truly blessed individual.

They landed in Winnipeg, Manitoba, where those traveling on were required to pass through customs. An announcement was made over the public address system when it was time for the passengers to reboard the plane, and after another exciting departure, the final leg of the flight began. Someone a few rows in front of Alfred began to sing "California Here I Come," and while Alfred found the tune pleasant, he had no idea what the words meant. He returned to the solitude of his own personal thoughts. *What if Hans isn't at the airport? He doesn't have a phone, so how will I find him?* But among his many thoughts, the most significant of all was, *Will I really be accepted, and how will I fit in to this entirely new environment?* Another young lady in a tailored uniform asked him another question that he didn't understand, but this time he nodded affirmatively. And this time, within a few moments, he was served a delicious meal.

* * *

Alfred was awakened from a nap by the pilot's voice announcing their descent. He could hear the thrust of the mighty engines soften, and when he glanced out the window, he saw the lights of Los Angeles, twinkling, flashing, seemingly stretching in every direction for miles and miles. While the sight was breathtaking, it also provided another moment of anxiety. Alfred had lived his entire life in a town with no more than four thousand residents. Below him was a major city with millions of people, all in one place—the concept itself was daunting.

As the wheels of the huge jet touched down on the runway of Los Angeles International Airport, most passengers applauded enthusiastically and shouted "Bravo!" Alfred closed his eyes and offered a silent prayer: *Dear Heavenly Father, I ask You to be with me and guide me in this new land. My will is in Your hands, and I promise You I will give it nothing but my very best and humbly ask that You send Your blessings my way and keep watch over me, as well as my family. Amen.*

Alfred entered the terminal and was directed through customs, where he showed the customs official his passport and the forms he'd filled out before leaving Germany. The man smiled and said, "Welcome to America." *Maybe he really means it,* Alfred thought, realizing he'd not noticed any suspicious stares. *Maybe I really am welcome here.* The room had American flags on display everywhere, and pictures of President Kennedy adorned the walls. While the enclosure was relatively stark, filled with travelers hustling in every direction, it also had a warm and comforting feeling.

Alfred was enormously relieved when he finally located a beaming Hans, who was waiting in the arrival area. They shook hands vigorously, sealing the lifelong friendship on which they were about to embark. Alfred collected his suitcase from the baggage area and then followed Hans to the parking garage. He smiled broadly as he saw Hans' car: a Volkswagen Beetle, exactly the same kind of car that Alfred had used to obtain his driver's permit back in Germany.

The fifty-mile trip to Hans' apartment seemed to pass by in a instant—there was so much to talk about and so little time. Everything was different here—the language, the brilliant lights everywhere, the wide streets and freeways, the thousands and thousands of people, the large cars with enormous tail fenders, the smells, the huge billboards competing for attention, the abundance of everything. Each time Alfred asked a question, Hans would answer briefly and then ask one of his own. "What's going on at the mill? How's Mr. Thieroff doing? What did the other workers say when you told them you were coming to be with me?"

The apartment complex was at the end of a short, dead-end street at 232 South Avenue in an area called Highland Park. Tall, green eucalyptus trees dotted the landscape. The complex had its own swimming pool, which Alfred would learn was heated and well lighted at night. Alfred was amazed by the opulence and stared, his mouth agape, at his new surroundings. Hans laughed, telling him, "Just you wait until this weekend, when all the girls are at the pool."

Alfred's new home had originally been part of a military barracks, consisting of four buildings with eight apartments in each—four at ground level and four above. "Most of the tenants here are bachelors, single women, and couples without children," Hans explained. "During the day, the place is deserted, but on weekends it comes alive."

The apartment was small but tidy and well kept—a compact kitchen with a counter separating it from the living room, and a door leading to the bedroom, which had an adjoining bathroom. There would be plenty of room for the two of them. "First things first," Hans announced as he poured two glasses of Pabst Blue Ribbon beer, the American variety. When they raised their glasses, Hans offered with a smile, "Here's to your success in your new town." The clinking of those two glasses touched off a monumental moment that neither one of them could possibly have imagined.

They finished their beer and then continued their conversation as Alfred unpacked his suitcase and began to put his things away. When he finally reached the bottom of his bag, he suddenly stood motionless and completely silent, seeming unable to speak.

"What's wrong?" Hans asked with concern. "What is it?"

Alfred felt tears well up in his eyes as he reached into his suitcase and gently held up a crucifix, the one that had been on the wall of his home since the day he was born.

* * *

Seeing Los Angeles—or "L.A.," as he soon learned it was called—in the daytime was an entirely different experience from the previous evening. Unlike Selbitz, there were no people on the street—no one seemed to be walking anywhere. Everyone rode in busses or cars, some remarkably exotic-looking and obviously expensive. Hans continued to pepper

Alfred with questions as he drove onto the Pasadena Freeway at Avenue 52, merged effortlessly onto the 101 South Freeway, exited on Wilshire Boulevard, and made their way to the Manhattan Die Company on West Seventh Street in downtown Los Angeles.

Being intimately familiar with the grand scope and size of the Bodenschatz mill, Alfred was astonished when he first saw his new place of employment. The shop itself was enclosed in a relatively small area, about twenty by forty feet. The building was sandwiched between a tavern on one side and a pawnbroker on the other. Hans noticed the concern on Alfred's face as they approached the door. "I know what you're thinking," he assured his friend, "but the work is steady, the customers are intensely loyal, and the quality we produce is among the best in the business." As they entered the front door, they were met by a portly man with thinning hair. "Mr. Gannon, this is Alfred Langer," Hans began. "Alfred, this is your new boss, Mr. John Gannon."

Gannon extended a large paw of a hand and clasped it around Alfred's. His boisterous voice sounded welcoming as he spoke to Alfred, and Hans translated his words: "Glad to have you aboard, son. Call me Johnny."

"Yes, sir," Alfred replied in his best English.

"You can forget all that 'sir' stuff. It's Johnny. Keep your nose clean, do a good job, and you'll do just fine." Hans translated again, and Alfred nodded. Then Hans introduced him to the only other worker in the place, a man he referred to as "Little Hans."

Johnny turned to Hans. "Show him the ropes, and teach him how to talk," he directed.

As Hans led Alfred to the far side of the building, Alfred was beginning to question his monumental decision. He'd left the relative security of a company that employed more than three hundred people to begin at one that employed just three. Hans again noticed his concern and explained, "Everything's going to be just fine. You'll make more money here than you ever would in Germany. Trust me."

When Alfred saw his workstation, he felt he was taking a step back in time. In a small area in the corner of the building was one old milling machine, a small lathe, two drill presses, a bench-mounted brass-and-steel rule bender, a table saw to cut wood, a band saw for metal cutting, and welding equipment. Alfred judged that the area was so small, that with the equipment and four people working at the same time, it would be impossible to get anything done without tripping over each other. Unlike the extreme cleanliness of his workplace in Germany, the floor in this place was covered with sawdust and carried a foul odor.

Being the newest employee, his first assignment was to clean all the machines and sweep the floor. *I am a trained, expert machinist*, Alfred thought. *What on earth am I doing sweeping the floor in a dump like this?* He did as instructed without objection, however, and thanks to his efforts, the distasteful odor disappeared. As he performed what he considered to be a demeaning job, he reflected on the words of Plato, which he'd read in the past: "The beginning is the most important part of the work."

His next assignment was to master the new and difficult forms of measurement. In Germany, everything was on the metric system, measured in ones, tens, and hundreds. Here, the measurements were confusing—an inch divided into eighths? A foot that had twelve inches? A pound with sixteen ounces? Alfred feared he would never understand.

The primary work at Manhattan Die was to manufacture radio-frequency sealing dies and steel-rule cutting dies, neither of which was particularly challenging. In general, sealing two or more pieces of plastic together was done with heat sealing, but radio-frequency sealing took less time, resulting in increased productivity and increased profits. Plastic that was heated with radio frequency cooled much faster, which made it safer to handle and kept its shape longer.

The steel-rule die was manufactured from razor-sharp, pre-manufactured steel rule blades that came in strips or a coil. The rule was bent to specific shapes and then welded together, much like a large cookie cutter. Seeing this machine brought a warm smile to Alfred's face. This was the same type of machine that his mother had operated when she worked at the Ludwig Shoe Factory. He fondly remembered the very first time that he and Rudi walked past the machines on their first at the factory. His own words to Rudi now echoed in his head: *"Someday I'm going to own a machine like this."*

Johnny seldom took part in producing any of the dies; he preferred to take care of any welding that was needed. Alfred didn't understand the great pride that Johnny seemed to have in his prowess as a welder—in truth, it was little more than melting pieces of steel together.

Later that afternoon Alfred was introduced to Nancy, Mr. Gannon's wife. He was delighted to learn that she also was from Germany, having lived in Karlsruhe. She brought a snack of coffee and cookies and enjoyed speaking with Alfred in their native language. While the exchange was pleasant, Alfred knew he had to learn English if he was going to survive and accomplish everything he wanted.

At Hans' direction, Alfred did busy work, familiarizing himself with the antiquated machinery and cleaning up his workstation, a job that took the better part of three days. This working environment took some getting used to. In his previous work experience, he'd been expected to stand straight and tall, with his chest out and chin tucked in and his hands kept out of his pockets. He knew to respectfully address his superiors, never becoming familiar. Here, everything was much more relaxed, but what troubled him was referring to his new employer as "Johnny."

Johnny was kind-hearted and gentle, but he had two addictions that Alfred had never seen in an employer in Germany: Johnny smoked constantly—a cigarette always dangled from the corner of his mouth. He even smoked while eating a sandwich during the lunch hour—and he had a propensity for alcohol. It was normal for him to disappear from the shop following lunch and not return until closing time. More often than not, either Hans or Alfred would have to go next door to the dingy neighborhood tavern when Johnny was needed for an important phone call or to help a customer who was waiting in the shop.

Little Hans was another interesting person—pencil thin with unkempt hair, he was quite unlike anyone Alfred had ever met. With Hans translating, Little Hans thought to impress Alfred by saying, "I'm an L.A. kinda guy, man. I live in the fast lane. Chicks dig me." Little Hans bragged about the bevy of girlfriends who chased after him because he made good money and drove a 1960 Thunderbird convertible. Alfred stared, with his mouth agape—even with the translation, he still had no idea what Little Hans was talking about.

In addition to Johnny's constant drinking and Little Hans' constant bragging, one other thing was consistent: the poor quality of the equipment. Not one machine in the entire shop was new, and this was difficult and unfamiliar for Alfred. Johnny felt he could save money by purchasing second-hand equipment. Although Hans—and later, Alfred—often suggested that Johnny would be much better off in purchasing new precision machines that would produce much better products, the concept was ignored.

The chain of command was relatively simple. Johnny would tell Hans what needed to be done, and Hans would translate and explain it to Alfred. Alfred performed far above Johnny's expectations, and the man was pleased with his decision to hire Alfred. He jokingly told Hans that he liked Alfred because he was full of "piss and vinegar." When Hans related the comment to Alfred, he didn't understand—until Hans explained it to him—that in America, that was a compliment.

Alfred wrote a letter to his parents within the first few days of his arrival, telling them all about Hans, their apartment, and his new job—although he omitted any comments on Johnny's fondness for alcohol. He told them what an incredible place California was and that he was doing well. He was more than happy with his decision to move to America, he assured them, and they had nothing at all to worry about. He asked after the other family members and sent his love. It was a very upbeat and positive letter that ended with his thanking his mother for the family crucifix; he let her know how much it meant to him.

A week later Alfred received a letter from home, telling him all the local news, along with greetings and well wishes from everyone he knew. They were all concerned about him and wanted to know as much as possible. Another letter was enclosed within the envelope, this one from the German government. Upon opening it, he discovered it was his official draft notice from the Bundeswehr, instructing him when and where he was to report for active duty.

Alfred smiled as he read the note. The timing of its arrival couldn't have been better—or more ironic. Prior to leaving Germany, he'd discovered that on the day he was permitted to enter America as a permanent resident, he would be eligible to be drafted into the U.S. Army. As a result, as he was now on American soil, his first obligation relative to military service was to the United States.

* * *

On September 1, 1961, less than two weeks after his arrival in America, Alfred enrolled in a beginning English class at the Highland Park High

School, where evening classes were held Monday through Friday. The instructor was as proficient as he was patient, spending whatever time was necessary to make sure the twenty-five students learned their lessons well. At the beginning of the first class, the instructor asked everyone to introduce themselves in English, an exercise that provided many outbursts of laughter and served to bond the students together in their common quest. During each class, they would learn a new series of words, and each day, Alfred did his best to use those words in conversations with others. He was surprised and pleased that so many people—sometimes even strangers—were helpful and understanding, willing to assist him in his effort to learn English. He was issued a workbook to use in class and for study at home. He also studied during his lunch break at work and during the time spent walking to and from the class each evening.

He went to see German films subtitled in English, making notes of new words and using them whenever possible. He listened to the radio to help him learn to correctly pronounce words, and he repeated them over and over. In his quest to master the language as quickly as possible, he discovered other valuable, if surprising, allies: the girls at the pool.

SEVENTEEN

THE BASS GUITAR POUNDED OUT A DRIVING RHYTHM, AS the volume on several radios was turned up simultaneously. The entire sun-baked crowd that surrounded the pool joined in with the Beach Boys, as "California Girls" blasted from numerous speakers. Countless others came out of their apartments and onto their balconies and sang along with great enthusiasm. It was not an unusual event; it was just a normal Sunday afternoon at the apartment complex.

It was late September, and Alfred could not contain the grin on his face as he thought about home. If he were in Selbitz, the ground would probably be covered with snow. And if he were in Selbitz, he would no doubt be wearing a German Army uniform, marching around in the freezing temperatures. If he were in Selbitz, he would not be surrounded by attractive females, all adorned in the two-piece swimming suits that they referred to as bikinis, a word he'd never heard before. In his clear baritone voice, Alfred joined in with the others as best as he could, even though words were as confusing as the music was captivating. This, however, was exactly how Hans' original comment concerning "the girls at the pool" became completely understandable. The girls were very willing to assist Alfred with pronunciation, elocution, and definition. The fact that Alfred was an attractive young man with a finely trained physique was not lost on the young ladies who helped him at every available opportunity. Their kind assistance proved to be a valuable asset, helping Alfred narrow the learning curve of a language that was remarkably difficult to master.

Within less than a month, Alfred concluded that the descriptions of California that Hans had sent in his letters were exactly correct; California was indeed a slice of heaven. Together, he and Hans made short trips to see the magnificence of the ocean, the majesty of the surrounding mountains, and the timeless beauty and endless solitude of the desert. His assimilation into his new world was taking place much faster than he imagined possible.

With the second letter from his parents, Alfred became troubled. His mother asked, with clear and expectant optimism, the name of the new church he was attending and how much he liked his new priest. Her words embarrassed Alfred; he had not yet joined a church. The problem was one of logistics. Los Angeles was so large and spread out that there was not a Catholic church within walking distance, and his one attempt to use public transportation had resulted in his ending up far away from his desired destination.

In order to alleviate his mother's understandable concerns, however, he wrote back: "There are many wonderful churches from which to choose, and I have not yet decided which one would best suit my needs."

* * *

Alfred's salary at the Manhattan Die Company was one dollar fifty cents an hour. That, plus overtime, earned him about the same amount of income that he'd earned at the Bodenschatz mill. But raises for performance were promised, and because of his skill and ability to adapt, they were delivered. When Johnny learned that Alfred was also an experienced and certified welder, he assigned him that task as well, and with it came another small raise. Even though temptation was abundant in this new land, Alfred followed in the tradition of his father and grandfather by saving his money in a miserly fashion. With small and minor exceptions, he spent it only when absolutely necessary. He and Hans cooked at home, eating out only on very special occasions. He bought some new clothing but only after extensive comparison-shopping. His expenses consisted of food, rent, tuition, and an occasional visit to the movies. Time was at a premium, as he worked five and a half days a week, spent five nights a week in school, and studied during his free time. The exceptions were the day trips to see the magnificence of the surrounding area and, of course, Sunday afternoons at the pool. Spending time at the pool was a pleasurable experience, but he viewed it as part of his educational process. To the disappointment of several of his young and attractive tutors, dating was an expense that Alfred was not yet prepared to undertake.

Johnny continued to be impressed with Alfred's work ethic and professionalism. Alfred, on the other hand, continued to be amazed that Johnny would spend most of each day in a nearby tavern, working only when it was an absolute necessity. One day, these two opposing attitudes came together in a most unusual fashion. Alfred was hard at work, concentrating as he leaned over a lathe and prepared a part for the precision piece of machinery.

"Hey, kid!" Johnny shouted from across the room.

Alfred looked up from the lathe, pointing to himself with a questioning look on his face.

"Yeah, you," Johnny said. "Over here."

Alfred walked to where Johnny stood and patiently awaited further instruction.

"How long 'til you finish that piece you're workin' on?"

By now, Alfred had learned enough English that he could usually converse about things pertaining to his work. "About five minutes," he answered.

"Good. Come with me."

As Alfred followed Johnny out the door, he looked at Hans and shrugged, having no idea what was going on. Then it struck him as if he had been hit with a two by four—he was going to be fired, and Johnny was being polite enough to not do it in front of the others! Panic coursed through his mind. *What will I do? Where will I go? Will I have to go back to Germany and be in the army?* His face became covered in sweat that dripped onto his shirt collar. The painful thoughts were magnified as Johnny opened a door and instructed Alfred to enter an establishment called Blarney's Castle. He'd been there several times in the past, when it was necessary to get Johnny to come back to the shop, but he'd never paid any attention to the place. Now, this time was different.

This time, as they walked the full length of the bar, he noticed it was dark and dingy and had a foul smell of stale beer and people who needed to bathe more often. Everything appeared to be very old—not antiques, just worn out. Johnny knew every one of the afternoon patrons seated at the bar and called each of them by name. They knew him as well. As Alfred and Johnny reached the end of the bar, Johnny pulled out a stool and indicated for Alfred to sit. *Here it comes*, Alfred thought desperately. *I'm a goner.*

The bartender moved in front of them. "Afternoon, Johnny. Same as usual?"

Johnny turned toward Alfred and casually asked, "What kinda cocktail you want?"

Alfred had seen the word "cocktail" hundreds of time on signs outside other places of business but had no concept of what it actually meant; he'd but never asked Hans to explain it. Now, he shrugged.

"Bring him a Mai Tai," Johnny said. "I'll have the regular."

Alfred waited nervously for his life to be disrupted beyond comprehension, for the shame and embarrassment of failure that most certainly would follow. Johnny lit one cigarette from another and stared straight ahead, making the wait even more agonizing. The bartender set the drinks on the bar and moved away. Johnny took a long sip of his and motioned for Alfred to do the same. After taking a deep breath, Alfred lifted the glass to his mouth and discovered it tasted good. Really good. But it certainly was not the type of drink one would have in the middle of a working day. Johnny finally looked at Alfred and broke the silence. "So, ya like your new job?"

"Very much," Alfred replied, waiting for the worst.

"You're a good worker. Really know your stuff. I'm glad you decided to come over and work for me."

By now, Alfred knew enough English that he at least thought he understood about half of what Johnny said. He nodded and replied, "Thank you."

"How's your drink?"

"It's very good."

Johnny nodded as he lit another cigarette. "Finish up. Got lots of work needs to be done over there."

Alfred downed the remainder of his drink, got up, and as he turned to leave, said, "Thank you, Johnny."

Johnny nodded and then added, "One more thing." Alfred froze where he stood, still expecting the terrible news. But instead, Johnny said, "You doin' anything special this weekend?"

Alfred was confused. "No, sir."

"Good. I want you to come to the beach with my family and me. We'll pick you up on Saturday morning about eight. Got a swimsuit?"

"Yes, sir."

"Bring it along. We'll go for a swim." And with that, Johnny shooed Alfred away and indicated for the bartender to bring him another drink.

When Alfred returned to the shop, he thought about an American phrase he'd recently heard: "Go with the flow." He realized that he'd worked himself into a frenzy over something that never happened, and he decided then that he would adopt the phrase. From then on, he would do his best at whatever he was doing and let the rest take care of itself. He thought then of some words of wisdom that his father had once shared with him: "You can't control what you can't control. But you are in charge of the way you react to it." He also reflected on the familiar words recited in his nightly prayer: "Thy will be done."

* * *

"Why do you suppose he asked you to go to the beach with them?" Hans asked, a slight hint of jealously in his voice.

"I have no idea," Alfred replied. Then he offered a sheepish grin. "I'm just going to go with the flow."

At eight o'clock sharp on that Saturday morning, Alfred waited in front of their apartment complex as Johnny pulled up. Alfred was relieved to see Nancy, Johnny's wife—she would be able to translate anything he didn't understand—but less than relieved to see Ronnie, their son. The boy wasn't a bad kid; he was just a bit of a pest, always interrupting, always wanting to know what's going on. Alfred smiled politely as he got in the car, reminding himself, *Go with the flow.*

Johnny eased the car through heavy traffic, eventually taking the free-way that indicated they were heading for San Diego. After an hour or so, Johnny pulled off the freeway and into the parking lot of the Orange Grove Restaurant, where Johnny said they'd have some breakfast. The restaurant was ornate, decorated with bright colors and fine leather chairs. The breakfast was delicious, but when Alfred offered to pay his share of the bill, Johnny said, "We invited you. This trip's on me."

Upon leaving the restaurant, Johnny led everyone across the road to the grounds of the Mission San Juan Capistrano. As a devout and dedicated Catholic, Alfred instantly felt a strong and reverent sense of belonging. The rustic ruins of the Great Stone Church and the soft serenity of the ten acres of breathtaking gardens were spectacular; the fountains and structures awe-inspiring. Walking among hundreds of other tourists, Alfred learned that this timeless place, referred to as the "Jewel of the California Missions," was founded in 1776, the same year that America itself was born. He stood in the midst of the grace and charm of nature, combined with the elegance and richness of California history. But more than that, he felt in his heart that he was in the presence of God, the same one who had carefully and gently guided him and his family through the darkest of hours, the worst of times, and the seemingly endless pit of despair. Alfred wished with all his heart that his parents could see this wondrous place, and he offered a silent prayer for their well-being.

Before leaving, they also visited the nearby little chapel, called Fr. Serra's Church, just north of the historic mission, where Johnny said, "This is where the swallows come back to."

"The what?" Alfred asked.

"The swallows. The birds. Every year, after they've gone south for the winter, they come back here on the same day to build their mud nests in the ruins of the old mission church. You know ... when the swallows come back to Capistrano."

"Why do they do that?"

Johnny scratched his own head. "Nobody knows," he finally replied.

Before Alfred could ask any more questions, Johnny suggested, "It's time to get back on the road."

Soon, he pulled off the freeway where a sign read "San Clemente," heading west, toward the ocean. They parked in a large lot and then entered a sprawling structure with the name "The Resort Hotel" displayed out front. Johnny checked them in, with a room for him and Nancy and another for Alfred and Ronnie. "Change into your swimsuits," Johnny ordered. "Let's hit the water."

The hotel was right on the beach, a large expanse of pristine, pure-white sand with an abundance of comfortable lounge chairs. When Alfred entered the water for the first time, he thought about Selbitz and the fact that soon, the river there would be frozen over. It was close to a year ago that he had skated on it with his brothers and other friends, wildly enjoying an enthusiastic game of hockey. And now, here he was, swimming in the magnificent Pacific Ocean. *The Lord certainly works in wondrous ways.*

Over dinner, Alfred learned that Johnny and his family lived in West Covina, a sleepy little town they referred to as "inland," about fifty miles from the ocean. The entire Gannon family enjoyed spending weekends on the beach, away from the hustle and bustle of work and neighbors. For them, several weekends each summer provided a series of short and relaxing vacations.

For Johnny, that particular weekend was more than just a vacation. He wanted to observe Alfred away from the shop. He wanted to see how Alfred interacted with his family and the strangers they encountered, and how strongly Alfred felt about certain things. Without being aware of it, Alfred was once again being tested. But this time, the test concerned his character rather than his competence.

* * *

Within a short period of time, Alfred learned to compensate for the inadequacies of the aged equipment in the shop. In doing so, his proficiency as a skilled machinist improved exponentially, and long-time customers began asking specifically that he and Hans perform jobs that called for precision workmanship. It wasn't long before Alfred and Hans were essentially running the company. Alfred and Hans worked extremely well as a team, understanding each other to the point that on most occasions, it was unnecessary for them to communicate verbally. When it came to work, they were in sync, usually completing jobs under budget and faster than expected. Their collective expertise, in addition to earning more money for the company, made it possible for Johnny to spend more time away from the shop.

Alfred always immensely enjoyed hearing from his parents, and count-less letters filled his mailbox. But one day, he received a piece of mail that wasn't from home, one that was somewhat expected, even though he wasn't looking forward to it. It was an induction notice from the United States Army. He found it somewhat curious that Hans, who had been in America two years longer than he, had not received the same "invitation."

"Why is it you haven't been drafted," Alfred asked.

"My father died from malaria when he was serving in the German Army in Africa," Hans replied. "There is an American provision stating that anyone who had only one parent wasn't required to serve unless there was some sort of a national emergency."

When they entered the shop, his face filled with remorse, Alfred showed the notice to Johnny and sadly told him, "I guess I'll be gone for a little while."

Johnny studied the letter, reading each word carefully, and finally re-plied, "Let me see what I can do about this." He folded the letter and put it inside his pocket.

Alfred was to report within three weeks and now wasn't quite sure what to do. "But what about—"

"I said, let me see what I can do about this," Johnny interrupted.

Alfred nodded and returned to work. He also returned to worrying. He didn't want to do anything that might invalidate his ability to stay in America.

He worried daily for the next two weeks, during which time Johnny never said a single word about the letter. Then, out of the blue, Johnny called him over and handed him a different letter from the army. Alfred still wasn't able to read English as proficiently as he spoke it, so he asked, "What's this?"

"It's called a deferment," Johnny answered with a smug grin. "I per-sonally went down to the local draft board and told them that Manhat-tan Die Company would not be able to operate or function without your services. I explained, in clear and certain terms, that my company would go out of business if my most experienced and proficient machinist had to leave for the required two years. The draft board was very understanding and granted you a one-year deferment."

"That's it?" Alfred said with a degree of disbelief.

"That's it," Johnny replied. His grin broadened. "Since I got you here for another year, you better get back to work."

* * *

From the time Alfred acquired his first bicycle, he'd felt a certain degree of freedom—he was able to go wherever he desired. Later, his Italian racing bicycle provided even more freedom, as he could ride longer distances. But now, in his new country, all that had changed. He was completely dependent on Hans for transportation.

But now it was time for a change.

Alfred decided he was finally going to get his American driver's license. He studied the brochure that detailed the various laws and regulations, and he passed that portion of the test with ease. He took the driving portion of test in a Corvair, a small, rear-engine car with an automatic transmission, which made this portion of the test a snap as well—he received a perfect score on exams.

Now, Alfred became more frugal than ever, saving money so he could purchase a car of his own and achieve the absolute freedom he so desperately desired. The expense of formal socializing was still out of the question, but one day, as summer approached, Hans made an offhand comment. "I heard about a group of Germans who get together down on Huntington Beach every weekend."

"What kind of a group?" Alfred asked.

"People our age—mostly kids who were born here to German immigrants, who just get together and have fun."

"How much does it cost to join?" Alfred asked, always concerned about money.

Hans smiled. "It doesn't cost anything. Let's go take a look and see what it's all about."

"Sure," Alfred replied, without particular interest.

His noncommittal attitude changed considerably when they reached the beach and located the group—it was easy to find them because they were singing German songs. Alfred instantly felt as if he were back at home, and in his mind were images of his instructing the exercise classes, riding his bike through the winding mountain roads, and the wind blow-ing through his hair as he competed on the track team. It was a genuinely warm feeling. When the song finished, the leader of the group, who was playing a guitar with a degree of proficiency, spoke in German, asking if he could help the two strangers staring at them with the silly smiles on their faces.

Hans replied, "We heard about your group and wanted to see what you were all about and what all you did."

Upon hearing Hans speak in such fluent German, the leader jumped up, extending his hand. "I'm Leo Kerz, and you're more than welcome to join us."

Hans and Alfred introduced themselves and were introduced to the group of about fifteen people, all of whom were about their own age. The boys and girls all had been born in America to German parents, and most spoke the language of the old country with a distinct American accent. Their purpose, Leo explained, was to maintain German traditions.

As they sat around an unlit fire pit, drinking German beer, they fired questions at Hans and Alfred: "Where are you from? How long have you been here? Where do you live? What sort of work do you do?" Everyone was exceptionally friendly; they were glad to welcome Hans and Alfred into their group, which they called *Donauschwäbische Jugendgruppe*, or the Danube Swabian Youth Group. The name came from the River Danube (*Donau*) that ran through the German state of Swabia (*Schwaben*). Most of their parents had immigrated to America in the 1930s, when times there were difficult, the result of the devastation in their country after losing World War I. At the time, even though Hitler was rising in stature and assembling a multitude of followers, many Germans foresaw more bad times ahead and left the country. Many of them came to America and established German neighborhoods, a large contingency of which settled in Anaheim, California.

When the golden sun began to slowly disappear into the ocean, the group lit a roaring bonfire and roasted hot dogs. Conversation, interspersed with singing, lasted well into the evening hours, as they shared stories from the old country. Hans and Alfred agreed to meet them again the following weekend.

During the return trip to their apartment, as Alfred reflected on the day, he was thrilled that he had gone along with Hans' suggestion. In addition to making a bevy of new friends and feeling comfortable with that group, he also discovered a fresh and eager source of educational influence: others who were willing and able to help him with translations, as he continued learning his new language.

As the size of *Donauschwäbische Jugendgruppe* grew larger, their activities became more varied. In addition to swimming, they also played volleyball and badminton at the beach, and one day, one of the members even brought a ping-pong table in the back of his truck, which resulted in a rousing tournament. In the evenings, as they had the first time Alfred and Hans joined them, the group would circle the fire pit and have boisterous sing-alongs in German.

Along with the group's growth came more organized events. The group would take day trips to nearby mountains, visiting places such as Big Bear, Lake Arrowhead, and Mount Baldy. On occasion, they would rent paddleboats and explore isolated areas, where they often saw a varied assortment of wildlife. The towering trees and clear blue lakes brought back many fond memories of Hermannstadt, the place Alfred always considered to be his hometown, his true roots.

EIGHTEEN

WITHIN A YEAR, ALFRED ACHIEVED A BASIC UNDERSTAND-
ing of his new language, but in the process, there were understandable errors in trying to express a thought he'd learned from someone else.
When Alfred related some of these to his English teacher at the conclusion
of their final class, the instructor chuckled. Then he said, "You've shown
diligence in learning a difficult new language, Alfred. I admire your enthusiasm and eagerness, particularly that you made a special effort to." Following his congratulations for working hard, the teacher asked, "In Germany, how far did you go in school?"

"The Volksschule had eight grades," Alfred replied.

His teacher nodded and showed great compassion as he explained,
"Here, in order to ever really get ahead and make something of yourself,
you need a high school diploma."

Alfred thanked him for the suggestion and asked, "How should I go
about doing that?"

The teacher offered clear instructions and wished Alfred the best of
luck; he knew without question that his suggestion would be followed and
that Alfred would excel.

By the end of that week, Alfred had enrolled in night classes at Frank-
lin High School in Highland Park. He was thrilled to learn that his classes
would include English grammar and composition, American history, biol-

ogy, typing, algebra, English literature, and social studies. He was fascinated by the fact that he would have different instructors for each subject. He was most excited, however, to learn that he could receive his diploma within eighteen months.

Each time he attended a new class, he enthusiastically received a new textbook for the subject. While some proved difficult to read and understand, he knew that his friends and instructors would assist him if he needed a translation. He looked forward, with intense anticipation, to each of his classes—with the exception of biology. While relatively interesting, he couldn't understand how the information would be beneficial to his future and his career.

Each evening as he walked to class on Figueroa Street, he passed a used car lot. And each time he passed the lot, he slowed down just a little, just enough to check out the shining merchandise under the bright spotlights. Several of the cars had considerable appeal but none seemed just right for him. Still, he knew that he would see the right automobile one night, and then he would achieve the unrestricted freedom he longed for.

* * *

The German group continued to grow to the point where they formed a choir, which would occasionally present concerts. To join the chorale, it was not essential to have a well-trained or even a good voice. Anyone who could sing loudly and express great gusto was warmly accepted into the fold. The choir would belt out a variety of popular German tunes, such as "*Hoch Auf Dem Gelben Wagen*," "*Mein Hut Der Hat Drei Ecken*," and "Rosamunde." Together, they would link arms and sway from side to side with the rhythm of the music, entertaining audiences both large and small.

"I have a fabulous idea," one of the members announced excitedly, following one of their concerts. "Let's put on a show for some kids. We could do it in one of the local elementary schools."

Members collectively decided the idea was worth exploring, and assignments were delegated. Someone had to get permission from a school that would be amenable to a show presented in German. Someone else had to come up with potential ideas for the show itself. Another person had to line up musicians and find a place where they could rehearse. Yet another had to design and create the scenery for the production. With remarkable ease, the project came together, and during the holiday season, the assembled cast and crew waited somewhat nervously for the auditorium to fill and the curtain to rise.

The show they decided upon was called "A Christmas Story," a classic German tale in which Santa Claus comes to visit the children of a poor miner's family. Alfred, to his great delight, played the role of the coal miner. His face was blackened with soot, his clothes were tattered and torn, and he wore a miner's cap and carried a lantern. His part consisted of telling his two young children about the true meaning of Christmas. He explained the story of the Star in the East, the Three Wise Men, Joseph and Mary, and the birth of their Lord, Jesus Christ, in a manger in Bethlehem. The production was entertaining but also educational and highly emotional—especially so for Alfred, as he reconnected and renewed his faith in the Holy Trinity.

All the children in the school sat in their seats, their faces filled with wonderment and awe. Alfred and the rest of the cast and crew were deeply touched by the reception they received, both from the children and the adults in attendance. Their work, effort, rehearsals, and time invested was worth more than any of them could adequately express. Alfred was enormously proud that he had been a part of something that provided so much joy and pleasure to so many.

* * *

Business at Manhattan Die increased in volume, to the point that it was impossible to perform it effectively within the confines of their limited space. In order to grow the company and satisfy their customers' needs, Johnny moved the shop to West Sixth Street, less than a mile away from their old establishment. It was a larger location, situated on the ground floor of the Teris Hotel, and there was a decent restaurant next door, where Alfred ate many meals while doing his homework for various high school classes.

Alfred's class at the school had a total of thirty-four students, all from different backgrounds. Some of the students appeared to be old enough to be his grandparents; others were his own age. Some were local residents, and some, like he was, were from other countries and still learning the language. They all shared one common goal: to graduate from high school and improve their station in life.

One crisp, cloudless evening in the spring of 1963, while walking home from school, he passed the used car lot and, as was his habit, slowed a little so he could check out the new arrivals. He stopped in his tracks when he saw the light-blue Volkswagen Beetle, with a sign in its window reading $460. On closer inspection, he discovered it was a 1957 model with black leatherette interior and brand new tires; it was in pristine condition. Alfred was torn—the price of the car was half his savings. But he loved the automobile, and his answer came without hesitation. It was finally time to free himself from his dependency on Hans.

Three days later, on a crystal-clear Sunday morning, Alfred drove his new car through a winding series of streets, past an abundance of colorful flowers, to a building that struck him as an architectural delight: St. Steven's. He parked his car, entered the church, and was both pleased and spiritually lifted with the service. As the parishioners left, Alfred introduced himself to the priest, adding that he would like to become a member. The young priest was delighted, as was Alfred's mother when she read the news in his next letter.

* * *

Over the next few months Alfred, in his new prized possession, explored and enjoyed the magnificent sights offered by California, Arizona, and Nevada. The price for a gallon of gasoline was about thirty-five cents, and that made travel inexpensive. The car performed flawlessly, whether in the blazing heat of Death Valley or the freezing temperatures of the Big Bear area, high in the San Bernardino Mountains.

Following the example set forth by his personal hero, Sir Edmund Hillary, Alfred went hiking and camping at such areas as Lake Mead, Nevada; up the waterfalls of Yosemite National Park; and the trails in Sequoia National Park. The newfound sense of freedom was exhilarating, but while it altered his outlook on life, it never interfered with his sense of responsibility to work or school.

Manhattan Die only had one real competitor, a company called Olson

Dies. And for a time, the two of them basically split all the die business in and around the greater Los Angeles area. But while Alfred and Hans put their heads together and created and manufactured new methods for making more efficient producing dies, Olson kept doing exactly what they had been doing for years. Within a short period of time, Olson Dies could no longer compete with Manhattan Die, a company that—based on Alfred and Hans' innovations—was experiencing unprecedented growth and success.

* * *

Even though he had a schedule heavily laden with work, school, studying, regular church attendance, and traveling, Alfred still made time for the German Youth Group, so much so that he was appointed to the position of director of publicity. A "German hour" was broadcast on radio station KPCC from Pasadena City College, and a German disk jockey would announce the upcoming activities of the German community. Advertisers for the program included German bakeries, butchers, grocery stores, and restaurants. In addition, the station also played a mixture of German hits and traditional Johann Strauss music.

Alfred's job was to regularly contact the DJ and ask him to announce various functions the Youth Group was planning. He also was responsible for creating and submitting ads, which were placed in the German newspaper, *Die Deutsche Staats Zeitung*. Once each year, the Youth Group sponsored a *Tag der Deutschen*, or German Day, held at an ethnic restaurant called the Phoenix Club, a place that catered heavily to the German community. Alfred worked diligently to encourage young Germans to attend the numerous events and participate in their group. The response was better than anyone expected, as they discovered a large number of like-thinking individuals who were interested in preserving German traditions and joining in the fun.

The Phoenix Club featured a band on Friday and Saturday evenings. Alfred attended regularly because he greatly enjoyed their food and the camaraderie. Being well trained in several different dances—a result of the lessons he took when he was sixteen—he often could be found on the dance floor. The girls enjoyed dancing with him because of his proficiency, but try as he might, he was never able to establish a meaningful relationship with any of the girls. Several friends took him aside and offered advice. "You have to be more aggressive." "You have to be slick." "You have to be a smooth talker."

Alfred found the situation troublesome; he could not erase the pain he felt from Inge's rejection back in Naila. And even though he would never mention it to anyone—especially not to Hans, because Inge was his sister—the hurt was so deep that he knew it simply wasn't his style to become more aggressive in the courting process. The potential for another rejection caused him to avoid even the possibility at all costs.

* * *

Johnny immediately noticed Alfred's depression as soon as he walked into the shop. "What's the matter, kid?" Johnny asked. "Got some sort of a problem?"

Alfred sighed heavily and handed Johnny a letter—another induction notice. With the increased business the company was experiencing, the timing could not have been worse. Johnny read it, patted him on the shoulder, and said with a sly grin, "Let me see what I can do about it."

Johnny's intervention had worked one time, but Alfred felt another deferment would be impossible. He was wrong. After three weeks, without mentioning another word, Johnny handed him another official-looking letter, this one from the government as well. He'd obtained a deferment for another year, citing the same reasons and explaining that his business would be forced to close if Alfred wasn't there. While that may not have been absolutely true, without Alfred's productivity and ability to turn out finished, high-quality work, the company certainly would have lost income.

The summer seemed to fly by, with more gatherings at the beach, more dancing at the Phoenix Club, more camping and hiking trips, more work, more studying, and more school. But as school was winding down, Alfred became acutely aware of approaching events that troubled him— the graduation ceremony and celebrations. Following their graduation, everyone else in his class had planned parties, some quite extensive and extravagant, for friends and relatives. Alfred felt this was a waste of money and time, but after a considerable amount of encouragement from several of his teachers, all of whom recognized the effort he'd put forth over the past eighteen months, he decided to rent a cap and gown and at least participate in the formal graduation ceremony.

He was pleasantly surprised to witness the number of people in the auditorium cheering on his fellow graduates. He was pleased with his decision to attend, and he listened closely to the commencement speaker, who stressed the importance of using their diplomas as a stepping stone to receive an even higher education and taking advantage of the opportunities that lay in front of them. Alfred made an appointment to have an official photograph taken, which he proudly sent to his parents. As most his fellow graduates moved on to attend various parties, Alfred returned the rented cap and gown, drove to the shop, and went back to work.

After graduating in June 1964, Alfred attended the fall semester night classes at Los Angeles City College, until November of that same year, when life took him in a different direction. As Manhattan Die continued to grow, the world was changing; specifically, a war was escalating in a far-off place called Vietnam. Alfred was aware that even though his deferment period was not yet up, if there was an emergency, he could be called to report at any time. The thought of being sent to that distant land and participating in a shooting war was abhorrent. As a youth, he had personally experienced the ravages and horror of war; it was most definitely not a situation he wished to repeat.

"Johnny," Alfred said one afternoon. "Got a minute?"

Johnny noticed the concern on Alfred's face. "What's up, kid?"

"I could use some advice."

Johnny didn't say another word; he just took Alfred by the arm and they walked to the restaurant next door. After they were seated, he asked Alfred again, "What's up?"

Alfred sighed heavily. "I'm concerned about being called up. A few people I know, who also have deferments, got notices to report."

Johnny rubbed his chin, now equally concerned. "Any options?"

Alfred shrugged. "If I join the National Guard, I'll only be gone for six months ..."

"And you'll probably stay stateside," Johnny said. He ordered a drink, and Alfred had iced tea. "Casualties are goin' up on a daily basis. Not a pretty sight, that's for damn sure."

"Think you can get along without me for six months?"

Johnny grimaced. "It'll be tough, but that's a hell of a lot better than two years. If I was in your shoes, and I'm sure glad I'm not, I'd go the Guard route."

In November 1964, Alfred took his induction notices, along with the two deferment papers, to the local recruiting station. He filled out what seemed to be a ream of paperwork and was told by the stern-faced sergeant seated behind a desk that he would be contacted soon.

Within a week, he received formal notification from the Selective Service, instructing him to report to the armory in San Pedro, an oceanfront community located across Los Angeles Harbor from Long Beach, which had a large and growing naval base of its own. Alfred wrote his parents, informing them of his decision. Rounds of rapid good-byes took place with all his friends.

By joining the National Guard, he would attend a six-month basic training program and then return home, committed to spending two weeks each summer at an assigned army base for further training for the following five and one-half years. Had he been drafted, he would have had to serve at least two years of active duty and then be on standby for an additional four years, in case of an emergency. The decision was simple and the thought process clear. If he had been drafted when his deferment ran out, there would have been a better-than-average chance that he would have been sent to the deadly and relatively unpopular war.

Most of those who were in the National Guard basic training program were assigned to Fort Ord, a base near Monterey in northern California, one of the most beautiful and scenic areas of the entire state. The base, however, was in quarantine as a result of an outbreak of spinal meningitis, and no one, other than doctors and medical personnel, was allowed to enter or leave the premises.

When Alfred and five other recruits reported at the armory, they were ushered onto a bus and driven to Los Angeles Airport, where they boarded a Delta jet, with their final destination a base identified as Fort Polk in the state of Louisiana. Alfred was assigned a window seat during the cross-country trip and was amazed as he discovered the scope of America from thirty thousand feet above it. On this November day, he was able to see majestic snow-capped mountains, barren deserts, endless forests, and mile after mile of fields bearing crops, as well as several large rivers and more cities than he could count. He'd seen America in maps and books and even globes, but actually seeing it firsthand was breathtaking.

The large jet made a perfect landing in Shreveport, and as the six of them passed through the terminal to another gate, Alfred was confused by many of the conversations he overheard. Most of the words sounded as if they were English but had a remarkably strange sound. Several of the words he couldn't understand at all. After asking one of his fellow travelers, he learned that what he was hearing was referred to as a "Southern accent."

"It sure sounds different," Alfred replied.

The other recruit smiled knowingly and said, "Just give it a little time down here and you'll be talkin' just like them."

Alfred shrugged, thinking to himself, *No way. Learning English is hard enough. I'm not going to learn it all over again.*

They located the correct gate, walked down a flight of stairs, and found themselves on the tarmac facing a very small, twin-engine prop plane with military insignias. Alfred had only flown in two airplanes in his entire life, both quite large, and he was hesitant about entering what appeared to be little more than a toy. A stern-looking man wearing a brown uniform with two stripes on his sleeve erased any hesitation, as he ordered the six onto the plane. The airplane they'd taken to Shreveport had seating for about a hundred fifty people; this one looked as if it could carry twelve passengers. Four of the seats were already filled and both engines were running, their screaming noise making conversation impossible. An overhead sign came on, informing everyone to fasten their seatbelts, and the plane began to taxi toward the runway. Like his first takeoff, Alfred gripped his armrests quite firmly.

It was a short hop to Alexandria, a city close to Fort Polk, but the pilot seemed intent on pulling stunts. He tipped the wings rapidly from side to side, and he would pull the nose of the plane up and then reverse direction, as if he was going for a crash landing. As they approached the landing strip, the plane flew so low over the rooftops and trees that the passengers were convinced they were going to make contact with protruding chimneys. Fortunately, and to the relief of the passengers, the plane landed smoothly and came to a stop; the door was opened and the group was instructed to deplane. They stood on the tarmac as a military bus pulled up, and a tall, trim man in a brown uniform—another with several stripes on his sleeve—and wearing a flat, wide-brimmed hat with a yellow band motioned for the group to form a line in front of the bus. His posture was perfect, and he had a stern look on his tanned face—a permanent scowl.

Once the line was successfully accomplished, the man began to pace back and forth in front of them, not making eye contact. He spoke in a low, authoritative, and gravely voice, that rose in volume with each spoken word. "My name is Sergeant Chavez. You will address me at all times as either Sergeant or sir." He hesitated, staring directly into each person's eyes as he passed. "Now, I know that a lot of you boys just left your mamas and joined the National Guard so you can avoid that nasty old war. Because you think this is gonna be easy. Because you think this is gonna be light duty. Well, let me make something perfectly clear." The sergeant got nose to nose with one of the new recruits and screamed at the top of his voice, "You're wrong! You are in the United States Army now!" He began pacing again. "For the next six months I'm gonna be your mama and your daddy and your worst enemy. Do you understand me?"

"Yes, sir" came the weak reply.

"I can't hear you!" he screamed.

"Yes, sir!" By now, most of the ten young men standing at attention were shaking in their shoes.

"You came here as boys, and I swear that as God is my witness, when you leave, you'll be men—proud and well-trained members of the California National Guard. I'm gonna change your lives in ways you can't begin to imagine. From now on and for the next six months, your ass is grass, and I'm the meanest and baddest lawnmower you ever did see! Get on the bus, ladies, the party has just officially begun!"

NINETEEN

THE SHRILL SIREN ON TOP OF THE COURTHOUSE IN THE center of town began to blare. Its screaming announced that all within the vicinity should seek cover and safety as rapidly as possible. Rudolf, working in a nearby field, hurried his ox along as fast as he could, back toward the barn. Elsa and Frieda, their maid, assisted the children in putting on several layers of warm clothing. The basket by the front door was already packed with assorted items of food and blankets. Even though they'd experienced the drill numerous times before, it was still unnerving, still frightening, still impossible to realistically comprehend. As Rudolf dashed through the back door, he nodded to the others, and as a group, they left quickly through the front door, across the road, and into the shelter of the nearby forest.

The family huddled closely together. They could hear the deadly and destructive bombs exploding in the distance, some close enough to make the ground shake and increase their unstoppable and unforgettable feeling of terror. Even covered with jackets and blankets, the children were trembling, immersed in cold sweat.

Alfred snapped awake from his nightmare, with the same cold sweat covering his body, but the sound that filled his ears was not that of distant bombs. It was the crashing together of two garbage can lids and the deep, raspy voice of Sergeant Chavez as he screamed, "Get your ass up, ladies! You lazy, worthless piles of pond scum! Fall in at attention at the end of your bunks!" As the new recruits stumbled out of their warm beds in a state of total confusion, Chavez continued his screaming as he marched down the center of the room. "Faster! Faster! Ain't no rest in this man's army!"

Forty disoriented men scrambled, doing their best to follow instructions, wiping sleep-filled eyes, not even aware that it was still pitch dark outside.

Chavez stopped in front of a frail-looking youngster, who was yawning and appeared to be shaking. "You afraid of me, boy?"

"No, sir" came the soft, trembling reply.

Initially, it appeared as if the sergeant might at least smile at the response, but instead, he continued screaming. "Well, you sure as hell better be! Hit the deck, asshole! Gimme twenty!"

The youngster dropped to the floor and began doing push-ups as rapidly as possible, anything to avoid the further wrath of the man now obviously in charge of his life.

"You ladies are gonna shape up, and I mean right now!" Chavez stared at another wide-eyed recruit. "Chest out, suck in that chin, soldier! Arms straight!"

Alfred stood straight and tall, a position with which he was intimately familiar. Like the others, he was wearing an olive-green T-shirt and matching boxer shorts. He stared straight ahead as Sergeant Chavez continued his ranting. Although he didn't understand several of the words used by the sergeant, Alfred assumed they were of a foul nature—curse words he'd not yet heard but would soon grow to recognize. The men were instructed that they had twenty minutes to take a dump, shower, shave, dress in a T-shirt and fatigue pants, make up their bunks, and fall out in front of the building.

Pandemonium superseded confusion, as the men jockeyed for position, screaming, pushing each other out of the way, and rushing to be the first at everything. Any sense of privacy was gone. The latrine at the end of the room had ten sinks, ten toilets, and a shower area large enough for ten men. Working as a unit, the order could have been concluded successfully, but they were not yet a unit. This first morning of their training, they were still individuals, a situation that over a brief period of time would alter dramatically.

One by one, they eventually found their way down a flight of stairs and lined up in front of the two-story, wood-framed, whitewashed building. Their formation left much to be desired. Only then did many of them realize that it was still dark. Sergeant Chavez waited impatiently, staring at his wristwatch rather than at the men. He had an assistant, another sergeant, who lined the new soldiers into four straight lines of ten each, many of them still yawning. Chavez tapped his watch and held it to his ear. "According to my watch," he began, "it's been twenty-five minutes since I told you to fall out in twenty." He glared at one of the men in the first row. "How 'bout you, moron? Can you explain to me why you didn't follow my orders?"

The man looked at the ground and meekly offered, "Well, sir, there were so many of us and—"

"*Shut up!*" Sergeant Chavez screamed. "Drop and give me twenty!" As the man fell to the ground and began his push-ups, Chavez continued, "When I talk to you, boy, you better damn well be lookin' me straight in the eye! When I give you an order, it better damn well be followed! This is *my* army, ladies, and in *my* army, there are no excuses! Do you understand me?"

"Yes, sir" came the timid reply.

"I can't hear you!" he screamed.

"Yes, sir!" the men screamed back.

The man finished the push-ups and got to his feet, breathing heavily. The sergeant, in nearly a civil tone, asked, "Any o' you girls want some breakfast?"

"Yes, sir!" the men shouted in unison.

Chavez looked at his assistant. "Now they can hear me." Then he said to the men, "Good. First let's do us a little exercise." For the next thirty minutes, the sergeant put them through a series of push-ups, jumping jacks, and knee bends. For those not in shape, it was nearly unbearable, causing aches, cramping, burning muscles, and throbbing temples. During one of the several sets of push-ups, one of the men couldn't raise himself from the ground. Chavez walked over and glared at the motionless body. "You dead?" he asked without emotion.

"No, sir" came a weak and breathless reply.

"You tired?"

The man could barely be heard. "Yes, sir."

Chavez sounded almost compassionate. "Would you like a little rest?"

"Yes, sir."

The sergeant returned to form, screaming. "I'll get you some rest, you weak-ass sissy! I'll get you three days in the brig with a healthy diet of bread and water! How's that sound?"

"Not very good, sir," the man replied, struggling to get to his feet.

Chavez offered an icy stare. "I ought to stuff my hand down your throat and rip out your liver, but I got a better idea." He looked at the rest of the men. "Hit the deck! Everybody!" The others followed instructions without hesitation. He stared at the man who was literally shaking in his boots. "Here's the drill, wise-ass. Your new buddies are gonna do an extra twenty-five push-ups in your honor while you watch." The soldier started to speak, but Chavez cut him off. "And to make it even better, you're gonna count 'em out to make sure they do every single one."

"I'll do the push-ups with the others, sir," the man said.

"Not one chance in hell! You will stand there, at parade rest, and count as all your new friends watch you. I'm sure that sometime later, they'll be more than happy to show their appreciation for you being such a screw-up. Now count!"

The man took a deep breath and began the count. And as he did, the other soldiers on the ground, with aching muscles and glaring eyes, stared at him, waiting for the opportunity when they would be able to show their "appreciation," up close and personal. Once they finished their extra punishment, the sergeant paced back and forth in front of them as he explained, "For the next four weeks you will not think. The army will do all of your thinking for you. Right now, the majority of you are weak, sissies, Mama's boys. But when I'm through with you, you will be lean, mean, fighting machines. My orders are law. The words I speak are the words of God. You will follow them without question or hesitation, or you will pay a price you can't even begin to comprehend."

As the majority of the new recruits stood in abject shock and terror, he instructed them to return to their quarters, put on a shirt, and rejoin ranks so they could to go to the mess hall.

* * *

Following a hearty breakfast, during which no one was allowed to speak, the group reassembled outside and awaited further instruction. Sergeant Chavez appeared and casually suggested, "Let's all take a little walk. Right face!" The men turned to their right, not together, not anywhere near in unison. "Forward, march! Hut, two, three, four. Hut, two, three, four. Quick time! Hut, two, three, four. Hut, two, three, four. Double-time! Hut, two, three, four. Hut, two, three, four." The men were now jogging down a dirt road toward the nearby forest.

Before long, Alfred could hear many of the others around him beginning to breathe heavily, some even gasping. Chavez led the group, still calling out the cadence. As others began to experience pain, Alfred actually was enjoying himself. The run brought fond memories of time spent as a member of the track team. For him, this was a walk in the park, not even enough to break a sweat. As he ran along with ease, he thought about the last twenty-four hours and all that had transpired: the vision of the vastness of America below the large and comfortable jet; the exciting plane ride from Shreveport to Alexandria; the forty-five-mile bus trip to the fort, during which he was shocked to see the abject poverty of many black people, who lived in little more than cardboard shanties. He thought of the extensive physical examination, with blood being drawn; receiving a series of shots; having his head shaved; and being issued a set of fatigues consisting of underwear, pants, shirts, belts, jackets, combat boots, a helmet, a complete dress uniform, a poncho, shovel, canteen, and backpack. After enjoying a decent supper, during which no one was allowed to speak, they had exercised until dark and were then assigned a footlocker and a bunk, where sleep came easily. The last thing he thought he remembered was the soft sound of someone moaning on the far side of the room.

During his brief time as a new resident of the base, Alfred discovered many things. Fort Polk was located in west central Louisiana and covered an area of nearly 100,000 acres, the majority of it sheltered with thick forest. It was established in 1941 and named in honor of the Right Reverend Leonidas Polk, the first Episcopal bishop of the diocese of Louisiana and a Confederate general. It was officially referred to as "Fort Polk, Home of Heroes."

Thousands of soldiers had learned the basics of combat here during the World War II Louisiana Maneuvers, before being deployed to Europe. After being closed for a short time the post was reopened for training during the Korean War and then closed again. It wasn't until the 1961 Berlin

Crisis that Fort Polk reactivated on a more permanent basis and in 1962, it became an infantry-training center. Subsequently, it was selected to conduct Vietnam-oriented training, which included airborne, medical, heavy artillery, and jungle maneuvers.

* * *

The group concluded their "little run," which was more like five miles, and ended up back in front of their barracks. During the run, Alfred noted that the dirt beneath their feet was soft, dark-red clay that stuck to their boots when wet, making the run even more difficult. During the outing, many of the men stopped to throw up the breakfast they had just eaten or fell by the wayside, a result of complete exhaustion. Those who finished stood at attention, most still gasping for air, until the stragglers caught up with them and joined the rank. Sergeant Chavez wasn't even breathing hard. It was apparent that he was in excellent condition. "Fifteen-minute break!" he shouted. "Clean off your boots, wash up, and report back here! And this time, when I say fifteen minutes, I mean fifteen minutes!"

This time, no one was late. The sergeant inspected each of their boots. Those whose boots weren't clean enough for his satisfaction did an extra twenty-five push-ups and then cleaned them again. They spent the balance of the morning in drill instructions, learning how to march correctly, and learning the commands and the proper responses. They were allowed one mistake each. Following that, if someone did anything incorrectly, he was taken aside and individually punished, usually in the form of physical training, or PT.

Understandably, the forty men did not achieve the perfection the sergeant required. Before the morning came to a close, every single one of them had made several mistakes and, as had been promised, painfully performed the extra PT. Alfred faced more of a challenge than his fellow soldiers. He had a reasonable understanding of English as it was spoken in California. Now, in addition to learning many new and unfamiliar military terms, he had difficulty deciphering the orders when they were spoken in a Southern accent. His learning curve resulted in countless extra push-ups.

Because he was in such excellent physical condition, the additional, forced exercises didn't bother him in the least. They only served to add to his physique, a fact that was not lost on Sergeant Chavez. During one of his many series of push-ups, Chavez casually observed, "You look like you're in pretty good shape."

"Yes, sir," Alfred replied, looking straight ahead.

Chavez noticed the accent and asked, "Where you from, boy?"

"California, sir."

"Don't sound like no California accent to me! Stand up! Where you really from?"

Alfred jumped to attention. "I was born in Germany, sir."

Chavez assumed a parade rest and his voice was deadly serious. "You one a them Nazi bastards we kicked the hell out of, boy?"

"No, sir. I'm an American, serving in the California National Guard."

Chavez didn't change expressions. "Good answer. Give me another twenty-five."

Alfred was unaffected by the Nazi slur. In his brief period of time at Fort Polk, he'd already determined the sergeant's plan was to erase all individuality by any means necessary, in order to develop soldiers who would act as a unit and follow orders explicitly. For purposes of self-preservation, Alfred decided to "go with the flow."

Following the morning drill exercises, the men ran to the mess hall, had a palatable lunch in silence, and formed ranks back outside. To their dismay, they went for another run, during which many lost their lunch and several were unable to finish with the others. Then the pattern from the day before was repeated: Fifteen-minute break. Clean your boots. Wash up. Fall back in. More marching drills. More PT. This continued until supper. After supper, there was more marching until the sergeant finally called them to attention and told them, "Return to your barracks. In the morning, there will be an inspection. Your boots *will* be shined. Your belt buckles *will* be polished. Your footlockers *will* be in order. Lights out at ten. Dismissed!"

The men wearily made their way up the stairs, several wondering if they'd make it. Many collapsed on their bunks, while others began their assigned tasks. They were well aware that if they were not completed to Sergeant Chavez' satisfaction, a severe price would be paid. Other than a few mumbled complaints, there was little conversation. There was too much to be done to waste time on such a worthless endeavor.

Alfred performed his duties without assistance. From his youth, he'd learned the lesson of following instructions and seldom questioned them. He wrote a letter to his parents, explaining he was doing well, that the food was good, and that the sergeant in charge of their group appeared to be a good and able instructor.

After lights out at ten o'clock, and following his evening prayers and even offering a kind word for Sergeant Chavez, Alfred was fast asleep. Several others were still in the latrine, where the lights remained on, still shining boots or buckles. Their transgressions would be paid for the following day.

At 5:30 the next morning, the screaming began again, along with garbage can lids banging together. The men jumped from their bunks as quickly as they were able and stood at attention. Sergeant Chavez walked down the aisle with his assistant, who carried a clipboard. Chavez looked at the first pair of boots, then the owner. "You call these clean?"

"Yes, sir," the man replied unenthusiastically.

Chavez threw the boots on the floor. "Do 'em again! And next time, I better be able to see my face in 'em!" He turned to his assistant. "Two demerits." The assistant made a mark on his clipboard. No one knew exactly what demerit was, but they were relatively certain it wasn't good. Chavez grabbed a belt buckle from another man. After close inspection, he snarled, "This what you consider polished?"

"I'll do it better," the man replied, embarrassed.

"Two demerits," Chavez barked to his assistant. He opened a footlocker, looked inside, and then stared at the owner. "This is crap! Worthless! Do it over!" To the assistant, he snapped, "Four demerits!" He grabbed the footlocker and turned it upside down, emptying its contents all over the floor. There were more demerits handed out as the sergeant continued his inspection. Only a very few passed to his satisfaction.

The men formed ranks outside, conducted thirty minutes of exercise, grabbed their shirts, and ran to the mess hall. During breakfast there were muffled whispers. "Think we'll have to do another run?" someone questioned.

"Naw. We'll probably go lie by a pool and get some rays," another one sniped.

A third man exhaled heavily, shook his head, and said in total seriousness, "I don't think I can do it."

Alfred turned toward the man and whispered, "Of course you can. You can do anything you put your mind to. You just have to believe in yourself. You're not alone here."

The rest of the men at the table looked at Alfred in disbelief, as if he was mentally disturbed.

Following breakfast, the group was pleasantly surprised when they ran in formation to a building identified as the armory. Once inside, they formed a single line, and one by one, each was handed an M-1 rifle. A clerk behind a table noted the serial number of the weapon and to whom it was assigned. Alfred was somewhat uncomfortable, for it was the first time in his life that he had ever held a weapon. The group was then directed into a large room filled with tables and instructed to take a seat. Within moments, another sergeant entered the room and walked briskly to a raised platform in front of the tables. He held up the M-1 in his left hand and said in a flat but serious tone, "This is your rifle." Then he grabbed his crotch with his right hand. "And this is your gun." He held up the M-1 again. "This is for shooting." He grabbed his crotch. "And this is for fun."

A few of the new recruits snickered, but the sergeant sternly explained, "You learn that lesson well, gentlemen, and someday it just might keep your ass alive." He held up the M-1. "This is your best friend. You're gonna learn more and know more about this weapon than you do about your wife or your girlfriend back home." The man walked to the first table and explained, "You will learn how to field strip this weapon until you can do it in your sleep. You will keep this weapon spotless at all times because if you don't, it could misfire and kill you." With that, the sergeant effortlessly and completely disassembled the weapon within a matter of seconds. The soldiers watching the demonstration were very impressed. "In time," said the sergeant, "you'll all be able to do what I just did." Then, with the same effortless ease he reassembled the weapon. "And you'll learn how to do that as well."

Few within the confines of the room believed they'd achieve that degree of expertise, but Alfred, always fascinated with anything mechanical, looked forward to the challenge. For the balance of the morning, they practiced. Over and over and over. Taking the weapon apart. Putting it back together. They became familiar with the stock and the barrel, and the bolt, and the springs, and the trigger, and every single moving part. Some were more proficient than others, but within time, they would all become experts. It was clearly explained, in no uncertain terms, that their lives depended on it.

At lunchtime, the men were instructed to carry the M-1's with them as they ran to the mess hall. Following lunch, they ran to the front of their barracks for marching drills, this time with the rifles on their shoulder, for the rest of the afternoon. They learned the lessons of "Right shoulder arms, left shoulder arms, present arms." They also learned a new form of PT. Now, when someone fouled up, in addition to the normal push-ups, he was instructed to run around in a circle, double-time, while holding his rifle over his head. At first, it seemed like a simple enough task, but after a few minutes, the rifle felt as it if weighed a hundred pounds. Weary arms would lower the weapons, causing even more time to be spent on the circular treadmill. While remarkably painful, it proved to be a good lesson, one that caused the new soldiers to pay closer attention to what they were doing, as well as encouraging others to follow their example. The result, which had been honed over decades of training, caused the men to become closer to each other and work together as a unit.

Then it was supper, no talking, more marching, and back to the barracks. In addition to polishing boots, shining buckles, and straightening footlockers, the men were now assigned the critically important task of practicing taking their weapons apart, putting them back together, and cleaning them to a state of perfection. As it was the previous night, several of the men were in the latrine well after lights-out, performing their assigned tasks.

Following breakfast, the routine was always a surprise. The men might find themselves in a classroom two or three times a week, learning correct military protocol, proper behavior, how to represent the United States whenever in uniform, adhering to the proper chain of command, and court-martial procedure. They learned that a squad has ten men, usually with a staff sergeant in charge. A platoon has four squads with a second lieutenant in charge. And a company is composed of four platoons, commanded by a captain. The fact their platoon was commanded by a master sergeant, also referred to as a drill instructor, was because they were in a basic training unit.

Long, exhausting power marches were often taken, normally while carrying rifles and full backpacks, including C-rations, which they ate when they stopped for lunch. Alfred smiled to himself as he ate from the green cans. A recruit beside him noticed the smile and asked, "What the hell's so funny?"

"I used to eat this stuff when I was a kid."

"Why?" the man asked.

"Because that's all we had."

Sometimes the platoon was pleasantly surprised as the mess truck brought warm food when they were far away from the camp. They never hiked anywhere without full canteens, adding to the weight they carried. Other times, they would ride in trucks to various sections of the camp. One area was the rifle range, where Alfred fired a weapon for the very first time. Initially, he was not very good, but over time and with practice, he became quite proficient. They also went to the grenade-exercise area, where instructor explained, "Pull the pin, count to three, throw the sucker as far as you can, and hit the deck." The explosions shook the ground, bringing back other unpleasant memories for Alfred.

There were nighttime exercises, marching through the forest in total darkness and total silence, wondering what, if anything, might take them by surprise. They were instructed in hand-to-hand combat, both with and without their rifles, with a bayonet attached to the barrel. But the most frightening of all the exercises was crawling through the red mud, underneath barbed wire, while live machine-gun fire flew over their heads. While nerve-racking and terrifying, the entire platoon successfully completed the ordeal.

To Alfred's amazement, Sergeant Chavez never seemed to talk—he always appeared to be screaming at the top of his voice. While a little frightening at first, the men grew used to his foul attitude and abusive demeanor. Even though Alfred drew more than his share of extra PT and KP—kitchen patrol, which normally consisted of peeling several large bags of potatoes, scrubbing pots and pans, and cleaning the grease trap—he knew from prior experience that the sergeant had his best interests and safety uppermost in his mind.

TWENTY

AFTER A FEW WEEKS OF BASIC TRAINING, ALFRED WROTE TO Hans, describing his activities and inquiring about the shop; asking about Johnny, his family, customers, new jobs, the Youth Group, and of course, the girls at the pool. His letters were always light and upbeat, never offering complaint about the difficult training he was experiencing. He avoided telling Hans about the physical training, nonstop drill practice, and long hikes through with a full backpack. He never mentioned that field activities often took place during driving rainstorms, even with intermittent flashes of lightning. He did mention, with a small degree of pride, that he learned how to shoot a rifle, throw a hand grenade, and even fire a bazooka, an incredible weapon that launched a rocket and could do unbelievable damage to its target.

While in basic training, Alfred learned another uniquely American phrase: "A chain is only as strong as its weakest link." If one of his fellow soldiers was not being all that he could be, he could potentially put the entire platoon in a dangerous and perhaps life-threatening situation. One situation that certainly seemed to be life-threatening was the gas-chamber drill, an exercise with which very few had ever been comfortable. During the drill, each member of the platoon was given a gas mask, secured with snaps in a pouch carried on their belts. They would enter a windowless and sealed room, after which the door was tightly shut. The instructor would then pop open a canister of tear gas. When he let go of the can and it hit the floor, the tear gas began to escape. That was the signal to remove the masks from their pouches and secure them over their faces. This had to be accomplished without breathing and with their eyes tightly closed. After about five minutes, one by one, they each had to remove the gas mask, state their name, rank, serial number, and date of birth, and then rapidly exit the room.

If the men followed the instructions carefully and did as they were told—speaking without breathing in and squinting their eyes—all would go well. Unfortunately, some of the men did not follow directions and ended up gasping desperately for air, rolling around on the floor, and violently throwing up. The exercise was critically important because of the growing nature of chemical warfare in the various theaters of war.

* * *

After a few weeks, the men were allowed a small but well-earned amount of free time. Alfred attended chapel on a regular basis and with the encouragement of the priest—or Padre, as he was referred to—found great comfort there. The base also had a PX—a post exchange—which was like a convenience store and carried most items the men wanted. It was a popular gathering place to browse. The base also had its own fast-food restaurant that served burgers, pizza, shakes, and other items not available in the mess hall. But the most popular venue of all was the theater that showed first-run films. Several times while watching a film Alfred whispered to a companion, asking for a translation of what was going on or being said on the screen—Alfred learned much about American culture from his questions.

Alfred's first real leave, a brief period of time when he and the other men were allowed off base, came at Christmas. Some of the men who lived close enough were able to go home for the holidays, but around the base there was nowhere of interest to go. A reasonably large contingency scheduled bus trips to New Orleans, where they planned to experience a wild and exciting adventure. Those joining that excursion were carefully and explicitly warned against getting into any trouble, for the price to be paid would be steep and extensive. At the time, as a war was escalating, the last thing the army wanted was any form of bad or negative publicity.

The skeleton troops that remained on the base still had to have their basic needs attended to, the primary of those being the food service. To that end, several soldiers were afforded the dubious honor of serving KP while the others were away having a good time. Alfred was one of who was assigned such duty. In addition to peeling countless potatoes and scrubbing mountains of pots and pans, he also learned how to prepare a variety of dishes—although it was unlikely that he would ever have the occasion to duplicate it once he was home, as the meal was prepared for two hundred people.

During the brief but anticipated break, all was not work. During this time, to let off steam, several of the men would engage in friendly shaving-cream battles in their barracks. After much encouragement, Alfred participated and, like the others, enjoyed their freedom and the fact they were making an enormous mess. It struck him during one of these battles that it was the first time he had heard laughter in this place they called home.

* * *

Spring came early to central Louisiana. The evenings were still chilly but daytime temperatures usually reached high and uncomfortable degrees. The discomfort came in the form of rain. Buckets of rain. Rain that did not deter the PT, the long hikes, or the various field activities. More often than not, even with the protection of their ponchos, the platoon would return to their barracks soaked to the skin and their boots caked with the red clay. After the rain, during marches through the forest, mosquitoes became the enemy. While others complained constantly, Alfred's thoughts turned to the regular army soldiers, many of whom would no doubt be deployed to a jungle on the far side of the world, where mosquitoes would be the least of their concerns.

As the months slipped by, Sergeant Chavez never let down his guard or showed any emotion or favoritism toward any of the men in his platoon. He remained aloof, unshakable, unrelenting. His job was to train them to be efficient soldiers; if they were ever called into service, they would be prepared and ready for any challenge. In that regard, while not a well-liked person, he was successful.

For Alfred, the six months of basic training passed quickly, and during his time there, he learned volumes about people and the history and culture of America. His platoon consisted of recruits from all backgrounds and experiences. He had the opportunity of interacting with those whose nationalities were Spanish, Italian, and Canadian, as well as diverse religious faiths. For the first time in his life, he had the occasion to work side by side with African Americans and learned much about their culture as well. But the thing that most impressed him was the fact that not that long ago, all the men had come together as strangers, individuals, and now, after six short months, they were a unit—well trained, physically fit, and highly efficient. For this result, he praised and appreciated the efforts put forth by Sergeant Chavez, a "lifer" in the U.S. Army who, underneath his cold and callous exterior, felt an enormous responsibility to properly train his recruits.

Following a brief but formal graduation ceremony, a picture of the platoon was taken. Their dress uniforms were pressed to perfection, and their shoes were polished to a mirror-like shine. They were then dismissed for the last time, given individual orders concerning where they were to report for their monthly meetings, and then instructed to return to their barracks, pack their things, and return to their hometowns. Alfred and his fellow soldiers exchanged promises to stay in touch as they said their good-byes.

During the bus ride back to the airport in Alexandria, it struck Alfred that even though he'd seen Sergeant Chavez on a daily basis, he'd never learned his sergeant's first name. Alfred smiled, thankful for the guidance provided by his sergeant; thankful he had entered the Guard as a private and was leaving as a private first class; thankful for all he had learned; and most of all, thankful he had made the decision to risk everything he had and come to this amazing place called America.

* * *

Hans picked up Alfred at the airport. While Alfred was pleased to see his old friend, Hans seemed to be troubled, as if something heavy was hanging over him. As they walked through the terminal, Alfred talked about his past six months and commented that he was eager to get back to work. He had asked Hans how the shop was going, if they have any new customers, and how Johnny was doing. Hans stopped walking, took a deep breath, and suggested they enter a nearby lounge where they could have a drink. Alfred looked puzzled but followed his friend, and as they took a seat and ordered a beer, Alfred knew something was wrong. Finally, after another deep breath, Hans blurted out, "Johnny's dead."

"What?" Alfred replied incredulously.

Hans nodded sadly. "He had a massive heart attack."

"You're kidding," Alfred said, refusing to believe the words, even though he knew they must be true. He took a long sip of his beer, then another. "When?"

"About three weeks ago."

Alfred stared at him with even more disbelief. "Why didn't you tell me? Why didn't you write? Or even call?"

Hans looked down at the bar, avoiding eye contact. He cleared his throat. "Nancy and I decided you were probably too busy with your training and all. We didn't want to cause you any more burden than you already had."

Alfred took a deep breath as he tried to control his anger. "You should have *told* me."

Now Hans took a long sip. He set his beer on the bar and nodded. "You're right. I should have. I'm sorry."

Alfred's breath came in ragged bursts. He shook his head, trying to compose himself. "How's Nancy doing?"

"As well as can be expected. Some days are better than others. She wants to talk with us."

"Both of us? About what?"

"About buying the company."

Alfred looked perplexed. "I don't have any money. You know that. So does Nancy."

"She wants to talk anyway."

During the ride back to their apartment, Hans told Alfred that many of their customers had attended Johnny's funeral. It was a very nice ceremony, followed by a wake, during which large amounts of Irish whiskey were consumed. Alfred smiled, warmly remembering. "That would have pleased Johnny."

"Very much," Hans agreed. He also told Alfred that all their customers had been advised of Johnny's passing and that the shop would continue its operations with new management.

"As in ... us?"

"Like I said. Nancy wants to talk."

That evening, Alfred and Hans discussed the prospect of becoming owners of the business, but the reality was that they really couldn't afford it. Perhaps someone else could purchase it, they thought, and they could continue to at least work there. Alfred had been looking forward to sleeping in his own bed and waking in the morning without the crashing of garbage can lids. But that night, with his uncertain future ahead of him, sleep would not come.

When the two visited the Gannon household the following day, Alfred gently held Nancy's fragile hands and offered his sincere condolences. "Nancy," he said, "I can't begin to tell you how sorry I am that I wasn't able to attend the funeral."

"I completely understand," she replied. "And I want you to know how very proud Johnny was that you joined the National Guard." She indicated that they should sit down at the ornate dining room table. "Would you care for a drink?" When the two men politely declined, Nancy offered a warm, gentle smile and suggested, "How about if we have one for Johnny? He would have liked that." They returned the smile and nodded. Nancy poured just a touch of Irish whiskey into three glasses. "To Johnny," she said. Alfred and Hans repeated the toast, and they clinked their glasses and downed the warm liquid.

Nancy got straight to the point, suggesting that Hans and Alfred purchase the company. "It's been apparent for more than two years that you two have really been responsible for running the shop anyway. You might as well own it."

"We are, of course, interested in continuing to work there," Hans said, "but we don't have enough money to purchase the business."

Nancy smiled. "Yes, I'm aware of how much you are being paid, but there's something you don't know—for the last year, Johnny had been telling me that, God forbid, if anything should happen to him, he wanted the two of you to have the company."

"We both appreciate that, Nancy," Alfred replied. "More than you can imagine. But that still doesn't solve the problem of our not having any money."

Nancy held up her hand, as if to silence any more protests. "There's more," she said. "Johnny would never tell you this, but he loved each of you as if you were his own sons. Night after night, he would tell me how proud he was of both of you and that he wouldn't even have a company if it weren't for your hard work and the quality workmanship you provide for the customers." Alfred and Hans were overwhelmed and unable to respond. Nancy smiled at both of them as she continued, "I know in my heart, because of all the hard work you've both put in, that he would want you to have the company. We'll work out whatever we have to so it can be yours, and you can continue doing what you've been doing."

Still astonished and immensely honored, Hans and Alfred quickly agreed with Nancy on a fair price for the business. It was decided that they would pay in monthly installments out of profits earned by the company.

Later that day, as they walked through the front door of the shop, it was as the new and very proud 50/50 partners and owners of the Manhattan Die Company.

During Alfred's absence, Johnny had hired an additional machinist named Reuben to help out in the shop. Hans said he was reasonably competent and followed instructions well. Both Reuben and Little Hans were pleased to learn that Alfred and Hans were purchasing the company—that meant they would still have steady employment. The first order of business was to send a letter to all their customers, informing them of the new ownership and assuring them that their needs would continue to be met in a timely and professional manner. The two new owners soon decided to expand and enlarge the company, and so they also sent letters of introduction to potential customers.

As was required, Alfred reported to the armory, located in downtown Los Angeles on Hope Street, at 6:00 a.m. Following PT on the blacktop parking lot, the men were assigned various duties. Alfred was assigned to a section referred to as G-2, for the express purpose of interpreting topographical maps, the majority of them from Germany—maps left over from the war. He was given a desk on the third floor of the building, as well as an ancient Remington typewriter on which he would write various reports. He stayed on duty until 6:00 p.m. on Sunday, a schedule that would continue on a monthly basis.

As a result of the introduction letters sent out, Alfred and Hans acquired several new customers, and business was on an uphill rise. Alfred was pleased that everything seemed to be going so well—and then he received an urgent call from a non-commissioned officer, ordering him to collect his gear and report to the armory as quickly as possible. The call, although somewhat alarming, was not unexpected. It was mid-June and the Santa Ana winds were forcing the temperature to well over 100 degrees. The relentless heat, lack of air conditioning, high unemployment, and years of frustration fueled one of the most destructive riots in the history of the country. The riot broke out in an area of Los Angeles known as Watts, a portion of the city whose population consisted primarily of African Americans. The National Guard was activated because the police were unable to control the rioting, looting, destruction, and violent mobs that were roaming the streets and setting indiscriminant fires—fires that were springing up at an alarming rate throughout the sprawling neighborhood. When fire department trucks arrived to put out the blaze, rioters fired at them with rifles and pistols.

There was understandable concern that the growing and out-of-control mob would attack the armory and gain access to the weapons stored there—that was a potential disaster that had to be avoided at any cost. As soon as Alfred arrived he was quickly ushered into the main room of the armory, where he was issued an M-1 rifle with a bayonet and live ammunition. With several others, he was ordered to the roof of the building, where they would stand post, protecting the facility with deadly force, if necessary.

He could see nearby plumes of smoke billowing into the sky, shrouding the smog that normally blanketed the downtown area. The sound of screeching police and fire department sirens could be heard from all directions. A sergeant standing nearby had a walkie-talkie radio, and Alfred could overhear reports from hospitals in the area, as scores of people with gunshot wounds filled their emergency rooms. Alfred gripped his rifle, pointing over the edge of the building, fully prepared to shoot if he were ordered to do so. His mind flashed back to the many hours he'd spent on the rifle range at Fort Polk—hours spent perfecting and honing his proficiency as a marksman. He wondered if today was the day he would be called upon to exercise that skill.

Rioters fired on police cars as they tried to control the looting and protect the fire fighters. They even fired on the helicopters that flew overhead, trying to report the activities and movements of the marauding mobs. High-ranking officials called for a citywide curfew, but it was only observed by those sheltered in their homes far away, who watched the madness on their television sets. By nightfall, it appeared as if the entire city was ablaze.

As more and more Guardsmen arrived, they were issued weapons and given assignments, one of which was to set up barricades in a parameter around the armory to prevent anyone from approaching without proper authorization. They could see the glowing night sky and hear random gunshots from where they stood guard. Nerves were on edge. Trigger fingers, which might only touch a weapon once a year, were itchy.

There were far too many people coming in and out of the armory for anyone to consider the mechanisms of feeding the men. Instead, on a rotating basis, the Guardsmen were given vouchers, a brief amount of time, and instructed to eat at nearby restaurants. That night, because of the volume of soldiers and the shortage of cots, they slept in shifts on the floor wherever space was available. Alfred was among many of the soldiers assigned the duty of riding inside an armored personnel carrier and into the midst of the rioting—the use of open Jeeps was far too dangerous. Their purpose was to disperse the crowds and hopefully bring order. Alfred witnessed several groups running from stores with looted merchandise and even some who were throwing Molotov cocktails—bottles filled with gasoline and a lighted wick made of cloth. As the devices were tossed through storefront windows, they exploded, causing even more fires.

The officers in command were explicit in their orders that none of the soldiers were to fire their weapons, unless they were fired upon first. With sunrise, the devastation was clear, and it was overwhelming. Countless streets resembled a war zone. More soldiers were activated to quell the continuing violence, until finally, three days and two nights after it began, it came to a halt. When the entire area was finally secured, all participating army units assembled to listen to glowing praises from the commanding general, the mayor of the city, and the chief of police.

Alfred was totally spent—exhausted physically and emotionally. The radio reports listed the number of deaths, along with noting the probability that there would be more. Alfred shook his head at the news. *It's so sad*, he thought, *that innocent people lost their lives for no reason*. It brought back tragic memories of the war, the one in which, as a child, Alfred had been unfortunate enough to be an innocent victim himself.

Once he reached home, he showered, changed clothes, and drove to the shop. As he walked in the front door, he forced himself to alter his mind-set from devastation and death to the fact that he and Hans now owned their own company, were responsible to customers and employees, and must do everything in their power to make it a success.

TWENTY-ONE

THE DOOR HAD NOT YET CLOSED BEHIND HIM BEFORE HANS, Little Hans, and Reuben surrounded Alfred. They had seen the riots on television—the looters, the roaming mobs, the military, the shooting, the burning buildings—and they were overflowing with questions: "Did you shoot anybody? Did you see any of the mobs? Was anybody in your unit killed? Did you get shot at?"

Alfred answered in a calm and steady manner, expressing the same resolve and restraint he'd shown during the horrendous days and nights of the riot itself. They clung to each word, yet peppered him with more questions before his answers were completed. Alfred patiently and clearly defined the experience through his own eyes, not showing any degree of emotion. "I was only doing my job as a soldier. Following orders. Protecting others."

Little Hans stuck out his chest and smugly announced, "Wish I'd been there."

Alfred looked him squarely in the eye. "No, you don't."

"Were you afraid?" Reuben asked.

"Of course I was," Alfred answered without hesitation. "But I pushed it out of my mind because I knew I had a job to do."

"Who did you talk to?" Hans questioned. "Anybody important?"

Alfred was reflective, staring into the distance as he quietly replied,

"Yes … yes, I did. Mostly, I talked to God."

Little Hans suppressed a snicker. "God? You talked to God? How long you been doin' that?"

"Since I was old enough to talk."

Now Little Hans' smile was clearly evident. "And just what does God have to say these days?"

Alfred knew that Little Hans was poking fun at him, but he wasn't bothered in the least. In fact, he answered as if he thought Little Hans' question was sincere. "God doesn't talk to you in words. You feel it in your heart. If you listen closely enough, you feel it in His presence."

Reuben leaned closer, totally serious. "What did you feel?"

Alfred looked into Reuben's eyes and quietly replied, "That I was safely in God's hands." Then, with polite firmness, he explained there would be plenty of time to talk later. Now, it was time to return to work. The first order of business was to huddle with Hans and discuss the jobs in process and any new ones that had come in during his absence. The letters they sent to prospective customers continued to prove to be beneficial, with more wanting to give Manhattan Die a chance at their business. There was much to do, and it had to be done as quickly as possible.

If they were to grow and satisfy new customers, the two men decided, they would have to obtain a larger facility. They also needed to replace much of their equipment and obtain new, precision machinery as well. Once their plans were solidified on paper, the challenge seemed daunting, but when they broke it down into smaller parts, they felt that with hard work, it could eventually be accomplished. They began by scouring ads in several newspapers for a new location. When any place sounded remotely workable, Hans would check it out to see if it would be acceptable for their needs. Unfortunately, the rents charged for the amount of space they needed were prohibitive. For the time being, they would just have to put in the necessary extra hours and make do with what they had.

* * *

When Alfred reported for his second monthly weekend of duty at the armory, he was told to report to a captain's office. *What is this all about?* he asked himself with great concern. He thought perhaps he was going to be relieved of his duty or—even worse—activated and shipped overseas. With understandable apprehension, he knocked on the door, and a deep, authoritative voice from the other side announced, "Enter."

Alfred opened the door, walked to the front of the desk, snapped to attention, and said, "Private First Class Langer, reporting as ordered, sir."

The captain was middle-aged with graying temples. He looked up and spoke clearly. "You impressed your commanding officer when you were here last month." Alfred stood straight, wondering what was coming next. The captain noticed his concern and ordered, "At ease, Private." Alfred relaxed, but just a little, as the captain continued, "Your efforts with regard to following orders were also noticed during the riot. The army has decided to grant you a secret clearance. This means you will be assigned to work in a special and secure map room, interpreting and explaining the writing found on a series of maps and documents. This is a classified position and as such, you are not allowed to tell anyone else, not even fellow soldiers, where you are working or what you are doing. Is that clear?"

"Yes, sir," Alfred replied, although it was not really clear at all.

"Good. Report to where you were assigned last month, and they'll give you further instructions." The captain returned to the paperwork on his desk, and Alfred wasn't really sure what to do. The captain looked back up. "Oh, yes," he said. "One more thing." He handed Alfred a stripe. "Put this on your sleeve. With the secret clearance comes a promotion. You're now a corporal. Congratulations. Dismissed."

Alfred saluted, left the office, and returned to the room where he had worked the previous month. After presenting himself to a first lieutenant in charge of the area, he was led to another room, which was clearly marked: "Classified Area. Security Clearance Required." Once inside, he was introduced to a number of other men, all officers. Alfred was the only soldier in the room who was not an officer. His job, as the captain explained, was to interpret German writing on a series of maps. His secret clearance was necessary because he was working side by side with officers who were planning a series of wide-ranging strategies—hypothetical actions against a potential threat. The concern, however, was not for another German uprising rather, the exercise was to prepare for the possibility of any troop movement or other unusual activity by the Russians.

Alfred set to work, explaining which parts of the map represented freeways, interstate highways, country roads, railroad stations, creeks, rivers, streams, lakes, cities, towns, villages, airports, and smaller landing strips, as well as identifying the borders of the states within Germany. While his new assignment seemed insignificant at first, he rapidly grew to understand that the United States was deeply involved in a Cold War with a well-armed and remarkably dangerous enemy, whose stated purpose was the destruction of the country he had grown to love. In overhearing the potential strategies of the officers in the room, Alfred determined that even in a small way, the work he was doing was integral protecting America, a fact of which he was very proud. Whenever questioned about his work with the National Guard, he continued to tell friends and associates that his job was simply to translate old and outdated documents, which had little or no significance. The consequence of his secret clearance status became clear to him when he received a letter from his parents. They told him investigators from the U.S. Army visited Selbitz and interviewed several of his friends, checking on his background, questioning his character, determining his loyalty. The questions asked most often concerned whether he or any members of his family were ever involved, in any way, in the Nazi Party or the Hitler Youth.

* * *

Alfred's life was consumed with work and planning for the growth of the company. Still, he recognized the need to occasionally create personal time—time to be alone with his thoughts and try to analyze various situations on his own. He discovered a restaurant called the St. Stefan's Club, a place originally founded by members of a successful German soccer team and later sold to a private owner. Many Germans frequented the establishment for the authentic cuisine and hearty German beer. A large contingent of Americans who loved real German food and the pleasant, genuine atmosphere were also regular patrons.

Alfred would often go there by himself after work, eating fine food as he made copious notes on his ideas for the company. The people who ate and worked there were open and friendly, and most of them equally fluent in both German and English. One special evening—September 16, 1965—a new waitress approached his table to take his order. He'd eaten there often enough to know all of the employees and the menu by heart, so he looked up from his notes and was surprised to see a new employee. She had dark hair and brown eyes and was remarkably attractive.

"Have you decided, sir?" she asked in a soft voice.

Alfred thought her voice sounded as if it came from heaven, and he was so taken with her beauty that he could barely speak.

"Sir?" she repeated, offering a warm and engaging smile.

Not taking his eyes off the young lady, Alfred gave his order and watched closely as she walked away toward the kitchen. He noticed the owner of the restaurant circulating among the patrons—the two had become well acquainted—and he called him over. "Who's the new waitress?" he asked.

"Her name is Irene," the owner replied. "Christina's sick with the flu, and Irene's filling in for her. I think they're roommates. Why do you ask? Did she do something wrong?"

Alfred shook his head and smiled. "Absolutely not."

The owner nodded sagely and walked away, and Alfred stared intently as Irene delivered food to other tables, sharing her glowing smile with other patrons. He had a strange feeling in the pit of his stomach. *Could it be*, he asked himself, *that I'm actually feeling jealous that she's spending precious time with others?* His mind suddenly flashed back to the number of letters his mother had sent him, each one asking if he'd found a girlfriend yet. And with each return letter, he'd replied in the negative. Now, he was wondering how he would respond when the question was next asked.

And then she was at his side again, delivering his food and saying sweetly, "I hope you enjoy it."

He smiled politely, a little nervously, only able to nod in response. He ate the large plate of bratwurst and sauerkraut mechanically, never taking his eyes off her, completely mesmerized with each measured movement she made. Several times while she was serving other tables, it seemed as if she was looking back at him, making sure he was still in his seat. It was a feeling he enjoyed, even though he cautiously assured himself that it couldn't possibly be true.

Finally, after what seemed like hours, she appeared at his table and asked, "Would you like something else?"

He really didn't but found himself ordering another beer, just so he could extend the time spent looking at her. As she went to retrieve his beer, the owner returned to Alfred's table and sat down. "You like her, huh?" he asked knowingly.

"She's very attractive," Alfred answered.

"A bit of advice ... if you're interested, you better do something about it soon, 'cause I don't know how long Christina's gonna be out." And with a slight smile, he returned to the kitchen.

Later, when Irene brought Alfred his check, he found himself tongue-tied, unable to say anything except, "Are you going to be here again tomorrow?"

She smiled that smile. "Yes. Are you?"

He was thrilled with the response. "Yes!"

"I'll see you then."

Later that evening, Hans wanted to talk about a new customer and their future plans for the company, but Alfred had trouble concentrating; his mind was on Irene. And he had just as much difficulty focusing on work the next day. Thoughts of Irene consumed him, and he counted the minutes until he would see her smiling, radiant face again.

When she approached his table the next day to take his order, he called up all his courage, offered his hand, and said, "My name is Alfred Langer."

She took it in hers and, with a warm smile and a firm but gentle handshake, replied, "And mine is Irene Aragon." Her dark eyes sparkled as she spoke her name, obviously proud of herself and her heritage.

Alfred's mind raced, not wanting her to leave. "How ... how long are ... you ... you going to be filling in for ... for your friend?" he stammered.

"Just a few more days. She's feeling much better."

"I'm glad to hear that," he said. "At least, I'm glad that your friend is feeling better." His mind continued to race, searching for anything to keep the conversation going. "You know, I really love going to the beach," he blurted out, and then immediately thought, *What a stupid thing to say.*

"Really?" Irene said, her smile widening. "I love the beach, too."

"No kidding?"

Irene nodded.

Summoning more courage, he continued, "Would you consider going to the beach with me this Sunday?"

Without hesitation, she said, "I'll have to check to see if my family has any other plans."

At least her response wasn't an absolute or definitive no, he thought, feeling somewhat confident. That feeling stayed with him throughout the night, the next day, and into the evening, when he returned to the restaurant. Try as he might, he could not erase the memory of the enormous pain of rejection he'd experienced when he was sixteen. In the back of his mind, he worried that Irene might do the same. To his enormous relief, however, when he repeated the invitation that night, she replied that she would be delighted to join him.

The following Sunday, Alfred arrived at Irene's apartment, where he met her roommate, Christina, and then, after a scenic drive up the coast, they shared a pleasant afternoon on the beach at Malibu. While walking along the sand, Alfred learned that Irene worked in the office of Gaffers and Settlers, a firm that manufactured stoves; and that her family had emigrated from Mexico in 1956; and that she was the oldest of five children. They shared their experiences of growing up, both their families struggling to make a new beginning with very limited means. They each seemed fascinated with the other. Alfred had never felt as comfortable with a girl as he did that very day. After driving her home and walking to her front door, he asked if she'd like to get together again the next weekend. She offered that magnetic smile and replied that she would. He thanked her for a wonderful time and warmly shook her hand—and when their hands touched, Alfred felt as if he had been struck by a small bolt of lightning.

Later that evening, when Hans asked Alfred how his date had been, Alfred replied with one simple word: "Perfect."

* * *

After much searching and many excursions to look at potential space, Alfred and Hans finally found a workable location in a place called South Gate, about seven miles south of Los Angeles. The building was owned by Herbert and Margaret Lippincutt, a delightful couple in their late seventies, who had run their own pottery business in the building before retiring. It had a large glass storefront and was in a good location on a major thoroughfare, close to freeways, and still centrally located in the L.A. area.

During their very first meeting, the Lippincutts felt an immediate affection for both Alfred and Hans. They had a daughter from whom they were unfortunately estranged, and they looked at the boys as if they were extended family; the feeling was reciprocated. The Lippincutts offered to rent them the location for a very reasonable amount per month, as well as offering their assistance whenever the boys needed their help.

Alfred and Hans worked at night, diligently preparing the new shop. Although they did most of the work themselves, they hired an electrician to professionally install all the outlets, and they hired a moving company to transport the machines and equipment and install them in the proper location. The layout and the manufacturing method were now similar to the way that Hans and Alfred had been taught while working at the Bodenschatz facility.

Having to make do with the antiquated equipment for several months because of their financial situation, replacement was now a necessity. Using credit based on their growing list of impressive customers, they were able to purchase the new equipment they needed, and machines were set up to minimize the change-over and set-up time.

Little Hans had decided to return to the East Coast, his original home. With the increase in business—and now one less worker—the workload for Alfred, Hans, and Reuben became a viable challenge. They worked late into the night and most weekends. They tried to replace Little Hans, but good machinists were difficult to find—part of that was due to the fact that North American Rockwell, located nearby in Downey, had obtained government contracts to develop the space shuttle. As a result, that company hired the vast majority of the qualified machinists and engineers within the surrounding area. Alfred and Hans interviewed numerous people who had limited background as machinists and found a few whom they felt could become proficient with proper training. Two new workers, Frank and Jose, adapted well, learned quickly, and soon became an integral part of the company.

In the mid-1960s the plastics industry was in its infancy but was growing and expanding rapidly. Manhattan Die was one of only two heat-sealing die makers west of Chicago. As a result, the majority of customers who needed specific and precision dies had little choice in selecting a supplier. Manhattan Die's continued efforts to provide quality service for a fair and reasonable price resulted in steady growth; the downside of their success was limited free time, especially on weekends. Alfred spent one weekend each month with the National Guard, and two weekends working at the shop. On his one free weekend, however, he explored the grandeur of the country he was protecting. One weekend, he and Hans drove to the Grand Canyon, pitched their tent in the campground, and planned to hike down to the Colorado River the following morning.

Early the next day, they began down the trail, after having been advised that the trip would take about three hours. They were not aware that typically, only a few of those who began the trek actually made it the entire way. They arrived at the river, expecting there would be somewhere to buy food, but there was nothing in sight—other than a magnificent and breathtaking view of the canyon.

After cooling their feet in the river, Alfred and Hans began the hike back up—and the trip back up took much longer than the trip down. That day, they hiked for more than eight straight hours without food. Fortunately, they were able to get water by sipping the cool liquid as it trickled out of rocks. Too late, they realized, as they watched others on the trail, that they could have ridden mules for the long excursion. When they finally reached their camp, they were completely exhausted and collapsed on the ground. Later, as they rested and rubbed aching feet, a park ranger stopped to chat with them. With a large smile covering his face, he observed, "Not very many people have accomplished what you two just did."

During the ride back to L.A., Alfred thought about the only other time he'd seen the Grand Canyon—out of a plane window from thirty thousand feet, on his way to Fort Polk. He wondered how many other Americans had experienced the vastness or the beauty of the country, as he and Hans had just had the opportunity to see and touch.

But most of all, he wondered what Irene was doing.

Alfred and Irene began to date steadily, discovering more about one another with each encounter. They both were devout Catholics and had practiced their faith since they were children. As their relationship developed and became more serious, Irene invited Alfred to meet her family. She did her best to calm his nervousness by explaining, "My parents are going to love you." She smiled warmly and added, "After all, I do."

When they entered the front door of the quaintly decorated, three-bedroom house in Norwalk, Alfred was greeted by Irene's father, Don; her mother, Delores; and her siblings, Manuel, Molly, Rudi, and Mary. During the hellos and handshaking, Alfred couldn't help but think about his own family and how long it had been since he'd seen them.

Within moments, Irene's reassuring words proved to be true. Her father was a machine operator in a machine shop, which meant he and Alfred had much in common. Her mother worked in the kitchen in the Norwalk Community Hospital and was rumored to be an excellent cook. She was greatly amused when Alfred shared the story of getting stuck with KP during the Christmas vacation while stationed at Fort Polk.

Alfred was positive that Irene's parents were both measuring him, seeing if he might possibly be "the one" for their daughter. Irene noticed Alfred's unease and told her parents, "He doesn't have any skeletons in his closet—at least, none that I know of." The others laughed, but Alfred was not familiar with the phrase and was troubled, wondering, *Why on earth would I have any skeletons in my closet?*

Irene's siblings just stared at Alfred, intrigued by the young man with perfect posture and a buzz haircut. He was a bit unnerved as they examined him and greatly relieved when Irene's father finally announced, "Let's have some food." The group moved into the backyard, and Alfred discovered the offhand comment was an understatement. The "food" was more like a feast. The elaborate barbeque consisted of *menudo*, a spicy Mexican soup that had been simmering since the day before to let the spices fully absorb; flat-iron steaks on corn tortillas with homemade salsa; Spanish rice; refried beans; corn on the cob; and an abundance of ice-cold beer. Dolores was indeed a wonderful cook.

Conversation was nonstop. Fascinating stories—telling of experiences in Hermannstadt and Selbitz and Mexico—flowed as freely as the beer. Alfred avoided saying much about the bad parts of the war and the painful transgression his family was forced to endure—these memories were painful enough in his mind, let alone actually speaking them out loud. The spirited and enlightening conversation was accompanied in the background by ranchero and mariachi music from outdoor speakers. Alfred was introduced to songs by Pedro Enfante and Jorge Negrete, Mexican singers who were idolized as if they were national heroes. While Alfred couldn't understand any of the words, he could most definitely feel the passion in both the music and the voices.

On the drive back to Irene's apartment, Alfred said, "I really enjoyed meeting your family. They're very nice people."

Irene smiled. "They liked you, too."

Alfred wasn't convinced. "Are you sure? At first, I felt like I was on trial or something."

"They've heard me say so many good things about you, they wanted to see for themselves if it was true."

Alfred grinned. "Think I passed?"

Irene touched his hand, returning the grin. "With flying colors."

* * *

It didn't take long for Alfred and Hans to realize that the commute from their apartment in Highland Park to the shop in South Gate was a tremendous waste of time. They were spending far too many hours on the road, time that could be spent much more productively in their shop. As long as they were going to move, they also decided it was time for them to each have their own places. Alfred moved into a three-room house on San

Juan Street in South Gate, and Hans located a three-room house of his own on Elizabeth Street. Now, they were both within a ten-minute drive of their company.

As the radio-frequency sealing industry expanded, the demand for heat-sealing dies grew exponentially. The Bridgeport milling machines and other equipment they'd purchased were able to meet the demand and stay ahead of the curve with far less downtime than they'd previously experienced. Their business was completely unique—if anyone wanted to manufacture anything from flexible or rigid PVC, a type of polyvinyl chloride, it was necessary to have a die.

One item that added tremendously to the coffers of Manhattan Die was a simple thing called a waterbed. The product itself had been around for a long time, but in the mid-1960s, the fad exploded and became a huge industry. Waterbeds were healthy, they were comfortable, and they were fun. Fueled by creative advertising, thousands of people wanted to own one. Companies sprang up overnight, and all that was needed to manufacture the beds and make piles of money was one thing: a reliable die.

Early one morning, Alfred entered their small reception area and found a rather scruffy-looking gentleman sitting on their desk. He had an unkempt beard and was wearing grease-stained jeans. "My name is Simmons," the man said in a raspy voice. "Your company was recommended by the people who sell the radio-frequency sealing machines as having the best reputation to produce quality dies to manufacture waterbeds." He showed Alfred a very rough drawing of what he had in mind. Alfred had a brief consultation with Hans, and they determined what it would cost to produce the die. Together, told Simmons they could provide him with dies he needed.

Simmons reached into his pocket, produced a large wad of cash, and calmly asked, "How much of a down payment would you like?"

At that moment the floodgates were most delightfully opened. Manhattan Die became the first die maker in the country to design and manufacture the tools necessary to produce waterbeds. Initially, they developed a simple vinyl bag that could be filled with water from a garden hose. It was available in different sizes, ranging from twin to king size. Their popularity grew as motion pictures featured the beds, with people sloshing around on them and having great fun doing it. As the fad grew more popular, it was necessary to design and manufacture dies for bed frames that would hold the bags. Then heated waterbeds became the new craze, popularized by advertising that the new and improved heated beds could potentially eliminate back problems. Next came the addition of vibrators, and the comfort and pleasure that could be found by sleeping on vibrating water-beds. Alfred and Hans had to hire more machinists to keep up with the demand. Business was booming, running smoothly and efficiently. Alfred felt a sense of relief that things were going well, as he was about to take a two-week "vacation."

TWENTY-TWO

DRESSED IN FATIGUES AND CARRYING A FULL DUFFLE BAG, Alfred reported to the armory at the appointed hour. A total of two full platoons also arrived, and once they were checked in, they moved to the parking lot, where they stood in formation. In the distance were several canvas-covered two-and-a-half-ton trucks. A sergeant moved among the men and chose several at random, Alfred among them. The select few were ordered to get into the trucks and drive them through a marked course without error or destroying any of the yellow cones that had been arranged in a zigzag pattern on the pavement.

Muffled laughter broke out, as some of the drivers couldn't even figure out how to start the engines. Others failed to control the large machines and destroyed several of the cones. Once the course was completed, the sergeant approached those who had successfully driven through it—and Alfred was one of them—and instructed them without emotion, "You soldiers are now qualified to drive trucks." Alfred was taken slightly aback and waited patiently as the sergeant initialed several pieces of paper and handed one to each of the new drivers. It was a certificate, officially signifying their prowess and competence to operate the beastly vehicles.

The new drivers were ordered to gather their gear and return to the trucks; the other soldiers were ordered to get into the rear of the trucks. After a loud blast from a whistle, they were off. The convoy of army vehicles drove north for more than three hours, finally leaving the freeway and traversing on smaller roads, until they passed under the main gate of a facility known as Fort Irwin. Summer camp had just officially begun.

The convoy passed several large buildings, many of them obviously barracks, and continued deep into the desert. Once they reached a remarkably isolated area, they were ordered to a halt, and everyone exited the trucks, glad to finally be able to stretch their legs. Their rest period was short-lived, as a small group of supply trucks joined them, and the soldiers were ordered to unload the equipment and items they carried. They spent the remainder of day erecting camouflaged tents for headquarters, a kitchen, a mess tent, a shower and latrine facility, and tents for the troops. Complete utensils for the kitchen were put into operable order, desks and tables were placed into the headquarters, and cots were assembled in the troop tents. It was instantly apparent that this exercise was not going to be what some had originally referred to as light duty. They were there to work, to train, and to become better qualified and more efficient soldiers.

Following dinner, the men learned that Fort Irwin was a training facility for combat troops. It comprised an area of approximately a thousand square miles, the majority of it barren desert. In addition to infantry soldiers, sometimes referred to as "ground-pounders," light and heavy artillery units and tank troops also trained there. The purpose of the two-week training period was to conduct a series of war games in which various groups would compete with each other in combat situations, but obviously without live ammunition. The word "games" was a misnomer—the training was intense and critically serious. They had to be ready and prepared to deploy at any minute, should there be a national emergency calling for their participation, just as they had been during the Watts riots.

Reveille sounded at 5:30 the next morning, and the men formed ranks in front of their tents. Able-looking sergeants were assigned different groups and issued orders to hit the latrine, shower, shave, and report back in formation in twenty minutes. The sergeant in charge of Alfred's group was not at all like Sergeant Chavez. He spoke in a normal tone of voice, rather than screaming. Even so, the men knew he was clearly in charge; he was a combat veteran who had faced death on a daily basis. His reputation preceded him, and his men respected both his bravery and accomplishment.

Following a decent breakfast in the mess tent, the men once again formed ranks, and a first lieutenant carrying a clipboard joined them. He whispered something to the sergeant in charge, who then announced, "Corporal Langer."

"Yes, sir," Alfred replied.

"Front and center."

Alfred walked briskly until he was standing in front of the two men. He saluted the lieutenant, and it was returned. Alfred noticed that the nametag sewn on the officer's shirt read "Schulz."

The lieutenant waved his index finger, indicating that Alfred should follow him, and they walked to a Jeep parked nearby. Alfred stood tall, at perfect attention. Schulz noticed and calmly said, "Relax, soldier. No need to impress me." Alfred put his hands behind his back and assumed a parade rest position.

Alfred and Schulz were about the same age, both born in 1940. Schulz had short brown hair and kind but focused eyes—eyes that seemed as if they could see things that weren't there. He looked at the clipboard. "Says here you're a Spec 5."

"Yes, sir."

"Why's that?"

"Because I have a secret clearance, sir."

"What's the secret clearance for?" Schulz asked.

"With all due respect, sir, the secret clearance means I'm not allowed to tell anybody what it's for."

Schulz offered a slight smile and replied, "Good answer. You're from Germany, huh?"

"Yes, sir."

"What part?"

"Originally from a small town called Hermannstadt, but I grew up in Selbitz."

"That's in the northern part, isn't it?"

"Yes, sir."

"I was deployed there for a year," Schulz offered. "Nice place. Decent people."

"Most of us were very glad you were there, sir."

"Those Czech bastards give you a lot of trouble?"

"If you mean, did they steal everything my family worked their entire lives for and then force us into poverty and homelessness and near starvation, then yes, sir. I'd say those Czech bastards gave us a lot of trouble."

Schulz became very serious. "We left a lot of damn good men over there."

Alfred was equally serious. "So did we, sir."

"You ever kill anybody, Corporal?"

"Thankfully, no, sir. I haven't."

"I hope you never have to." He looked at his clipboard again. "Also says you're qualified as a driver."

"Yes, sir."

"Ever drive on the Autobahn?"

"Yes, sir."

Schulz rubbed his chin, apparently deep in thought. "What's your first name?"

Alfred was somewhat confused. All the soldiers had their last names sewn above the right pocket of their shirts and jackets, and in his six months of basic training and several weekends at the armory, he'd never heard anyone called by anything other than his rank or his last name. "Alfred," he finally said.

"What do people call you?"

Now he was more confused. "Alfred, sir."

"Sounds a little formal to me. Mind if I just call you Al?"

Not wishing to be argumentative, Alfred replied, "That'd be fine with me, sir."

With Schulz' next comment, Alfred's mouth nearly dropped open in surprise, as Schulz said, with perfect pronunciation, "*Geniessen sie ihre Zeit in der Armee, Korporal?*" Translated it meant, "Do you enjoy being in the army, Corporal?"

And with a completely straight face, Alfred replied, "*Jawohl, ich bin Stolz mein neues Heimatland zu Dienen.*" Or, "Yes, sir. I'm very proud to be able to serve my new country." The lieutenant nodded, smiled broadly, and patted Alfred on the shoulder. "Tell ya what, Al. I like your style. You've got a secret clearance, which means you know how to keep your mouth shut; a license to drive military vehicles; you own your own business, which means you have leadership abilities; and you can help me brush up on my German."

"With all due respect, sir, your German is quite good."

"Got a proposal for ya. How 'bout if I make you my personal driver for the next two weeks. Or, if you'd prefer, you can hike around in the desert day and night, carrying a rifle and a hundred-pound pack on your back. Which sounds better?"

Alfred suppressed a smile as he responded, "Where would you like me to drive you, sir?"

Schulz handed him the keys to the Jeep and told him, "Be right back." The lieutenant walked over to the sergeant and informed him that he was commandeering Corporal Langer for the duration of their stay. The sergeant nodded, and Schulz returned to the Jeep. In the background, Alfred could hear the sergeant ordering his men to get their backpacks. The last words he heard before he started the engine were, "Saddle up, ladies. We're goin' for a little walk."

Lieutenant Schulz sat down in the front seat, pointed forward, and off they went. After they'd driven about a mile or so, Schulz commented, "When we're around other people you'll have to act military. But when it's just you and me, we can drop all that formal crap. My name's William, but most folks call me Will. Fair enough?"

"Yes, sir."

Schulz smiled and shook his head. "Here's the drill. I'm in charge of maneuvers for one of the tank groups. Naturally, I've got a commanding officer who gives the orders, but I'm the front-line guy who's supposed to make sure they're carried out. Basically, I watch what the guys in the tanks are doing and then report back to my C.O. on a daily basis. Questions?"

"No, sir."

"Listen up, Al. When it's just us, you can call me Will. Think you can handle that?"

Alfred smiled and replied, "Not a problem, Will. From now on I'll just … go with the flow."

Now Schulz smiled. "Works for me. Think we're gonna get along just fine."

When Alfred returned to his unit that evening, he found his fellow soldiers collapsed on their cots. While he was out having a leisurely and pleasant drive, the rest of them had taken a twenty-mile hike with full packs. One of the men explained that the sergeant told them he was going to spend the first few days getting them into shape. When Alfred was asked what he'd done all day, he said that he was assigned duty as a tank observer; that his job was classified and he was not permitted to discuss it.

* * *

The "war games" were designed to not only improve the skills of the regular soldiers but also the commanding officers' skills concerning military strategy and troop movements. Somewhere on the far side of the camp, two groups—one called the Red Army and the other called the Blue Army—were training. Once the games officially commenced, the commanders of each group would try to outmaneuver the other, using an element of surprise—counter attacks, various offensive and defensive strategies, night-time raids, and full-scale assaults.

Independent judges, mostly high-ranking officers, traveled throughout the "conflict areas" and determined which team won various battles and skirmishes. All elements of personnel were involved: infantry, artillery, and "rolling stock," such as troop carriers and tanks. While Alfred's unit spent hours conducting long marches and practiced on the rifle and hand-grenade range, he was driving Lieutenant Schulz to the far corners of the desert, from Barstow to the edge of Death Valley. They would normally take a position high on a ridge and, through binoculars, oversee various tank groups as they went through maneuvers. Alfred was fascinated by the huge machines as they lumbered at great speed across the desert in perfect unison, as if it were an enormous ballet with the encore being that of potential death. He remembered vividly the first tank he'd seen as a child—the one in front of their house that had mowed down their fence and shrubbery. He was intimately familiar with the destruction of which they were capable.

Will was what in military terms could be called a lone wolf, one who preferred the solitude of the desert to crowded places. He loved the thrill and exhilaration of going very fast, flying over hills and ridges, completely trusting Alfred's driving skills and ability. Each time they became airborne Will would let out a whoop, not unlike a child at play. He had a wild side and enjoyed tempting danger but, to Alfred's relief, Will was always controlled, always in complete charge of any situation.

One day, the two of them were parked on a hilltop, surrounded by saguaro cactus and tall Joshua trees, and looking down on a unit of eight tanks moving in a tight formation through gleaming sand. Will was on the radio, listening attentively. He closed the conversation with, "Yes, sir. Over and out." He pressed a few numbers into the radio and within seconds. Alfred heard him say, "Angel One to Bullet One. Come in. Over" After a brief wait, he said, "Right two-sixty. Increase speed to twenty-five knots. Repeat. Over." He finished with, "Roger. Over and out."

The tanks, in perfect unison, turned slightly to their right and increased their speed. Will stared at them and commented with a degree of awe, "Beautiful, aren't they?"

"Amazing," Alfred replied. "What's more amazing is what they're capable of doing."

"That's the whole purpose of war," Will said in a flat tone. "To break things and kill the enemy."

In the time they'd spent together, Alfred and Will had reached a point of being able to talk about anything. After deep thought, Alfred asked, "Think you'll be sent to Nam?"

"Probably," Will replied without emotion

"How do you feel about that?"

"A little scared. Anybody who goes into a shooting war and isn't scared is either remarkably naïve or just plain stupid."

"I don't think you'll be scared," Alfred replied.

"Truth is, I probably won't have time to be scared. I expect I'll be promoted to captain either just before I go or right after I get there. That means I'll be responsible for a lot of men—responsible to keep them alive. The sad reality of it is that a lot of 'em probably won't be coming back. That's a tough load to carry, but that's what I signed up for."

"Permission to speak, sir."

Will chuckled at the unnecessary formality. "Say what's on your mind, Al."

"I think you'll be a fine captain, and I'd be proud to serve with you."

"Al, I hope to hell you never have to."

As the war games continued, Alfred drove Will to various locations, observing the maneuvers and directing the tank movements. But one night everything changed. The sergeant in charge of their group walked into their tent and announced, "O'Malley, Simpson, Gonzales, Langer. In your fatigues. Bring your weapons. Front of the tent in five minutes."

The men followed the orders without hesitation and after they reported, as instructed, the sergeant said matter-of-factly, "The four of you just volunteered for a mission. Our commanding officer informed me that intelligence reports tell us there's an enemy camp about four miles southeast of here, planning a full-scale assault on us tomorrow night. They're traveling light, with three trucks filled with supplies and support materials." He handed each of the men a piece of chalk. "When you locate their camp, mark their trucks with a large X on the side, indicating you blew the truck to hell. They'll probably have guards all over the place that you'll have to avoid. Langer, since you got the extra stripe, you're in charge. One more thing: if you get caught, no one will acknowledge this was a sanctioned operation. You're on your own. Questions?" There were none. The sergeant dismissed them with, "Go. Make us proud."

The men eased their way, single file, through the desert terrain, traveling under a moonless sky as quickly and quietly as possible. Alfred took the lead, staying on course by using a hand-held compass with a dial that glowed an eerie shade of green in the darkness. No one spoke above a whisper. After about two hours, they saw a faint light in the distance, obviously their objective. They moved slower, closer, staying low to the ground. Alfred held up a closed fist, a signal to freeze where they stood. An enemy guard was patrolling in front of one of the trucks. They could hear him, as he was speaking in a normal tone of voice. "Hey, Taylor. Got an extra smoke?"

An unseen voice replied, "Come and get it. You already owe me a whole damn pack." The guard casually swaggered toward another truck, leaving his own unguarded. Quickly, Alfred led the others to the first truck and placed the X on its side. When the guard returned to his truck, the four of them froze again. Alfred signaled to one of his men and, together, they sneaked behind the truck, crawled to the second one, and placed a mark on it as well. Other soldiers were walking to and fro, not paying much attention to anything that was going on. Alfred whispered to the soldier with him, "You feeling lucky?"

The man smiled and softly replied, "That's my middle name." He crawled from under the truck and walked among the other soldiers—the enemy—casually saying things like, "How's it goin'? Gonna kick us some ass tomorrow night"—just as if he was one of them. He slipped underneath the third truck, reached up, made his mark, and then softly disappeared back into the cover of darkness. The four men gathered together and quietly moved away from the camp, heading back toward their own. They were tired, but enormously pleased with themselves as Alfred reported to their sergeant, "Mission accomplished."

At the end of two weeks of summer camp, as the men were packing their trucks, Lieutenant Schulz approached Alfred. "Just heard about your little midnight mission the other night. Why didn't you say anything about it?"

"It was supposed to be a secret," Alfred replied.

"From what I hear, you did a pretty damn good job."

"Just following orders, sir."

Will smiled and shook his head. "You do that well, soldier. Real well." He stuck out his hand. "You take care, Al. I'm gonna miss ya."

Alfred shook Schulz' hand and, with great sincerity, added, "And I'm going to miss you, Will. You're going to be a fine captain."

Alfred had two recurring thoughts on the drive back to L.A. First and foremost, he thought about Irene and how much he was looking forward to seeing her. And he thought about Will, hoping that Will would never have to make the trip they discussed—but if he did, Alfred prayed that Will would return home safely.

* * *

Irene flew into his arms, thrilled to see him. The two weeks had seemed like an eternity. They opted against the Phoenix Club and the St. Stefan's Club, choosing instead to go to a quiet and intimate restaurant where they would not be interrupted. They wanted to be able to share what they each had experienced during their separation and just be alone. After Alfred's return from summer camp, he and Irene spent more and more time together, and their relationship grew stronger. One starry Saturday night, they went to a local theater to see *The Sound of Music*. They both enjoyed the movie immensely, and while walking back to Alfred's car, holding hands, Irene commented on the location where the movie was filmed. "The Alps are gorgeous," she said. "Absolutely and literally breathtaking."

Alfred looked deeply into her bright eyes. "Someday, I'll take you there so you can see them yourself."

Irene's smile came from the bottom of her heart. "Promise?"

Alfred responded with the only word possible. "Promise."

As the reputation of Manhattan Die grew, so did their customer list. In addition to the workload of manufacturing dies for waterbeds, they were also creating dies for ring binders for Avery-Dennison Corporation, sheet protectors, and vinyl sleeves of any kind that could be purchased in stationery stores and major outlets, such as Staples or Costco, and buoyancy compensation dies for diving suits for Scuba Pro, Soniform, and U.S. Divers. They made dies for door panels and seat embossing, to be supplied to companies that restored classic cars, and for blood bags, urine bags, drainage bags, colostomy bags, and almost anything available in hospitals and pharmacies. They made dies to produce life vests, available at REI and Sports Chalet. When Nintendo, Microsoft, and Sony came out with the enormously popular videogames, they made clam-shell tooling for Wii, Xbox, and PlayStation components. They made dies for virtually anything that could be made from flexible vinyl.

Alfred and Hans were often challenged with unusual and unique projects but seldom failed to meet or exceed their customers' satisfaction. On rare occasions, they were given extensive blueprints of exactly what a customer needed, but most of the time, they were offered little more than an idea or a rough outline, often drawn on the back of a napkin. Alfred and Hans had to carefully analyze each customer's request and then advise and convey to the customer what could or could not be done. The experience they gleaned over the years was critical in order to process someone's idea and then develop and create a functioning die.

Even with the volume of business they were creating, the company continued to run smoothly—at least to the point that Alfred and Hans felt they could take a few days off for a much needed break.

* * *

Destination: Mount Whitney, the highest summit in the contiguous United States. Located between California's Inyo and Tulare counties, it stretches from the Sequoia National Park to Sierra, Nevada. The peak was named after Josiah Whitney, the California state geologist.

Alfred, Hans, and Bernhard, a friend from the Youth Group, made the long drive in Bernhard's Ford Fairlane to Lone Pine, the base of the summit. Seeing the remarkable and challenging sight before their eyes was daunting, even threatening. Excitement mixed with trepidation consumed the three as they parked the car and donned their backpacks, which were filled with food, other supplies, and sleeping bags. After a moment of silence, Alfred said, "Let's do it," and they began the difficult and demanding hike.

Reaching the base camp about halfway up the mountain was relatively easy—the incline was not anywhere near as steep as that which lay ahead. Several other people, wearing warm jackets, had pitched tents and built campfires. It was July, but at an elevation of seven thousand feet and with the nonstop, biting wind, the temperature was barely forty degrees. After a brief discussion, the three decided to press on so they could spend the evening resting closer to the top.

They made it to the nine-thousand-foot mark and found a wind-protected spot, where they could spend the night comfortably in their sleeping bags. Within a short period of time, however, the temperature was flirting with the freezing mark, and they realized why the base camp was located where it was. They wanted desperately to build a fire, but at that elevation they were above the tree line, and there was nothing available that could be burned. Constant movement was the only way they could maintain any body warmth. But with constant movement, they traded away the ability to sleep.

Tired and shivering, the three packed their things and began anew before the sun rose. The trail was difficult, narrow, slippery, and considerably more treacherous in the dark. Several times, they had to keep one hand on the rocks on one side for balance, because the other side of the trail provided the potential for a precipitous fall that would result in certain death. In addition to the cold and the difficult terrain, another obstacle faced them. At more than ten thousand feet elevation, the air is so thin that breathing becomes strained, more of an irregular gasping that saps strength and tests one's will.

After sunrise, a few other hikers passed them on their way down the mountain. On those rare occasions, few words were exchanged other than a breathless, "Good luck." Each step became more laborious, as breathing became increasingly difficult. They continued on with what seemed like a monumental effort, and when they reached the eleven-thousand-foot mark, Hans and Bernhard could no longer continue. The three of them sat down on a rock and discussed what they were going to do. Hans and Bernhard decided to go back down the mountain; their limit had been reached. They turned toward Alfred, awaiting his decision.

His chest heaved at a rapid pace, but his mind raced as well. He thought about Sergeant Chavez and his six-month basic training; how his sergeant had pushed him to his own level and then forced him to surpass it. The screams of "You can do anything you put your mind to, soldier! Never stop! Never give up!" echoed in his ears. Barely able to force the words from his mouth, he finally replied, "I'm going to the top."

Hans and Bernhard wished him well and said they'd wait for him at the base camp. Alfred looked up at the gray, foreboding, billowing clouds that covered the top of the mountain, making it impossible to see his final destination. Summoning all his strength, he stood up, took a deep breath, and began the culmination of an unspoken goal he'd held deep inside for a long time.

With each step, his legs ached, his chest burned, and his temples throbbed. It was necessary to stop every three or four steps to catch his breath. No other people were in sight, and he felt as if he was alone on the mountain, not unlike the time he was separated from his parents at the train station in Prague. Pain consumed him, but he continued to press forward, determined to reach his goal. The minutes seemed like hours, each one taking its toll, each one telling him to stop. But the voices in his ears and the pictures in his mind told him to go on. The most vivid picture was that of Sir Edmund Hillary and his guide, never stopping, never quitting, never giving up as they conquered Mount Everest, a summit nearly twice as high as the one he was on.

Finally, thankfully, Alfred reached the top of the mountain, not really sure if he was capable of taking another step. There were a few other people there and as was the tradition, they greeted him with warm hugs and extensive congratulations. Many had tried but few had succeeded. Alfred was now an official member of an elite club—those who refused to submit to intensive pain or the uncompromising elements. A brass marker placed on the ground stated the elevation of Mount Whitney was 14,497 feet. Alfred turned completely around, basking in and thoroughly enjoying the magnificence of God's majestic splendor.

TWENTY-THREE

BY HIMSELF, WITH HANS, OR WITH OTHER ADVENTUROUS souls from the Youth Group, Alfred explored the grandeur of several other breathtaking locations throughout the West. On each of these quests, he had the opportunity to meet people from all over the United States and, for that matter, the entire world.

His encounters with total strangers were always enlightening, always fascinating, as he discovered others' thoughts and feelings, especially those concerning his newly adopted country. In virtually all cases, the people with whom he came in contact were equally amazed with the beauty of the land and the absolute freedom of those fortunate enough to live here. The lessons, while often unspoken but always prevalent, made a lasting impression and served to deepen his sense of patriotism, his feeling of belonging and acceptance. For the first time in his life, he felt as if he was no longer an outsider, an outcast, a *Flüchtling.*

In addition to long, grueling hikes and conquering rocky, treacherous summits, Alfred faced two major challenges at ground level. The first was to ensure that Manhattan Die satisfied their present customers and continued to grow. The building they were renting from the Lippincutts was already bulging at the seams. Even so, they managed to manufacture the necessary dies on a timely basis and move on to the next.

The Lippincutts now were both in their late seventies. Margaret was in poor health, confined to a bed. Herbert was totally attentive to her needs, but whenever possible, he would visit the shop and busy himself cleaning the machines or sweeping the floor. Having something productive to do seemed to give meaning to his life. He loved the companionship he found with Alfred and Hans and, in turn, he was equally gratified whenever either of "the boys" would visit Margaret, bringing a small gift or just spending time talking with her.

Within a short period of time, Herbert was no longer able to care for Margaret at home, and she was moved into an assisted-living home, across the street from St. Francis Hospital in Lynwood. Alfred and Hans visited her there as well, and it became apparent to them that her pain increased with the same level and intensity as did her depression. The sweet, frail woman could never comprehend why their daughter had abandoned them nearly twenty years earlier.

Margaret's funeral was well attended by friends from the neighborhood, but it was clear Herbert's heart was broken, not only from the loss of his wife but also by the fact their daughter had not shown the respect her mother deserved. After Margaret's death, Herbert spent more and more time in the shop, busying himself, trying to be helpful. It seemed, tragically, as if his own will to live was diminishing on a daily basis. Alfred and Hans did everything they could to cheer him up and make him feel as if he was needed but sadly, it was to no avail.

Alfred's second challenge, on a much more personal level, concerned how deeply he felt about Irene. It was an odd feeling because when it came to matters of business, he was capable of making decisions instantly. He knew, without question, that he was in love with her, and even though she told him that she loved him as well, he was still hesitant about asking for her hand in marriage. The rejection he'd experienced over ten years ago still weighed heavily on his mind. The remote possibility of her saying no to his proposal was frightening—terrifying.

Ultimately, it was very spur of the moment. Alfred and Irene were having a quiet, intimate dinner. The moment was serene and perfect. Alfred picked up his wine glass and held it forward, as if offering a toast. Irene followed his lead, and as they clinked their glasses, Alfred looked into her eyes and softly said, "Irene, you know how much I love you and want to spend the rest of my life with you. Would you do me the great honor of being my wife?"

The following seconds seemed like hours, until she tenderly replied, "You know I feel the same way about you. And, yes. I would be proud to be your wife."

Following tradition, Alfred suggested, "I think we should wait to make an official announcement until I receive your parents' blessing."

Irene smiled and agreed, knowing full well their blessing would be little more than a formality.

They went to St. Emedius Church to talk with the priest about their plans, asking him to keep the secret until Alfred formally asked her parents for their blessing. The priest smiled politely, offered agreement, and over a period of weeks, conducted counseling meetings. They discussed the importance of marriage, finances, birth control, the responsibility of having children, what they should expect from each other, and how important religion would be in their relationship. It was all very positive and uplifting.

Late one afternoon, as planned, they went to the White Front Department Store and picked out an engagement ring. Both being prudent, a result of their backgrounds and upbringing, they made a very reasonable selection but one that Irene was eager to put on her finger. With the holidays approaching, they decided to take advantage of an upcoming special occasion.

The entire Aragon family was eagerly awaiting the Thanksgiving feast that Dolores was preparing. Irene, Molly, and even little Mary, who was only seven, were chatting among themselves, assisting with the varied assortment of dishes. The men—Don, Alfred, Manuel, and Rudi—sat in the living room discussing sports, politics, and business, their conversation inconsequential in that their true thoughts were concentrated on the upcoming meal. More than once, Alfred would appear to be listening to someone talking, but his mind drifted to long ago traditional family meals in Hermannstadt and Selbitz—the warmth and love the Langers each held for the other; the safety and protection they all felt in their comfortable home; the misguided belief that their future was stable and secure.

The men's eyes were glued to the dining room as the women brought plate after plate of food to the table, which was decorated with their finest china and tableware. Finally, to everyone's great delight, Dolores came out of the kitchen carrying the large turkey, placed it in the center of the table, and with a beaming smile of satisfaction announced, "Dinner is served."

Everyone took their seats in an orderly manner and reverently bowed their heads as Don offered a thoughtful and heartfelt blessing, thanking God for their family, their friends, their health, and for all the wonderful things they were able to achieve as a result of living in America. Alfred silently concurred.

The dinner was delicious. Once again, Dolores had outdone herself. Following a traditional and delightful dessert of flan—a baked custard, quite similar to crème caramel—the talk was light, mostly of family matters and plans for Christmas. Alfred looked into Irene's glowing face, and they shared a smile. Her eyes clearly indicated the question: *Well? Are you going to do it or not?*

Alfred's shirt collar felt as if it had become two sizes smaller. It also seemed his temperature was slightly rising. He had practiced the words at least a hundred times but now, because of the emotion of the moment, the words completely escaped him. After taking a deep breath, he reached out with his spoon and gently tapped the side of his water glass, capturing everyone's attention. He smiled warmly and looked at Irene's parents. After clearing his throat, he slowly began. "Don, Dolores … Irene and I have spoken about this, and she and I would like very much to get married. We … I … here in front of your entire family, ask for your blessings."

There was a remarkably uncomfortable moment of silence as Don looked across the table at Dolores. After what seemed like an eternity, Don finally broke into a wide smile and replied, "Well, it's about time."

Just as applause was breaking out, Alfred silenced them again with, "First things first." He took the ring from his pocket and gently slipped it on Irene's finger—they were officially engaged. The entire family was absolutely thrilled and showed their acceptance with hugs all around and friendly slaps on the back. Irene and her mother shed tears, even more so as she hugged her father. Alfred was welcomed into the family with a kindness and a graciousness he never expected. Being inexperienced in such matters, he decided he would let Irene and her mother make all of the arrangements for their wedding.

After arriving back at her apartment, they consulted a calendar and decided the wedding would take place on September 16, 1967, two years to the day since he first saw her.

That evening, with considerable emotion, he wrote a long letter to his parents to share the exciting news and express how happy he was. He explained with great clarity that he felt that God had miraculously blessed him with the perfect mate.

* * *

Alfred dressed in his rented tuxedo, checking his watch as he fastened his cufflinks. Any perceived nervousness was only because he and Irene wanted the wedding to go as perfectly as she and her mother had so diligently planned. Neither bride nor groom shared the nervousness most couples do, for they were both ready to settle down and enjoy a comfortable life together.

Irene went to her parents' house to dress for the occasion. As her mother assisted her, she was somewhat surprised that Irene was perfectly calm and looking forward to the ceremony. But Irene and her mother had been planning every detail of the wedding for the better part of a year, and she was completely prepared to be a bride.

St. Emedius Church was beautiful, decorated with an abundance of white flowers, which nearly all the hundred guests commented on. There were several members from the Youth Group, but the majority of the guests were Mexican. It was an eclectic mix, and everyone got along well, talking among themselves, anticipating the upcoming event.

As soon as everyone was seated, Alfred, his best man, Hans, and three groomsmen wearing white dinner jackets took their positions to the right of the priest. And the music began. The three bridesmaids and the maid of honor, all dressed in a pleasing shade of pink, walked down the aisle as the excitement mounted. The moment had arrived. Irene appeared on her father's arm and began to walk down the aisle—she was absolutely radiant. Upon seeing her in her beautiful flowing gown and veil for the first time, Alfred's thought was exactly the same as it had been two years ago, this very day. He remembered well the night he returned to his apartment from their first date and Hans had asked how it went. One word defined it all: "Perfect."

The reception was held at the Knights of Columbus Hall in South Gate, a true celebration of mixed ethnicity. A German band, wearing their traditional outfits, provided the entertainment. Their oompah music played as if they were in a *Hofbrauhaus*, delighting all and giving the guests a small insight into Alfred's side of the newly formed partnership. The wrapped gifts piled on tables provided all the necessities they would need to begin their new life together.

Alfred stood off to the side, by himself, a faraway look on his face. His new bride approached him and asked, "Is anything wrong?"

He slowly shook his head and forced a smile. "I just wish my parents could have been here."

"Me, too," she said, and then she brightened. "But I'll get to meet them."

Alfred turned toward her and asked, "Remember the time we went to see *The Sound of Music*?"

She nodded.

"Remember the promise I made?"

Irene nodded again. "That someday you'd take me to see the Alps."

"We'll do that. We'll save our money and a year from now, I'll take you there."

Irene smiled warmly at her new husband. "I never doubted for a second that you wouldn't."

As the festive evening drew to a close, Alfred and Irene bid a fond farewell to friends and family and then drove down the coast. They spent their wedding night in a place called the Resort Hotel, right on the beach in San Clemente, the same hotel where Johnny and Nancy Gannon had taken Alfred five years ago.

* * *

Business continued on an upward growth path, as did Alfred and Hans' knowledge and expertise. Whenever Alfred and Hans learned something beneficial, they shared it with their employees, helping them learn as well, making them feel as if they were an integral part of the company. Most of their contracts were a result of referrals from satisfied customers or others, who came to find out if Manhattan Die could make specific dies. But one day, Alfred and Hans received a blow that hurt them, both personally and professionally.

Without any advance warning, Frank and Jose, the first two men Alfred and Hans hired when they became owners, betrayed their trust. They secretly copied customers' names, addresses, and phone numbers, as well as detailed information concerning all their suppliers.

The personal loss was twofold: Hans and Alfred had trusted these two men implicitly and had shared the knowledge and experience they had gleaned over several years of hard work and education. To have that trust violated was a difficult and troublesome lesson, one that affected them deeply. But there was also the loss of time. Because Frank and Jose had left without warning, Alfred and Hans were now obligated to work seven days a week, for an extended period of time, in order to make up for the jobs the two men should have been handling. Free time became nonexistent.

From a professional standpoint, Alfred and Hans became far more cautious concerning how much they taught each new employee. They assigned different skills to different workers, never again allowing any of them to know the complete details of their operation or have access to their valued customer list. One point in the entire debacle was, at least, somewhat gratifying: While the new owners of S&M Die Company contacted all of Alfred and Hans' customers, telling them they could produce the same quality work for a lower price, few took advantage of their obvious disloyalty—the vast majority of their customers stayed with them.

As Alfred and Hans worked diligently to return their company to the level it once was, they never said a disparaging word about their new competitors. This was due to their keen business acumen, but also because they never viewed them as true competitors anyway. S&M Die might produce dies more cheaply but in doing so, they produced them with less quality. The majority of the customers who gave the new company a try eventually returned to Manhattan Die for their needs, most often with an apology in hand.

Alfred and Hans decided to alter their practices. The majority of their business came from referrals. They decided, however, to make personal calls on both customers and prospects, sometimes picking up or delivering orders; sometimes explaining to a potential customer exactly which services they provided. This hands-on understanding of their customers' needs helped them to learn the ins and outs of production and what improvements could be made, and the customers themselves could create more profits—it proved to be a remarkably educational process. Learning how to produce dies more efficiently and effectively caused Manhattan Die to stand head and shoulders above any competitors.

* * *

Herbert Lippincutt continued to come to the shop and do general cleaning work. Being in the company of others helped him to cope with the loss of his wife. It was apparent, however, that his health was deteriorating at a rapid pace.

Alfred was soundly asleep when the phone startled him at 11:30 one night. "Hello," he mumbled.

"Alfred ..." Herbert said weakly.

"I'll be right there! Don't move!" Alfred pulled on his clothes as he ran out of the house and then sped to the Lippincutt residence, where he found Herbert on the floor, gasping, unable to move. He helped the frail man into a chair. "You should have called 9-1-1," Alfred said.

"I'm not sick," Herbert gasped. "I fell down and couldn't get back up."

Alfred got him a drink of water, and soon, Herbert appeared to be breathing regularly. "You should be in a hospital," Alfred suggested.

Herbert weakly shook his head. "If I go to a hospital, I'll never leave."

This was not the first time Alfred had been summoned in the middle of the night. He helped the weak old man into his bed, covered him with a blanket, and held his hand. Then Alfred closed his eyes and offered, "Heavenly Father, surround this good man's heart and soul with Your healing and understanding. Give him Your strength, Your blessing, and Your peace. In Jesus' name we pray. Amen."

A week later, unexpectedly, Herbert asked Alfred and Hans to come to his home. They expected the worst but instead, they found him in a reasonably good mood. He asked them to sit at the same table where they'd first met and served them a glass of wine. "Boys," he began, "I have a proposition." In a voice that shook with age, he offered to sell them the property he owned, at a very reasonable price, with no down payment and without any interest on the balance. His only condition was that they allow him to live in the house until he died. They instantly accepted the proposal but assured him, to the best of their ability, that he was going to live a very long life. Sadly, the three of them felt, in all probability, that would not be the case.

Alfred continued to spend one weekend a month at the armory downtown, interpreting boring maps and other equally boring documents, as well as putting in his two weeks each summer, participating in war games. None of the subsequent summer camps came close to matching the interest or freedom of the first. Instead of driving a friendly, laidback first lieutenant named Will, Alfred was assigned regular soldier-type duties, including marching, conducting maneuvers, and maintaining his skill on the rifle range. Alfred actually enjoyed the exercises, although he missed Irene intensely during this time away. Still, it was an opportunity to get in shape, something than his constant work schedule didn't allow. He always returned home with a freshly rejuvenated mind and a renewed sense of creativity.

* * *

Alfred turned his long-ago promise into reality when in the fall of 1968, he and Irene took a three-week trip to Germany. They flew into Frankfurt, where they picked up a new car that he had ordered in the States and used that as transportation for the duration of their stay. Irene was thrilled with the prospect of meeting Alfred's family. She was a little concerned with language barrier but knew that Alfred would translate for her.

Their first stop was Bamberg, where they visited with two of Alfred's uncles and their families. Irene was fascinated with the wonderful new people she met, as well as with the countenance and beauty of the country. She proved herself to be a good sport when communicating by using gestures and the few words she had learned from Alfred. Her grace and generosity endeared her to the entire family.

Arriving in Selbitz, Irene was enthusiastically welcomed by all of Alfred's relatives and was accepted without reservation or prejudgment. Alfred had written letters praising her beauty, kindness, and unconditional love, creating a sense that he was bringing a queen for them to meet. Once formally introduced, everyone was impressed by her charm and worldliness; she became as much a part of his family as he did hers.

Together, they hiked the same trails that Alfred had as a youth, picking mushrooms and blueberries, enjoying nature at its finest and most pristine. He explained that the Frankenwald area was known throughout all of Germany for its magnificent forests and beautiful, rolling green meadows. He took her past the Hartenstein farm and told her of his youthful ambition in bundling and delivering wood, earning much-needed money for the family. Driving down the road he pointed out the area where his father turned the branches from worthless scrub trees into versatile brushes.

Irene finally got to see firsthand the Alps that had so moved her when they saw *The Sound of Music* together. The sight was so dramatic and breathtaking that it brought tears to her eyes. She couldn't remember ever being happier. The food she tasted was delicious and the people she met were all delightful. Several times, they visited local pubs where old friends of Alfred's would relate tales of their growing up together—more than a few of the recollections were slightly embarrassing. Irene found it both curious and interesting that in all the conversations with various people, not one of them ever mentioned anything whatsoever concerning the war. She assumed—and rightly so—that reflections of that dark time were far too uncomfortable and disconcerting.

The next day, Alfred had an appointment for a long-anticipated visit to the Bodenschatz mill. Herr Thieroff greeted him warmly and took him on a tour, allowing him the opportunity of saying hello to many old friends. While the majority of Selbitz remained the same, the mill was enlarging and improving. As they finished the tour and walked toward the front gate, Herr Thieroff said, "I hear you and Hans are doing well in your new country."

Alfred nodded and replied, "It's been a challenge, but we're doing fine."

"Do you like America?"

"Very much."

"What is it you like about it?" Herr Thieroff asked.

The answer was simple and came quite easily. "Freedom."

Herr Thieroff looked surprised. "We have freedom here."

"Thanks to the Americans," Alfred replied with a slight smile.

They walked a few more steps, and Thieroff asked, "Do you remember the time when we had to choose someone to attend the master machinist program?"

The question was like an arrow into Alfred's heart. "I remember it quite well."

Herr Thieroff cleared his throat. "It was my decision that you should go … but I was overruled."

They walked a few more steps in silence, then Alfred responded, "Thank you very much. I appreciate that."

As he walked back to rejoin Irene and his family, he contemplated how different his life would have been, had he been selected to attend the class. Smiling to himself, he concluded that the rejection for the position had been the best thing that had ever happened in his entire life.

One afternoon, Alfred suggested a meeting with Rudi and Willie, his older brothers. When they got together, Alfred mentioned the rather obvious fact that their parents still lived in the house between the railroad tracks. Rudi and Willie had no idea where he was going with the conversation—and then he calmly suggested, "I think we should find some way to move them to a better place."

Rudi and Willie stared at Alfred for a moment, until Rudi replied, "How on earth could we possibly do that?"

In a businesslike fashion, Alfred said, "The American dollar is very strong and the prices for property around here are still relatively inexpensive. You're both more familiar with the area than I am. Plus, the two of you are also experienced in electrical work and general contracting."

Willie shook his head. "I still don't understand what you're talking about."

Alfred smiled. "How about if the two of you look around and check with some of your business associates. If we can find a suitable property at a reasonable price, perhaps I might be able to buy it, and then you two could help and oversee building them a new home."

"It would cost too much," Rudi argued.

"I was thinking of a three-story building," Alfred explained. "Mom and Dad could live on one floor; Willie, you and your family could live on another; and we could rent out the third floor for probably enough money to make a monthly payment on the entire place." Then he became as persuasive as possible. "Look, after all they've done for us and all the sacrifices they've made, at least we can look into it."

Neither brother thought Alfred's idea was viable but agreed to look around and see if they could find anything suitable. Alfred, however, felt in his heart that someday, somehow, his dream of repaying his parents for all they had done for their entire family would come to fruition.

On the return trip to the United States, Alfred insisted that Irene sit beside the window so she could see the magnificence of the world below. A flight attendant delivered two glasses of wine, and as they touched glasses, Irene softly and tenderly said, "Thank you for keeping your promise."

TWENTY-FOUR

FEBRUARY 1969 BROUGHT THE ANNOUNCEMENT THAT IRENE was pregnant. Alfred completely lost his normally calm and calculated demeanor. Irene watched with amusement as he seemed flustered and asked rapidly, "When? Are you all right? Can I get you anything? Shouldn't you be in bed?"

Their happy news was dimmed for a time by another tragedy, although one that was not unexpected. Herbert Lippincutt passed away peacefully in his sleep. Alfred was saddened by his passing for two reasons: Herbert never had been able to take advantage of or enjoy the extra income he received from the sale of his property, and—just as had been the case with Mrs. Lippincutt—their daughter had not been there for him in his time of need.

Upon hearing the news of Herbert's passing and, more particularly, that he'd sold his property to Alfred and Hans, Bessie Long, an elderly widow who owned the property next door, contacted them and requested a meeting. Mrs. Long had a building on her own property, which was considerably larger than the one occupied by Manhattan Die. It was, as fate would have it, unoccupied.

"Look," Bessie explained in a no-nonsense manner, "I'm not receiving any income from the property, and I'm tired of paying taxes on the thing.

I'm willing to sell you the building and property at an extremely reasonable price and just be done with it." Already bulging at the seams and desperately needing larger facilities, Alfred and Hans immediately took advantage of the opportunity. Mrs. Long was so eager to dispose of the property and the tax obligations that she sold it to them without even requesting a down payment. After the necessary wiring was installed, the move itself was relatively easy—they laid pipes on the ground and rolled the milling machines to their new location. As before, Alfred and Hans hooked all the equipment up so everything was once again running smoothly.

By taking the time and making the effort to visit their customers and prospects, Alfred and Hans were able to see firsthand how careless some machine operators handled dies. A small nick in a cutting edge could make a die completely useless, and downtime for repairs was normally extremely costly. Because of their background, and especially the welding skills Alfred learned in Germany, both men could silver solder damaged sections on brass dies and blend in the cutting edge on the milling machines. Even A&S Die, the largest die manufacturer in New York, found repairing dies to be a nuisance and in most cases refused to do it. Yet product manufacturers didn't want their dies made by a die maker who was unwilling or unable to follow up and fix them, should anything go wrong or not work to their satisfaction. Because of this dilemma, customers from all over the country came to Manhattan Die, a company that earned a reputation for repairing dies better and faster than anyone in the United States. But with this additional work, and even with their new, improved, and larger shop, Alfred and Hans were once again pressed for adequate space.

The lot next to them was deserted and completely overrun with miscellaneous junk, shrubs, and tall grass. After a careful examination of their income and profit situation, Alfred and Hans managed to locate a woman named Mrs. Drummond, who owned the property. During a brief conversation, she explained she had no use or plan for the lot and would be more than willing to sell it to them. Again, just as they had done with Mrs. Long, they were able to purchase the property for a very reasonable price. After conferring with the city of South Gate about expanding their business space, they were told that if they paved and used the new lot as a parking area, they would be granted permission to expand and extend their own building, all the way back to the alley.

This was going to be major construction and would require a substantial amount of money. Alfred and Hans invested whatever personal funds they could afford and borrowed money from the company to provide the financing. They were risking virtually everything to expand their building and create the shop that could satisfy all the growth they could imagine. During the construction, they continued to manufacture high-quality dies in the portion of the building that was still operable. They struggled through the inconvenience as best as possible, but each day provided more challenges. When the expansion was finally completed, they created custom-built workstations for twelve employees, purchased more milling machines, and created a reception area and an adjoining office. The building had restrooms for both men and women, a twenty-foot-wide loading area gate, and air conditioning and heating units on the roof. Working at full capacity, which was exactly what they rapidly did, became a reality and a dream come true.

* * *

The National Guard summer camp Alfred attended that year did not provide the relaxation or extended exercise he normally looked forward to. This year, his mind was consumed with Irene and her condition, the new facilities of Manhattan Die, and their financial situation, all causing an unpleasant degree of stress.

When these thoughts entered his mind, he would often reflect back to his youth and how difficult and challenging those times had been, times when the family's very survival was at stake. He thought of his parents and their refusal to ever give up, to never give in, and to always keep going forward, following the adages of "This too shall pass" and "Thy will be done." They always believed that God would see them through any situation, no matter how desperate it might have seemed at the time. Now, Alfred, too, knew that somehow, someway, everything was going to be all right.

Many times, Alfred recalled the monumental efforts of Sir Edmund

Hillary and the fact that even while facing insurmountable odds—odds that had tragically taken the lives of many before him—Sir Edmund continued until he finally reached the summit. And with this as inward motivation, Alfred also remembered vividly that July day not that long ago when he, Hans, and Bernhard stood freezing on the rocky and ice-covered side of Mt. Whitney, completely spent, out of breath, ready to give up and go back down the mountain. His own words from that very moment rang true in his ears: "I'm going to the top."

Upon his return home with renewed vitality, Alfred found Irene also in very good health but showing the strain of upcoming motherhood. Her own mother had been an enormous help with cleaning their house and cooking while Alfred was away. The shop was running at full capacity, and their monthly expenses were being paid on a timely basis. While seemingly insignificant, this added greatly to their reputation, especially when it came to acquiring credit from various financial institutions.

After considerable discussion, Alfred and Irene determined that the house they were renting in South Gate was not suitable for raising a child. They wanted a house with more room, more privacy, and in a neighborhood they considered to be a little more upscale. They spent every weekend looking for a house that would meet their needs, attending countless open houses, stopping whenever they saw a For Sale sign that looked as if it might be an option. To their delight, on Santana Street in the city of Cerritos, they found a house they felt was right for them, a lovely three-bedroom home with a well-trimmed yard. They made an offer and began the process of purchasing the property. Irene left her job six weeks before her due date so she could relax as much as possible, and they moved into their house one week before the arrival of their child.

The overwhelming question on everyone's mind was whether the baby would favor the Mexican or German side of the family. That question was answered on September 23, 1969, when Irene gave birth to their beautiful daughter, Christine Ann, at Norwalk Community Hospital. The baby had dark hair, no doubt inherited from Irene's grandfather, who was 100 percent Yaki Indian, and light skin from her grandmother, who came from England. Her sparkling hazel eyes were exactly the same as those of her proud father. The delivery had been difficult, and as a result, Irene spent three days in the hospital, receiving friends and family and proudly showing off their new child. When Alfred first saw his daughter wrapped in pure-white bundling, he knew instantly and without question that his life had just been altered dramatically and had taken on a completely new meaning. Again, his prayers had been answered.

* * *

When meeting customers, Alfred always maintained a straight-laced and proper demeanor. In personal situations, he was more relaxed and spirited, but business was business, and for that, he kept his tone formal.

He met one afternoon with a prospective customer. Entering the man's cluttered office, Alfred extended his hand. "Hello, Mr. Thompson. My name is Alfred Langer."

Mr. Thompson, a portly man with thick eyebrows, shook his hand and replied with a quizzical look on his face, "Alfred, huh? What do people call you?"

The question seemed strangely familiar, as if he'd heard it before. "Alfred," he replied.

"Sounds a little formal. Mind if I call you Al?"

Instantly it came to him—Lieutenant Schulz had said the exact same thing during his first National Guard summer camp. Alfred smiled, remembering the exchange, and said, "Al would be just fine."

"Great. Most people call me Andy. Let's see if we can do some business."

When Alfred returned to the shop, he related the story to Hans and their employees. To his surprise, they all expressed basically the same thought: that "Alfred" was a bit stuffy, but they hadn't wanted to risk offending him by mentioning it. Everyone shared in the laughter, and Alfred decided then and there that henceforth, he would be known simply as Al.

That evening, after checking on Christine to ensure she was sleeping comfortably, and then crawling into bed with Irene, he chuckled to himself as he reflected on the transition of his name over the years. From the day he was born until he entered school, he had been called Fredi. Then, after school began and up until today, he had been Alfred. And, apparently, from this day forward, he would be referred to as Al. *Change is inevitable*, he thought. After all, when Christine was one year old, her pure dark hair began to change gradually to a gleaming strawberry blonde.

* * *

Manhattan Die continued to grow steadily and to prosper, a result of due diligence, extensive market study, quality and precision manufacturing, concern for their customers, and on-time delivery. Their keel remained steadfast, and their annual goals were met or exceeded. All twelve of their workstations were filled with machinists or apprentices who were learning their trade from recognized and respected experts in the field.

Because Al and Hans had relatives in Germany, they decided that, business permitting, they each would make a return trip every other year. These preplanned trips generally were for three weeks, and while visiting their hometowns, they would usually manage to arrange a scenic drive through the magnificent German, Austrian, or Swiss Alps.

Al's trip was planned for late summer of 1971, and his parents were especially thrilled that he and his family were coming because it would be their first opportunity to see Christine, who was not quite two years old. At that age, she didn't require her own ticket; instead, she would sit on Al's or Irene's lap. Once the passengers seated around them saw how polite and delightful Christine was, many of them asked if they could hold her. With the assistance of several friendly people, the thirteen-hour flight proved to be unexpectedly pleasant.

They arrived in Frankfurt, and Al picked up a new car he had ordered in the States—a silver Mercedes-Benz 280E, which he wrote off as a business expense and used as a tax deduction. At that time, a European delivery made a great deal of sense because the U.S. dollar was so strong. The savings made on the purchase of the car more than paid for the expenses of the entire three-week vacation.

Everyone fell instantly in love with Christine. The entire family was so intent on holding her that she barely had a chance to put her tiny feet on the ground. While she was delighted with the attention, she was equally confused with the unfamiliar language. Countless outbursts of laughter occurred as someone would say something to her in German, and Al would translate for her. By the end of the trip, the bright little girl was able to understand much of the language—she'd received her first real lesson in German!

The trip was timed so that Al could be the best man at Harald's wedding. Harald, his youngest brother, was marrying a lovely young woman named Margit, whom the entire family adored. Al felt a great sense of pride as he and Irene drove Harald, Rudolf, and Elsa to the church in the nearby city of Hof for the ceremony, which proved to be delightful.

During their time back in Selbitz, Rudolf and Elsa joined Al, Irene, and Christine on long hikes into the mountains, to the beautiful, scenic locations that Al had visited many times as a child. Al and Irene were pleased and excited by this, as Rudolf and Elsa, burdened with age and minor frailties, had not been active for quite a while. Al and Irene also provided another surprise by taking the elder Langers on a remarkably exciting, three-day trip through the German Alps. It seemed that just seeing Al, Irene, and especially Christine gave the old couple a new and more positive outlook on life. This alone made the trip enormously worthwhile.

Willie took Al aside and told him what a transformation he'd seen in their mother. "You know she's been in and out of the local hospital several times, but when she started to prepare for your arrival, her spirits seemed to soar." Al smiled with pride as Willie continued, "She even had her hair done a special way."

During their visit, Rudolf and Elsa always wore their Sunday best. The entire family knew Elsa was suffering and in pain, having to deal with thrombosis of the legs, high blood pressure, and diabetes, but she never showed it or offered complaint—she didn't want to do anything that would distract from the importance of Al and his family's visit.

When Al and his mother had time alone, Elsa would always ask him to tell her about the wonders of the remarkable world where he lived, a world she knew she would never be able to see. Several times, she expressed how much she would love to see his and Irene's house and his adopted country.

Al looked into the possibility of bringing his parents to America for a visit but was advised by her doctor that his mother might not be able to survive the connecting travel and the thirteen-hour flight.

Although Al insisted that he didn't want any special treatment while he was visiting, he and his small family were treated like royalty—everyone was enormously impressed with his business and life in America. Al was rather embarrassed by the attention, and he explained that with hard work and dedication, almost anyone could achieve his level of success in a place where freedom was the guidepost and mantle under which a business could grow and prosper.

One highlight of the trip was when Al discovered Willie had found a suitable property in a new development where they could build the house they'd discussed during his previous visit.. Al purchased the property and set the plan in motion. Only then did he tell his parents that within a short period of time, they would be able to move out of the house on Friedhof Strasse between the railroad tracks and into a brand new home. Willie, who was in the construction business and also a master bricklayer, would oversee the construction of the three-story building. As Al and his brothers had planned, the top floor would be for Rudolf and Elsa; the second floor would be for Willie, his wife, Brigitte, and their daughter, Antje; and the bottom floor would be rented. Rudolf and Elsa were extremely excited about the prospect, even though they expressed doubts to each other that Al would be able to follow through with the plan.

At the end of the three weeks, good-byes were difficult and highly emotional. Traveling in their new car down the Autobahn toward Frankfurt, Al was unusually silent, so much so that Irene did her best to alter the mood by commenting, "Everyone certainly loved Christine."

Al just nodded, concentrating on the high-speed highway and seeming deep in thought.

"The good news," Irene continued, trying to engage him, "is that we'll get to see them all again in just a couple of years."

He nodded again, but an unexplained and disturbing feeling in the pit of his stomach led him to feel that her statement might be less than accurate.

* * *

The following year, after finalizing blueprints and plans, construction began on the home Al had promised his parents. Willie, acting as the general contractor, did an excellent job of overseeing the entire building and finished it in record time. Willie was able to hire qualified and efficient labor in the area at such a reasonable cost that they completed the construction without Al's having to make a mortgage payment. Each day brought more excitement from everyone involved, but none was filled with more anticipation than Rudolf and Elsa.

Willie sent Al photographs of the progress on a regular basis, but the finest picture of all was the one showing their mother and father, with beaming faces of gratitude, as they officially moved into their new home.

* * *

In 1985, Al moved his young family into a larger and more comfortable house in Westminster. At the same time, Christine was excited to begin the first grade at Blessed Sacrament Parochial School, and Irene, who enjoyed being a stay-at-home mom, became more involved with church and school activities. When Christine joined the Brownies—part of the Girl Scouts organization, whose purpose was, among other things, to develop character and establish a sense of helping others—Irene became the troop's Brownie leader. Both the church and the school held a variety of fund-raising events, and Al and Irene were always an integral part of the effort. Irene usually participated in behind-the-scene activities, helping to make others look good and making sure things went as smoothly and efficiently as possible. Al, on the other hand, was quick to volunteer as the front man. Using his persuasive talents, he manned booths featuring various sorts of games. He could always be found standing in front of one the booths, urging others to play the game. "If you're lucky," he would call out, "you could win a fabulous prize!" The "fabulous prize" usually was an inexpensive trinket, but it was treasured by the youngsters—and win or lose, no child ever left a booth without a prize. Bingo games and socials provided additional funds for the church and school, but they also brought people together to work for a common cause, teaching the children, by example, that it's possible to share a pleasant experience and help their fellow man at the same time.

* * *

Al received the call at the shop on a Monday morning. The telephone service, which had been promised to Selbitz years ago, was still not fully installed, and as a result, the family in Germany had to wait until the post office opened before they could make the call and share the devastating news: Rudolf had passed away two days earlier.

Al's heart was broken and his knees trembled as he ended the call from Selbitz, but he knew that his emotions would have to be placed on hold for just a little while. He immediately phoned Irene to share the tragic news and then began to contact every international airline, desperately seeking arrangements for a seat on the next flight to Frankfurt. Unfortunately, the next available flight would not be for two days. Taking into account the nine-hour time difference and the train ride from Frankfurt to Selbitz, it would be physically impossible for him to arrive in time for his father's funeral.

Hans expressed sincere regret and condolences at Rudolf's passing. Al left the shop in a near state of shock. His parents had always been the rock-solid foundation of their family, and now, half of that precious duo was gone. There was a cavernous hole in his heart that he felt would never be filled. On his way home, Al stopped at his church, which at this time of day was completely deserted. He walked slowly to the front of the holy sanctuary and stood in silence, staring at the large crucifix on the wall behind the altar. He lowered his head, lit a candle and offered a silent prayer.

When he arrived at his home, he explained to Irene that it would be impossible for them to attend his father's funeral. They embraced, sobbing quietly in each other's arms. Al looked up at the crucifix on their wall, the crucifix that had provided him solace on so many occasions. He attempted to comfort his own grief with two thoughts: that his father had lived his entire life as an enormously proud man, filled with timeless Christian values that had been passed along to each of his children; and that their most unfortunate loss was heaven's blessed gain.

TWENTY-FIVE

I N 1980 THE ECONOMIC TIDES WERE TURNING, AND UNFOR-
tunately, they were turning in the wrong direction. People were more
frugal and hesitated to purchase many of the novelty items produced by
dies manufactured by Manhattan Die. Several companies went out of business and others began to order products from overseas. Many American
manufacturers found it impossible to compete with the inexpensive prices
offered by countries such as China, India, Korea, and Malaysia. When the
downturn in business began its spiral, Al and Hans were no longer able to
offer raises to their employees, and a few of their most experienced machinists left the company for opportunities elsewhere.

Their loyal customers, however, stayed with Manhattan Die, and by
spending ten to twelve hours a day in the shop, Al and Hans kept the business alive. They also fine-tuned their manufacturing to stay ahead of the
curve in the evolving radio-frequency sealing industry. It was a tremendous
challenge but one that, in a small way, prepared Al for what would prove to
be a life-altering experience.

Needing a short break from the stress at work, Al, Irene, and Christine—now ten years old—took a much-needed short vacation to Cancun,
Mexico. They experienced day trips with other tourists, traveling in ancient
busses at breakneck speeds down remarkably narrow roads, to visit such at-
tractions as Chichen Itza and Tulum, areas known for their Mayan ruins

of pyramids and temples. Experiencing the true flavor of old Mexico, the family spent several afternoons in the city, visiting specialty shops, interacting with the locals, and occasionally, relaxing at a sidewalk café. One day, as Al and Irene enjoyed a traditional margarita, Al's face brightened with a wide smile.

Irene looked at him, curiously. "What?"

"I just think it's interesting," Al replied.

"What's interesting?"

"When we were in Germany, I was the interpreter. Now that we're here, the roles are reversed."

"Yes," Irene agreed. "That seems normal to me. What do you find so interesting about that?"

Al cocked his head to one side, searching for the correct words. "Interesting in that no matter where we are in our lives, we always seem to need the help or assistance of someone or something else. And while that help or assistance is always available, so many times we seem to avoid asking for it."

On their last, sun-filled day, the family decided to enjoy the pristine beach and magnificent crystal-clear ocean. While Christine romped in the sand, Al told Irene, "I think I'll go for a little swim."

"Don't go too far," she cautioned.

He gave her a playful smirk. "Don't worry. I know how to swim."

She smiled. "That's reassuring to know. Just don't go too far."

After walking waist-deep into the warm and refreshing water, Al turned to offer Irene a comforting wave, then dove into the ocean. Initially, the swim was pleasant, relaxing, and exactly what he needed to clear his mind from the pressures of work and be at peace.

He was about a hundred yards from the shore when it happened: an undercurrent, often referred to as a riptide, caught him by surprise and began to sweep him farther from the beach. At first, he wasn't concerned; he turned and began to swim back. But now the current and the waves were too strong and continued to carry him farther away. Al increased the power of his stroke, going faster and faster, but his efforts proved of no avail. Drifting farther out into the vastness of the ocean, he realized he was in serious trouble. He screamed at the top of his voice but was too far away for anyone to hear.

Then, rather than panic, his mind turned to logic. It was apparent that trying to swim against the current would be fruitless. So, in order to con-serve energy, he began to tread water and wave his arm in the air, hoping that sooner or later, someone would see him. As he bobbed up and down, flowing farther out to sea, the moments seemed like hours. He closed his eyes and began to pray. *Heavenly Father, my life is in Your hands. Please help me.*

When he opened his eyes, he saw a man on a cliff far in the distance, waving back at him. His prayers had been answered. In his mind, it was a divine intervention. A wave swept over him, pulling him under the water. When he surfaced, the stranger on the cliff was no longer there. *Had he been a vision? An illusion?* Al's legs were growing tired, exhaustion was setting in, and breathing became more difficult. *With God, all things are possible*, he thought. Another wave pulled him under again. *Thy kingdom come, Thy will be done*, he repeated over and over. As he bobbed to the surface, he heard a voice—soft, distant, but definitely a voice. Was his mind playing a cruel trick on him? *With God, all things are possible.* The phrased echoed through his mind as the voice grew louder.

"Hang on!" the voice shouted. "I'm almost there!" The voice was real—it was a lifeguard, less than twenty yards away. Al tried to swim to-ward him, but his arms were too spent to move. Once the lifeguard was within ten feet, he threw Al a red buoy. "Grab hold of it!" he screamed. Al clutched the buoy, hanging on for dear life, as the lifeguard guided him to swim parallel to the shore to escape the riptide.

As they grew closer to land, Al could see a large group of people form-ing, shouting encouragement, screaming for the lifeguard to keep going and for Al to hang on. Al continued to periodically slip under the water but always came back up, spitting salt water, gasping for air. Finally, they made it to safety on the sand. Irene and Christine rushed through the cheering crowd to his side. The three of them embraced as never before.

Tears of joy and relief ran down Irene's cheeks. "I thought we'd lost you."

Breathlessly, Al gasped, "That was scary." He vigorously shook the lifeguard's hand, thanking him profusely for saving his life.

As they walked back to their hotel, Al looked up toward the cliff where he had seen the man waving. He knew in his heart that God had put the man in that place and at that time, to provide the lifeguard at precisely the right moment. He closed his eyes and offered a silent and remarkably sincere prayer of thanks.

* * *

In June 1981, business had returned to the point that the Langer family was able to make a return trip to Germany. The visit coincided with an annual four-day celebration called *Wiesenfest*, an event that included all the residents of Selbitz, as well as those from towns far and wide. There was a long parade through the center of town, with all the local clubs and organizations participating. Al was thrilled as he proudly marched in the parade alongside old friends and former members of the Selbitz Athletic Club.

School children performed traditional plays on the steps of the City Hall, to everyone's delight. There were booths, games, and numerous rides, and even a large area featuring bumper cars. The most-attended attraction, however, was a large outdoor dance floor, complete with musicians playing local music, performances of the men's choir, and a huge beer tent. It was filled to capacity with people singing along with a brass band, interlocking arms, and swaying side to side while standing on benches and tables.

Christine, now eleven, had a wonderful time with her grandmother, aunts, and uncles, and most of all, with cousins her own age. She had the opportunity to see the old Langer house between the railroad tracks, the Ludwig Shoe Factory, and the sprawling Bodenschatz facility. She went on several nature hikes, exploring the beautiful countryside, where her father once played. While holding her hand, Al would explain several sights and things he'd experienced when he was a child. Having a clearer picture of her father's background gave Christine a new perspective and respect of her family's history.

During that trip, several things left a lasting impression in Al's mind— there was the occasion of seeing beloved family members and old friends, of course; and the deepening of the bond between father and daughter, which was an exceptional blessing. But perhaps the greatest impression came when he first saw the house he'd proudly provided for his parents. The pictures Willie had sent failed to give the structure the justice it deserved. When Al saw the house, it exceeded his greatest expectations. He walked slowly up the flight of granite stairs to the third floor, appreciating the wrought-iron handrails and the wall of glass blocks that illuminated the staircase with a soft glow. He stopped on the landing on the third floor, where the entire wall had an oversized mural of a classically beautiful alpine scene.

The front door to his mother's home had a large panel of colorful opaque glass, and once inside, he marveled at the pristine marble flooring and ornate ceramic tiles on the walls that his brother Rudi had installed. The kitchen, while small, was extremely cozy, and the comfortable living room had a skylight in the ceiling that could be opened to let in sunshine, along with two more large windows on the front of the building. The bedroom was tastefully decorated with Elsa's distinctive touch.

Even though Willie and his wife, Brigitte, lived on the second floor, almost everyone seemed to gather on the third floor, where Elsa lived. She enjoyed having company and graciously provided her delicious meals to all who visited. She loved the house and was enormously happy living there. The only sadness Al felt was that his father had only been able to enjoy the house for three years before his passing. Still, Elsa frequently thanked Al profusely for providing it, often saying it was a dream come true. On countless occasions she would stand in her living room, staring out the window at the magnificent view of the lush green meadows and surrounding forest, reflecting on previous residences—the tiny two-room apartment over the shoe factory, the comfortable yet noisy house between the railroad tracks, and now this, an exquisite home of her own.

Leaving Selbitz and his family after a visit always proved an extremely poignant event, the emotions of which only lessened with the promise they would visit again in two years.

* * *

Upon the family's return to America, Al's routine began again—long work days, more strain, more stress, more pressure. Al knew that he had to make some dramatic changes in his life that would allow him to find the inner fulfillment he so desperately desired.

Al and Irene's shared faith helped them tremendously during the difficult times. Even though Al felt that God provided a positive direction and influence, he still had serious and troubling questions concerning his own spirituality, which he was unable to satisfactorily answer.

Perhaps it was a higher power that intervened and caused Al and Irene to become acquainted with Don and Chris Taugher; Al actually considered the Taughers' friendship to be a gift. He found it fascinating that Don and Chris always appeared to have absolute peace in their lives—a perfect balance of the spiritual and the secular. Many times, Al and Irene would privately discuss the Taughers, wondering what enabled them to exist in such serenity and joy. Although he wasn't sure he understood, Al felt that, somehow, God was urging him to seek the answers he desired and that Don and Chris could possibly be the instruments God had provided to help him and Irene grow stronger in their spiritual walk.

Al's feelings were validated one warm summer evening when he and Irene went out to dinner with the Taughers. Following a bite of Caesar salad and completely unrelated to any earlier conversation, Don asked, "Have you ever heard of Cursillo?"

Al and Irene both shrugged and shook their heads.

"We think it's something you might be interested in," Chris said.

"What is it?" Al asked politely.

Don and Chris explained that Cursillo was a Catholic weekend retreat, during which participants developed a deeper and closer walk with both their faith and their God.

Al leaned closer to the table, his interest rising. "What does *Cursillo* mean?"

"Loosely translated," Chris answered, "it means a short course in Christianity. Priests, deacons, and laypeople offer a series of highly informative presentations on how to discover a better and more fulfilled life. In my opinion, Cursillo evolved out of a need to answer people's questions."

Focusing on the word "answers," Al was now paying much closer attention. "The two of you have attended?"

Don and Chris both nodded, offering smiles of intense satisfaction.

"Would you say," Al asked, "that this weekend retreat had something to do with the way you both seem to be so at peace with everything; the way you seem to glide through life like you know something other people might not know?"

Chris leaned forward and said sincerely, "I can say, with absolute certainty in my heart, that I know it did."

Don briefly explained, "The retreat is designed to assist people in developing greater courage, making it possible to see things in a different light and overcome any challenges, and most important, remembering and understanding the fact that God made the ultimate sacrifice—His own son—for you." With unconditional belief, he related that the core purpose of Cursillo was to strengthen people's love for Jesus Christ and, as a result, strengthen themselves.

"We think you might find Cursillo informative and enlightening," Chris suggested.

"If you'd like to attend," Don continued, "you need to be invited by a sponsor." He smiled at Irene and Al. "Chris and I would be honored to sponsor you."

Almost before Don had finished speaking, Al began to ask a series of rapid-fire questions. "When is it? Where is it? How long does it last? How many people will be there?"

Don politely held up his hands in an effort to curtail Al's enthusiasm. "All your questions will be answered in good time. First, we'll give you some information about it, and if you decide you'd like to attend, let us know."

Later, when they arrived at home, Al and Irene eased onto a couch and began to read the material that Don and Chris had provided. And as they read, they began what would prove to be a road of personal and spiritual discovery.

Their first discovery was that Cursillo was born out of the pain and suffering of the Spanish Civil War, which ended in 1939. Spain was a Catholic country and in that war, Catholics were fighting Catholics. When the terrible killing ended, the country was nearly dead itself from a spiritual standpoint. Then the Holy Spirit took charge and a young Spanish Catholic lay group responded to a plea from Pope Pius XII to restore Christian values to their country. After prayer and discernment, these remarkable young people decided to gather 100,000 other young men and women to go on a pilgrimage to Santiago de Compostela (the burial place of St. James the Apostle). It was an arduous trip, and while enduring many hardships during their journey, they continued to encourage each other by saying "*ultreya*," which means "onward."

The Cursillo was formed during that pilgrimage and under the leadership of Eduard Bonnin and Juan Hervas, Bishop of Majorca, and the first Cursillo was held on the island of Majorca, Spain, in 1949. Its message was brought to the United States by two Spanish military exchange pilots, who were training with the U.S. Air Force in Texas. The first United States Cursillo was held in Waco, Texas, on May 25, 1957.

The movement spread quickly throughout the United States and the first English-language Cursillo was held in 1961. The first Orange Diocese Cursillo, the county in which Al and Irene resided, was held at the Blessed Sacrament parish in Westminster in May 1977. Worldwide, there were millions of people who had attended Cursillos; they referred to themselves as Cursillistas. Since its inception 1949, Cursillos have been held in virtually every major city in the United States and nearly every country in the world.

Al and Irene looked at each other in amazement. They were long-time members of the Blessed Sacrament parish and active participants in various church activities, and their daughter attended school there. They were both dumbstruck that this evening was the first time either one of them had heard the word Cursillo. With their interest increasing, they continued to read that the Catholic Cursillo had been so successful in bringing people to Christ that it found expression in other faiths. There was a Lutheran and a Methodist Cursillo and also a Protestant "Walk to Emmaus," which was essentially identical. Also coming from the Cursillo was the Kairos movement, which they learned was an interfaith Cursillo-type weekend for those incarcerated in prisons. Al and Irene read that many of those who had made their Cursillo retreat weekend likened it to a personal encounter with Christ—to being touched by the Holy Spirit.

Al leaned back on the couch, deep in thought. In a calm and serene tone, he said, "I have an unexplained feeling in my heart that this weekend retreat might be the experience that could provide some of the answers to questions that have been plaguing me for so long."

"What types of questions?" Irene asked gently.

"So many," Al responded. He sighed, finally willing to express his thoughts out loud. "What is our real purpose here on earth? Why are some people always so satisfied and happy, while others are so continually miserable and depressed? How is it that some find success and joy in their lives, and others wallow in failure and misery? What is our responsibility to other people? Where does true inner strength come from? How can I have a closer relationship with the Lord?"

Irene placed her hand gently over Al's. "So many questions, indeed. Don's information does explain that everyone experiences something different and is touched differently by the weekend retreat. Perhaps it would help to answer your questions." She pointed to the material they had spread on their laps and said encouragingly, "Look—read here, where it gives the stated purpose of Cursillo."

Al followed along where Irene had indicated and read:

> *Cursillo is a movement of the Catholic Church which, by means of a specific method, makes it possible for people to live what is fundamental for being a Christian, and to live it together.*
> *It helps people discover and fulfill their personal vocations.*
> *It promotes the creation of core groups of Christians who leaven their environments with the Gospel.*
> *It gives pride in being a Catholic.*

Al and Irene were intrigued and fascinated by the possibilities. Their conversation lasted well into the night, as they experienced intimate moments that revealed their innermost thoughts and feelings. "Maybe this is it," Al quietly said. "Maybe this is what I've been waiting for, looking for, hoping for."

Al and Irene reflected on the words Don had spoken: "All your questions will be answered in good time." They concluded that enough of their questions had been answered already, to the point that they were willing to take a profound leap of faith. They decided to attend the retreat.

The next day, Al phoned Don to accept his and Chris' offer to be their sponsor. The next Cursillo for men, he learned, would be held September 10–13, and the woman's retreat would be September 17–20. The first step was to fill out an application that would be reviewed by the priest at their parish. Following his approval and signature, they would be accepted as candidates.

As the weekend grew closer, Manhattan Die received several important rush orders that had to be completed. To his dismay, Al informed Irene that he didn't think he would be able to attend the retreat—there was too much work to be done at the shop.

"You're only going to miss one day of work," Irene countered.

"It's for a long-time and loyal customer," Al replied. "I can't let him down."

"If you don't go, I can't either," she argued.

Al was flummoxed. "Perhaps we can attend another one."

Irene was enormously disappointed and knew that Al was as well. She shared the news with Chris, who comforted her by saying, "Perhaps something will change. Just keep the faith and keep praying."

On Monday morning, four days before the retreat was to begin, the critically important customer phoned Al to say that the rush order he was working on had been delayed for a few days—it was no longer necessary to have the job completed that coming weekend. Al considered the unexpected call to be a miracle.

On the evening of September 9, 1981, Don called Al. "I'll pick you up after work and take you to a facility known as Marywood. It was once a high school but is now being used exclusively by the Orange County Diocese. Bring along a sleeping bag or blankets, a pillow, and clothing and toiletries for three days. Everything else will be provided."

Later, during the short drive to the facility, Don offered. "My final piece of advice would be to just relax and let it happen. Experience the experience."

Al and Don walked into the building and were met by a greeter, who welcomed them warmly and escorted them to a large gymnasium. It was separated into two parts by sliding curtains. On one side, the floor was covered with several mattresses, each with a chair beside it. Al smiled to himself, remembering the days as a youth in Naila, when he spent several weeks sleeping on a straw mattress on the floor in another gymnasium. He remembered fondly how his mother had safely protected the crucifix, which now adorned the wall in his own home. He thought that his life, perhaps, had come full circle, and that this moment and this time might possibly be the beginning of another.

The greeter assigned Al a place to sleep, and he then met several other men, all of whom seemed congenial and represented all age groups. Al could detect a universal sense of anxiety and anticipation among them, not unlike walking into a strange, unfamiliar room and not quite knowing what to expect.

When the group of chosen candidates was finally assembled, they numbered forty-four, all eager to begin a journey that they hoped would lead them down a path of enlightenment. The group was led to the other side of the gymnasium, where they found tables and chairs arranged in a dining-room configuration. Sandwiches, cookies, coffee, and tea were consumed during introductions and conversations. Without prior notification, someone rang a small bell, and all the sponsors in the room stood up. The candidates, following their lead, did so as well. Don turned to Al. "It's time for the sponsors to leave." They shook hands warmly, and Al could clearly see a tender glow emanating from Don's eyes. Don leaned closer and whispered, "You are about to experience the most wonderful weekend of your life." And with that, the sponsors left the area.

A well-dressed gentleman walked to the front of the room and introduced himself as the rector, the Spanish word for leader. With a warm smile, he said, "Welcome. Initially, I'd like you all to know and understand that you will receive from this Cursillo only that which you are willing and able to give. I ask that you open not only your minds but also your hearts. I further ask that you hear words that are not spoken and experience feelings that are not expressed." Following another reassuring smile, he continued, "I understand that these words may not be comprehended at this moment, but by Sunday evening, they will be."

TWENTY-SIX

Four days earlier, Al had looked into Don's eyes and seen an indescribable glow. Now, when Don looked into Al's eyes, the same glow was clearly evident. During the ride home at the end of the retreat, Don asked, "Were your questions answered?"

Al nodded and replied, "Every single one." Without encouragement, he went on to passionately and emotionally explain, "Don, I never realized that there were such truly giving individuals in the world. Each and every leader this past weekend served us with amazing spiritual guidance. The team members working in the kitchen spent hour after hour preparing meals for us, hardly sleeping at all, always eager to serve us with a genuine smile. And the messages I received from the presentations were ones I really needed to hear and take into my heart—messages that God is actually calling me to be His apostle; to go forward and touch environments; to be aware of the need in the world for godly intervention. And the greatest part of all is that He's giving me brothers in Christ with whom to travel on this glorious and remarkable journey."

Don smiled warmly at his friend. "Can you describe it in one word?"

And Al replied, "Transformational."

* * *

Irene greeted Al at the door and as he stepped into the light of the entryway, she could see he had become a different man. She peppered him with questions, wanting to hear every detail, eager to hear about what she would soon experience herself.

Al tried to explain, but words seemed to fail him. Finally, he said softly, "The words are in my heart but not my mouth. By this time next week, you'll understand that. All I can say is that the Cursillo is life-altering and that you just have to experience the experience."

Al walked around with a knowing smile on his face all week long, much to Hans' and the employees' confusion, fully aware of the wonderful adventure Irene was about to encounter. The smile grew even larger during the weekend as he eagerly awaited her return. On Sunday evening, when she walked through their front door, she returned the same smile that he had worn the weekend before, and tears rolled gently down her cheeks as she simply said, "Now I understand."

* * *

Al continued to be amazed by his altered mind-set and renewed outlook on life. Before his Cursillo weekend, his life evolved around his work. But now, with a much deeper understanding of God in his heart and how that feeling could impact others, he maintained a sense of bliss and transformed confidence. He knew, without question, that his purpose was guided by a higher power, and with that understanding, stress became much less of a factor.

On a normal Wednesday afternoon, Al was working on a milling machine, making precision cuts with a three-inch diameter slitter blade on a brass part. Whenever he received a phone call, his secretary would ring the buzzer in the shop two times. Now, he heard the buzzer, ring twice; Al turned off the machine and went to his workbench to answer it. By the time he reached the phone, however, the party who was calling had become impatient and hung up.

Al returned to the machine, and soon, the buzzer sounded again. In his haste to get to the phone so he wouldn't lose another call, he forgot to turn off the machine and the blade continued to turn. He spoke with a customer briefly; then, with the conversation still on his mind, returned to the machine and opened the vise to remove the brass part, using his right thumb and forefinger.

He felt a sharp and stinging snap at his forefinger and realized the slitter blade had caught a part of his finger—it had actually removed it! He knew instantly that it was a bad cut. Blood began to flow rapidly. He pressed his finger against his stomach to try to stop the bleeding, as he grabbed a nearby worker. "I need you to take me to my doctor's office right now. It's only about two miles away." By the time he arrived, the blood had completely soaked his light blue lab coat, even running down his pant leg.

The nurse rushed him into an examining room, and when the doctor saw the abundance of blood, he initially thought Al had been shot in the stomach. Quickly realizing the actual problem, he attended to the finger, numbing it, trying his best to stop the bleeding. "Where's the end of your finger?" he asked excitedly.

"I guess still in my shop," Al replied, fighting pain.

The nurse immediately phoned Hans and asked him to look for the tip of Al's finger. Fortunately, within seconds, Hans found it—on the floor with brass chips attached to it. He wrapped the finger in a paper towel and rushed to the doctor's office, where the doctor informed Al that the injury was too big a job for him to handle. "You need to go to the emergency room at the Downey Community Hospital," he said, handing him the severed part of his finger wrapped in ice.

Hans took Al back to their shop, where Al got in his own car and drove himself to the hospital. The emergency room physician gave Al a small brush and told him, "Go to the sink and thoroughly scrub the stump of your finger so you can remove all the metal chips." Once he looked at Al's finger and scrubbed stump, the doctor said nothing could be done, but after Al pleaded with him, the doctor finally agreed to sew the finger back on. "I'll do it, but it is unlikely the finger will ever grow back together." He told him in no uncertain terms, "It would take a miracle."

Driving home, his finger still throbbing, Al reflected on the time when, as a youth, he'd talked his brother Willie into holding a log while Al attempted to split it in half with an ax. He remembered the flowing blood and the screams of pain and panic. He also smiled, recalling that it had been only a flesh wound, leaving a minor scar. Now, in addition to everything else, they had yet one more thing in common.

The following day, word of Al's accident quickly spread throughout the Blessed Sacrament School in Westminster, where Christine was in the seventh grade. An announcement came over the public address system told the students: "Christine Langer's father was in an accident and needs all of our prayers for a quick recovery." There was a moment of silence as all students in the entire school reverently bowed their heads.

Although it might have surprised some, Al completely understood the power of prayer, when, in a relatively short period of time, his finger healed completely. The miracle that the doctor at the emergency room had suggested had become a reality.

* * *

The weather in February 1983 was different from that which Al experienced since first coming to America. Unlike the typically warm and sunny days of winter in California, the temperature this particular month seemed to be unusually brisk, and for days on end, the skies were leaden with thick, gray clouds—ominous, troublesome—putting most people into what was generally referred to as a "funk."

Friends told Al several times that he needed to lighten up, relax, and not be so serious. This attitude was also expressed with reference to talking on the phone. They explained that those on the other end of the phone could "hear the smile in your voice," and as such, would be more receptive.

Al decided to try to sound as if he was smiling on the phone, regardless of who was calling, so when the telephone rang at home, he picked it up and brightly said, "Hello."

"Alfred?" the female voice said, slightly trembling. "It's Gerti. I think you'd better sit down."

Al felt a jolt to his heart, but he followed his sister's advice, knowing with certainty unpleasant news was coming. After a deep breath, he softly said, "It's Mama, isn't it."

Gerti hesitated before saying softly, "Her suffering has finally come to an end. She's gone to be with Tata."

Al exhaled deeply as the blood drained from his face. "When's the funeral?"

"Day after tomorrow."

"I'll be there. I have to make some arrangements, and I'll call you back."

"Alfred?" Gerti said.

"Yes?"

"I love you."

"And I love you."

After an emotional but brief discussion with Irene and a prayer for the eternal souls of both his father and mother, Al was able to arrange a flight for the following morning. He called Hans, told him the news, and explained that he'd be away for a week or so. The thirteen-hour flight was unlike any he'd taken in the past. This time, there was no upbeat conversation with family members or fellow travelers. This time, he did not watch the in-flight movies. This time, he barely touched the meals that were presented. This time, he reflected on his mother's life and what an enormous influence she had been on his own. By her actions and example, she had provided strength, values, perseverance, and deeply seeded faith—faith that, in his own mind, had eventually led him to his Cursillo weekend and a much higher level of understanding.

Heinz, Al's younger brother who lived in Bruchsal, picked him up at the airport. They were thrilled to see each other, yet wished the circumstances had been different. As they reached the Autobahn, they exchanged stories about their youth and the difficulties they'd experienced and endured while growing up. They managed to overcome various hardships because of their parents' leadership, unconditional love, and the fighting will to conquer any obstacle in their path.

Like the skies that month in Southern California, the skies in Germany were ominous. They were also considerably more dangerous. At first, it was only light flurries, but within moments, the snow developed into a raging blizzard. Vision was totally obscured—it was a "white-out"—and Heinz' little Fiat was slipping and sliding all over the road, which was rapidly turning into a sheet of ice. They were forced to pull off to the side of the highway; trying to move forward would be perilous.

Accompanying the blizzard was flashing lightning and booming thunder, sending shivers down their spines. Al and Heinz waited impatiently for assistance of any kind. The temperature began to fall, and the Fiat became covered with snow. They waited for hours before a snowplow finally arrived to clear the way, followed by a salt truck, which melted the ice, making the road drivable again.

The family gathered that evening, but during their meal, there was little conversation, only contemplation that every life, no matter how cherished or important, would always culminate in death. Understanding that reality and inevitability brought little relief to their grief or the loss they all felt. Yet Al knew his mother had indeed gone to a much better place and was now held safely and with eternal love in the hands of their Lord. He explained to the others, from lessons he had learned during his Cursillo, that while this life was finished, their mother had just begun another life that would be filled with joy and celebration—one in which she would be truly able to walk without pain in the footsteps of Christ.

Elsa looked beautiful, lifelike, as if she could arise from her prone position on the altar and greet the mourners with her warm smile and generous, caring heart. Al stared at her from behind a glass divider, his forehead pressed against the glass, hiding his emotions from the family in the room behind him. Someone tapped him on the shoulder and whispered, "It's time to join the others in the chapel."

During the Mass, Elsa's body was placed into a coffin and transported to a gravesite near the church. When the Mass concluded, the family walked to the gravesite along a sidewalk that had recently been shoveled, with the snow on either side of the walkway two feet deep.

After the priest said his final words of consolation, Al said a brief, silent prayer and placed the first rose on top of the coffin, as was expected; then other family members followed suit. After the service was completed and the final farewells had all been said, the Langer children—Gerti, Rudi, Willie, Alfred, Heinz, and Harald—hugged each other, none pretending to hide their tears. As they shared perhaps their closest moment ever, they realized that they now had to carry on without their pillar of strength. Al calmly expressed his feeling that now, in their mother's absence, they were each required to be not only their own pillars of strength but to share that strength with others as well.

* * *

That fall, Christine enrolled in Mater Dei High School, one of the more highly respected secondary schools in the greater Los Angeles area, one that maintained high educational standards. She had an excellent background, coming as a student from Blessed Sacrament, where she not only earned good grades but also was a proud and loyal member of the Coronets, the school drill team—after an intense competition, she had been chosen as Miss Junior Drill Team of the city of Westminster.

While at Mater Dei, she continued to receive excellent grades and also competed on their swimming team. As a result of Christine's numerous activities, Irene also was constantly on the go, inundated by an abundance of church activities, carpooling, and taking Christine to swim, drill team, and soccer practice, and tennis and guitar lessons.

In addition, there were countless parades, football games, and other activities to attend. Even with his own church activities and monumental work schedule, Al supported Christine's activities to the fullest extent, attending at every opportunity. By Al and Irene's actions and deeds, other parents became more involved as well. Al and Irene, as they had been instructed, were leading by example to make a friend, be a friend, and bring a friend to Christ.

Christine, following her own parents' leadership and of her own volition, volunteered to assist others who needed practical help or positive encouragement. Time after time during family discussions, Al and Irene reiterated the simple but absolute fact that by helping and offering strength to others, they, in turn, helped themselves and increased their own strength. By their actions and willingness to give and share, Al and Irene made a lasting impression on their daughter.

* * *

Business began to increase on a steady basis since the downturn in 1980. It was a slow and agonizing process, but old customers returned and new ones were attracted. Al found the rebound in their growth stimulating, rejuvenating, and exciting. Hans, on the other hand, seemed to become more frustrated with each passing year. Competitors continued to encroach on their customers, which added to the stress of having to meet the demand for faster delivery with better quality and lower prices. Whenever one of their customers switched to another die maker, Hans took it very personally and would sometimes enter a state of depression for several days.

By 1984, the company was operating at full capacity. All twelve work-stations were occupied by experienced machinists or apprentices. Even so, Al could sense that Hans had lost his passion for the business. He seemed to have misplaced his drive and was no longer willing to go the extra mile that was occasionally necessary to satisfy a customer's needs.

Over the years, Al's and Hans' interests grew in different directions. Al was happily married, with a teenage daughter, and deeply involved with numerous church functions. He was also vitally interested in pushing forward and expanding the business. Hans was single, financially secure, and often complained that the stress was affecting his health. The two men had known each other and worked side by side for more than twenty-five years. They had gone on great adventures and built a successful business together. In all their years, they had always been able to resolve any minor disagreements with mutual respect and understanding, but when the filing of his tax returns on April 15, 1985, made Hans feel physically ill, he finally concluded that he could no longer continue—he wanted out in the worst possible way and offered to sell his share of the business to Al. His proposition came as no surprise; Al had felt it slowly building over the last several years. Because of their closeness and long association, it was an extremely peaceful transaction. With their attorney, they carried out brief negotiations and determined a fair and equitable price for the purchase. The details seemed to matter little to Hans; he just wanted out.

The prospect of running Manhattan Die as a sole owner was some-what daunting to Al, but it provided much-needed peace of mind. He no longer had to consult with anyone else before making a decision, nor did he have to put up with occasional personality conflicts. For his entire life, he had loved the challenge of making new dies; now he was now personally involved with every aspect of running the company. He had an elaborate brochure professionally created and sent it to all his customers and prospects. He had a Web master design a five-page website, demonstrating in an animated fashion the way in which his dies worked on the heat-sealing machine.

Once the business was running efficiently, Al hired a highly respected consulting firm to analyze precisely what he was doing and recommend what else could be done to expand the company to new levels. Two professional consultants spent a full week in the shop, listening, observing, charting, documenting. In their final report, they determined that Al, by himself, was doing the same jobs that other companies would require at least four additional employees to do. Al was in a position to double the size of the operation, but in order to do so, he would have to move into a much larger facility, purchase more machines, and hire department heads to oversee engineering, manufacturing, quality control, and shipping. He would also need to hire a computer-literate office manager and a sales staff.

While the prospect was exciting and challenging, he and Irene decided that taking a step of that magnitude would be like asking for a heart attack. Once that decision was reached, Al resolved to keep on going as they had been, except more efficiently.

To motivate the workers, he offered more overtime and conducted a series of creative meetings, in which they were encouraged to provide their thoughts about the efficiency of the company and how they could better themselves. Al exercised the practical concepts that had been learned and proven during his Cursillo weekend. He showed leadership skills, but he also, by including his employees in the process, demonstrated the concept that a chain is only as strong as its weakest link. Offering his employees three weeks of paid vacation and one week of sick leave also proved to be highly motivating, as did his paying up 25 percent of employees' salary into a retirement account. Other business owners would criticize that he was being overly generous and impractical, but Al calmly explained, "I've been through times when it was difficult to make ends meet. I know what it's like to go to bed hungry. I've had several workers who lived from paycheck to paycheck. When my business is doing well, I don't mind taking home a little less in order to share with others who really need it." Other than that simple statement, Al never felt the need to justify his actions to anyone; he didn't talk about his background or the fact that he had personally known abject poverty, not having a roof over his head, and not knowing when or from where his next meal was going to come. He kept that information to himself, knowing with clarity and a certainty that was true to the foundations of his faith that he was doing the correct thing for his employees.

To lessen his own responsibilities, he offered his most highly qualified employees the opportunity to become second in command, to slowly work their way to the point where they could run the shop if he ever had to be away. None, however, took advantage of the offer; none felt they had the talent required to deal with customers, accept orders, and produce dies that met the perfection that Al required and expected.

* * *

Now approaching graduation from Mater Dei High School, Christine applied for entrance at San Diego State University, the University of San Diego, and UCLA—she was accepted by all three. After intense contemplation, she decided UCLA—the University of California at Los Angeles—would best meet her educational needs. Al and Irene were pleased with her decision and proud of the professional and adult approach she had taken in making her choice. Their pride was only diminished by the fact that come September, their baby would be leaving the nest and beginning a life of her own.

Al and Irene decided it was time for a move of their own, to leave Westminster and find a new home. They searched for a larger house, one that would have room for Christine to visit whenever possible and accommodate friends from college that she might bring along for a weekend excursion in the country and near the ocean. They found the perfect house in the delightful community of Laguna Hills, located in the Saddleback Valley of Southern California.

From their new house, looking toward the ocean, they could see large earth-moving machines removing the top of a ridge that was higher than their own, obviously creating lots for another new subdivision. Al discovered semi-custom houses were going to be built and would be available sometime in 1989. Potential customers could place their names on a waiting list—the houses, based on their location, were expected to sell rapidly. Al and Irene were among the first to place their name on the waiting list. On several evenings, during the building process, they would drive to the construction site, sit on piles of lumber, enjoy a glass of fine wine, and be overwhelmed by the breathtaking view of the ocean and the valley. As soon as the floor plans were available, they chose one in a picturesque location with a spectacular view—without question, it would be the house of their dreams.

After Christine's graduation from Mater Dei, the family scoured Westwood for an apartment where she and some friends from school could live while attending college. After several visits, an agreement was reached and in late summer, Christine and three friends moved to a comfortable apartment close to the school. Since parking on the sprawling campus was by permit and a serious challenge, Al and Irene bought Christine a Honda motor scooter so she could safely get from class to class.

Al and Irene bid their daughter an emotional good-bye and drove back to Laguna Hills in silence, the only sound being an occasional, heavy sigh. Then, Irene smiled and said, "Remember when Christine was a Brownie?"

Al nodded. "And the times we took her to Germany."

One fond reflection followed another and continued long after they reached their home. They were tremendously proud of their young daughter, who had blossomed into a fine young woman. They had no question that she would continue life, based on the lessons she learned and the examples that had been shown.

Christine received excellent grades while at UCLA, through hard work, persistence, and dedication. She appreciated all the sacrifices that had been made for her and wasn't about to disappoint or let her parents down in any way. Her values and moral compass had been well formed and well directed.

TWENTY-SEVEN

I N NOVEMBER 1988, AL AND IRENE LEARNED THEY WOULD be able to move into their new home in nine months. Having a specific date for the move, they put their own house on the market immediately. They would now watch from their present home as their dream house was constructed.

Their plans were altered dramatically, however, when their house sold in one day, and the new buyers wanted to take possession within thirty days. "Everything happens for a reason," Al said philosophically. "This is just another small obstacle to overcome." They immediately found a two-bedroom apartment to rent until their own house was completed.

As they waited impatiently for their house to be built, Manhattan Die continued forward on a steady pace. Following suggestions from the consulting firm, Al upgraded his office with computers, a plotter, fax machines, and a wireless telephone system. New vinyl and vinyl-coated fabric was developed, requiring a different approach to making dies, calling for additional equipment. Vinyl zippers came out for Ziploc bags, with or without a slider. New anti-static vinyl was available for sensitive, electronic parts storage. Cold-crack plastic was used to produce ring binders and notebooks that would not get "fluffy" and would not shatter if dropped in the cold.

* * *

Al normally made pickups and deliveries himself because he enjoyed the close relationships with his customers. His knowledge with regard to precision die-making, however, meant he needed to spend the vast majority of his time in the shop. He placed an ad in a local newspaper for a driver. After interviewing several applicants, he was particularly impressed with one young man.

His name was Ramon, and he'd worked as a driver for Tomco, a company that manufactured carburetors. He was young, not yet twenty, but seemed to be extremely ambitious. He was sincere in his desire to earn more money to support his three children. After making monthly child support payments, he barely existed from paycheck to paycheck. He was also recently married and expecting another child. Coming from Mexico, he and his wife had work permits and had made applications to become permanent residents.

Al discovered that Ramon had a good driving record and could operate a manual transmission, a prerequisite to driving the company van. Ramon promised Al that he would be a good worker. He wanted to be able to move out of his two-bedroom apartment in a bad section of town, where drugs were prevalent, gangs ruled the neighborhood, and shootings were commonplace. When Al heard this, he was reminded of his youth, when his family first arrived in Selbitz as outcasts, having to make do with the absolute minimum of everything, living day to day in uncertainty. His compassion for Ramon and his family was heartfelt, and he wanted to help them, not only as a result of his own unpleasant memories but because it was the right thing to do. Once again, he practiced the principles from his Cursillo weekend.

In addition to his pickup and delivery responsibilities, Al also assigned Ramon a workbench and tools, teaching him the basics of producing special dies. As an added bonus, Ramon received overtime pay by staying after the shop closed to clean the entire area. He was thankful for the opportunity and showed his appreciation by being the good and loyal worker.

* * *

On July 4, 1989, Al and Irene moved into their new house in Laguna Niguel. The first object to enter the home was the crucifix that Elsa had given to Al on the day he left Germany for his new life in America. With pride, great emotion, and a lifetime of fond memories, he placed the crucifix next to their front door, so it would be seen whenever anyone entered or left the house. It was a visual and constant reminder that with God, all things are possible. Moving to a new neighborhood meant transferring their church membership from Blessed Sacrament in Westminster to the Mission San Juan Capistrano, where they continued to attend Mass on a weekly basis.

After they were settled into their new home, they had an *ultreya* and an open house for more than fifty close friends. The guests learned that the *ultreya*, which means onward, was to encourage them to persevere and evangelize the environment. It also represented a reunion of friendship groups to form a larger community through prayers and sharing of spiritual relevance. Father Bruce Lavery from St. Timothy's parish was among the guests and said a Mass. The Mass was held for the South County Cursillistas, those from the southernmost part of Orange County, who had attended a Cursillo weekend. During the Mass, Father Bruce Lavery offered a special blessing for the home and its new residents.

* * *

Time passed quickly, as if it were rapidly evaporating. It seemed as if it were only yesterday when Al and Irene had dropped off Christine to begin her four years of college. And now, almost in the blink of an eye, they were sitting in the Royce Hall auditorium on the UCLA campus, attending their daughter's graduation from college.

The commencement speaker was Barry Diller, one of the most highly successful and respected businessmen in America. He was the founder and driving force of Fox Television and then built a television empire of his own. He spoke to the graduates and those in attendance of the undisputed and unquestionable power of having a clear and unshakable vision, of using persistence and dedication as a moral compass, which would overcome all obstacles, and that by following the dreams in their hearts, they each had the opportunity to achieve the American dream.

Al smiled to himself as he listened attentively to Mr. Diller's powerful presentation. It was a description of his own life; a life of overcoming obstacles, of being steadfast and unwavering in his absolute belief that a higher power was offering him guidance and understanding. It described a detailed map of the path Al had taken to achieve his own American dream.

At the close of the address, and as the orchestra played the traditional "Pomp and Circumstance," Al and Irene watched with indescribable pride as Christine, in cap and gown, walked across the stage and received her bachelor of arts degree in economics.

Prior to her graduation, Christine had been offered a position with Merck Pharmaceuticals as a sales representative, calling on doctors, hospitals, and clinics to present their products and services. She accepted the job and acquired a sales territory that was quite large, covering the western part of Los Angeles. She was paid well and had a company car and an expense account, but within two years, she reached the conclusion that Merck would not be able to provide the opportunity of working in the field of finance and economics, her area of expertise.

* * *

At Manhattan Die, Ramon, keeping his promise, continued to be a good worker and a fast learner. He was always willing to go the extra mile and do whatever he could to help Al and the company. In 1992, he approached Al and explained, "With the increase in gangs and all, our living conditions have become much more dangerous. I'm very concerned about the safety of my wife and sons."

Al was empathetic. "What can I do to help?"

"I was wondering if you would consider renting us the house behind the building next door." It was the home where the Lippincutts had once lived.

As fate would have it, the people who presently were renting the house were planning on moving, so Al agreed to Ramon's proposition and went the extra mile himself. Reflecting on his own childhood in Selbitz and so being able to relate to Ramon's children, Al had the house completely remodeled.

The rent he charged was much lower than that for comparable properties, and he even made the company VW van available for Ramon's use. The children enjoyed freedom, privacy, and finally, security in their backyard, which was surrounded by a six-foot-high brick wall. They referred to Al as "*el patron*," and Ramon called him "*compadre*." The children often visited the shop, and Al was generous with giving Ramon time off to attend to family issues, such as taking a family member to the medical clinic.

In exchange for Al's kindness and compassion, Ramon was a loyal worker for Manhattan Die for eighteen years. But Al didn't feel he had done anything special—in his own heart, he was merely expressing the lessons and principles he had learned from that memorable Cursillo weekend in September 1981. Al's expressions and generosity were not singular; they were shown to many others over the years.

And through those years, Al strongly felt his greatest contribution was that he and Irene personally sponsored other couples to attend a Cursillo weekend. As a result of the overwhelming pleasure those people received from their own experience, they, in turn, sponsored others, all becoming part of a movement in which they could more effectively share their love of Christ with their fellow man.

* * *

Christine recognized the value of furthering her education and submitted applications to several graduate schools—she was accepted by all. But again, following logic, well-respected advice, and her own inner voice, she came to the best choice: Northwestern University, located in Evanston, Illinois, a suburb just north of Chicago. Northwestern was widely known and acknowledged as one of the most respected and prestigious business schools in the country. While her parents were pleased with her decision to get a graduate degree, Al and Irene were somewhat uncomfortable with the fact she was going to be so far away.

Christine adapted well to her new environment and vastly enjoyed her classes, but during her first year she had difficulty with one of her marketing courses. She went to her advisor, who suggested she hire a tutor. The Kellogg School of Management, part of Northwestern, provided tutorial assistance to those who wanted their experience and expertise. Christine appreciated the suggestion.

Being both popular and attractive, she never had a shortage of dates, but she never had a serious relationship. While the boys and men she met were acceptable, she felt none was what she would consider "marriage material." Then, one day, all that changed.

* * *

Christine walked into the office of the student from Kellogg who was to be her new tutor. When he stood up and offered his hand, her heart skipped a beat. If ever there was such a thing as love at first sight, this most certainly was it. As they touched hands for the first time, she knew with certainty that her skipping heartbeat was not an accident.

His name was Todd Dow, and he'd been born in Canada. He had graduated from Princeton and was in his second year at Kellogg, working toward his master's degree in business management. In addition to being tall and handsome, he also—as Christine soon discovered—had a warm and caring heart. Beyond his tutoring, they spent time together learning all they could about each other.

When Christine phoned home and spoke with her mother, Irene could tell that something about her daughter was different, unusual. When she asked, Christine simply said, "I met a very nice guy."

Irene smiled, remembering the words her own mother had spoken to her several years ago. "Is he the one?"

Without hesitation, Christine replied, "I think so."

Sad news followed good, however, when Gerti phoned a few days later to inform Al that Willie had died. He was only fifty-seven but, like their father, had been a smoker all his life; throat cancer was the cause. Al was troubled, especially because he had asked Willie time and time again to stop smoking … but the habit had been too strong to break. Al was comforted in the fact his older brother would be in heaven with their parents and their God.

* * *

Although he started out as her tutor, Todd's personal relationship with Christine eventually took precedence as it grew considerably more serious. After Todd's graduation in 1994, he moved to New York City and began working as an investment broker. Christine received her master's degree the following year and soon after, they announced their engagement. Al and Irene fell in love with Todd on their first meeting, finding him to be considerate and caring. Their only regret was that Todd had taken a wonderful job in a far-off location, where the happy couple would relocate after returning from their honeymoon.

Many of Todd's relatives and friends came from Canada for the nuptials, and Al was thrilled that Gerti, Harald, and Harald's wife, Uschi, were coming all the way from Germany for the event.

The wedding was held at the Mission Church in San Juan Capistrano and was presided over by Father Martin Benzoni, one of Christine's favorite teachers from her days at Mater Dei. Nearly two hundred guests attended the wedding and the following reception, which was held at the golf resort of Marbella. For their honeymoon, Todd and Christine spent a romantic week on the island of Bora Bora.

When they returned to Los Angeles after the honeymoon, it suddenly appeared to Al and Irene that they were always saying good-bye to their daughter. But this good-bye would be different from all the others because this time, she truly was going off to begin a new life. Once in New York, Todd and Christine moved into a high-rise building near the office where Todd worked, and after receiving several job offers, Christine chose to work as an associate branch manager for Chesebrough-Ponds, a division of Unilever.

* * *

Al and Irene continued to volunteer their services for various Cursillo weekends, whenever time permitted. Acting as assistants, they would help prepare and serve the food, make sure all the speakers had everything they needed for their presentations, and basically do whatever they could to assist. In addition to making many new friends, they also found bliss and an inner joy in being engulfed by such an enormously spiritual environment.

But perhaps their greatest blessing came at the end of each weekend, when the candidates completed their instruction and had a new and clear comprehension of how and what they should do to become better Christians. Seeing the look of excitement on their faces, the shining glow in their eyes, and a new understanding of their personal relationship with Christ in their hearts was indeed a gift from God.

* * *

Blessings continued in the spring of 1998, when Todd was transferred to the Bay Area. Al and Irene could now visit them in their apartment in San Francisco by taking a short hop by plane or a one-day car trip.

The following year, Christine and Todd invited Al and Irene to join them for a tour of the wine country in Napa Valley. Al and Irene were exceptionally pleased to learn the invitation also included Todd's parents, Joyce and Carl, from Toronto. Following an insightful and informational tour of several large and well-known wineries, they went to San Francisco for a fine dinner in an exquisite restaurant. After they were seated and wine glasses filled, Al expected someone to make a toast. Instead, Christine, with an ever-so-slight smile, said, "First, we have something for you." The parents all looked at each other with blank faces, as Christine handed her parents a nicely wrapped package, and Todd did the same with his. Their collective shrieks of excitement filled the room as they opened the package to discover a book titled *How to Be a Good Grandparent*.

Later that year, Al and Todd stood on either side of a table in the delivery room of the California Pacific Medical Center in San Francisco. They each held one of Christine's hands, breathing nearly as hard and rapidly themselves as she was during her contractions. Finally, and with a giant sigh of relief, a precious infant made her entrance into the world with a loud squall—Samantha Grace Dow announced to the world that she had arrived.

* * *

Each day, the 102-mile round trip that Al made between home and office became more difficult. Traffic was much worse than it had been when they first moved to Laguna Niguel, which extended his time on the road to an hour and a half in each direction. Many times, while making the long commute, he felt perhaps the suggestions offered by the business consultants had been correct—perhaps he should have sold the building he owned and built a larger one closer to where they lived.

This thought plagued his mind until 2000, when business in general at Manhattan Die took a downturn. Overseas competition was cutting prices to the point that several of Al's customers had no other choice but to go elsewhere. He, in turn, was forced to cut back on overtime, which caused his employees to earn considerably less than they had grown accustomed to. Workmen's compensation for tool and die makers skyrocketed. New laws and regulations required that companies with more than nine employees must offer health insurance. The sales tax in Los Angeles increased again, and it seemed as if small-business owners were becoming tax collectors for the city and the state.

While still profitable, it was necessary for the company to again tighten its belt and operate more efficiently. More than once, Irene suggested that Al retire and sell the company. Each time she suggested it, however, his standard reply was, "I'll know when the time is right to retire, and right now is not the time." Al felt a great sense of responsibility to his employees, as well as to loyal customers, who had stayed with him even when others had offered lower prices for services.

It was also suggested that he work less and take on fewer jobs, to which he replied, "How can I refuse serving a loyal customer who has consistently given me die work for the past fifteen or twenty years? How can I not be available when the customer sends me a damaged die by FedEx or UPS from across the country?" He couldn't—and he wouldn't. He loved his work and what he was doing far too much.

Al had a strong and valued reputation for honesty, fairness, and high-principled values—lessons learned over a lifetime and solidified during his Cursillo weekend—and the people Al dealt with were more than merely customers or business associates; they were friends. One of his guiding principles was the continual and living example of the Golden Rule: "Do unto others as you would have them do unto you."

* * *

Al pulled into the garage in the rear of his shop and turned off the radio, a classical station that provided a sense of relative calm and serenity. When he entered the machinist's area, instead of finding the usual hustle and bustle of men at work and equipment grinding away at manufacturing dies, he discovered the vast area filled with silence and a profound degree of tension. All his employees were huddled around one specific workstation, the one occupied by an employee named Stefan, who had a portable television on the corner of his bench. Al approached the group, wondering what on earth was going on and why everyone was so transfixed. From his travels, he immediately recognized the Twin Towers in New York City— and a large plume of smoke billowing out of the side of one of them.

"What's going on?" he whispered to no one in particular.

"A big plane just crashed into the side of the building," one of his employees replied.

"Was it an accident?" he asked.

"No one's said," another man answered, concern in his voice.

The words were no sooner out of the man's mouth when they watched in abject horror as a second plane crashed into the second tower, creating a huge ball of flame. Everyone took a step back from the TV, as if the explosion could reach them through the screen. Several of them made the sign of the cross and bowed their heads. Others stared, with their mouths wide open. After a long moment of silence, one of the men finally said, "It wasn't an accident."

Al grabbed the nearest phone and called Irene. She answered on the first ring. "Are you watching it?" he asked.

"Yes," she replied, fear in her voice. "And I'm praying for the poor people inside. Are you coming home?"

"Not yet. I'm going to call Christine, and I'll call you later."

Al hung up and immediately phoned Christine to make sure that she and her young family were all right, fearing that perhaps areas on the West Coast were being targeted also. As he was on the phone with her, someone in the shop called out with a degree of urgency, "Al! You better see this." He said good-bye and quickly returned his attention to the TV set, watching in total disbelief—as did much of the nation—as the first tower began to crumble to the pavement below.

"Sweet Jesus in heaven," one of the men whispered. "How can this be happening?"

The TV station announcer said, in a voice as grave as any of them had ever heard, "While it has not yet been officially confirmed, there is a strong possibility the United States is presently under attack by an enemy nation." After a short while, that possibility was confirmed as a third plane crashed into the Pentagon Building. Estimates of the dead rose by the minute, estimates that were impossible to comprehend. Within a half an hour, another airplane crashed into a field in Pennsylvania, this one hijacked like the other three and supposedly on its way to Washington DC for yet another round of death and destruction.

All planes in the air were ordered to immediately land at the nearest airport, and people on the ground remained glued to their TVs, radios, or computers, compelled to watch the horrific pictures and frightened by pundits' suggestions of other potential targets. During the ordeal, the overall mood of the country changed from fright and alarm to panic—where or when would the next strike occur? The entire country was in a state of confusion, chaos, and terror.

Al and his employees remained at the shop that day but very little was accomplished. Like their fellow Americans, they continued to watch and listen to the breaking and worsening news, concerned for those dead and still in peril in New York, as well as for themselves and their own families on the West Coast, wondering if they might possibly be the next and most logical targets. A few questions were quietly asked: "How could this happen? Why did this happen? Who would do such a terrible thing?" But there were no answers.

Al went to his office and placed his hand on the Bible that was always on his desk. His mind was swimming with the senselessness and devastation of war. Visions—vivid and horrific—flashed in front of him: the mindless destruction of their Maria Hilf Chapel in Hermannstadt, the unexplainable deaths of millions of people to justify the whims of a madman, a riot of insanity in the streets of Los Angeles that took lives without reason or purpose, and now this. "Dear Heavenly Father, why?" he asked. But in his heart, he already knew the answer. God gave man the responsibility and opportunity to possess the free will to make choices—for either good or evil; to help or to hurt; to bring up or to tear down. Al's heart was deeply saddened by the thought that so many people chose the latter of all three.

That evening, along with millions of others across the nation and the world, Al and Irene watched television as the news worsened. They continued to offer prayers for everyone who lost their lives, the families of those left behind, and the first responders who were doing everything possible to assist. With the destruction of the Twin Towers and the offices and records kept within them, the financial future of the entire country was in extreme jeopardy. The potential to affect virtually every business in the United States was incomprehensible.

Al considered closing his shop until things became a little more settled, but after reflection and prayer, he decided that doing so would only serve the wishes of the terrorists who had done such a despicable act. He had seen in the past what happened when others cowed to the wishes and desires of tyrants. He knew firsthand what it was like to be forced into submission and lose everything that people had worked for their entire lives. He also knew that God would give him, as well as the entire country, the strength to go on, to continue, to defeat the enemy. From a more practical standpoint, he also knew that closing the shop would cause extreme hardship to those who depended on him for their livelihood.

On September 12, 2001, Al was the first one at his shop, reassuring his employees as they joined him and comforting them that their safety was in the hands of a higher power. The strength he shared came from an inner voice that calmly consoled him that his decision not to hide from life or his beliefs had been correct.

Work was accomplished that day, even though many would stop periodically to listen to and watch the discouraging words and pictures on the television. As had been anticipated, however, most businesses and even entire industries decreased productivity, a result of caution and uncertainty. Manhattan Die was among those affected, and it took the better part of six months before they were once again operating at full capacity.

TWENTY-EIGHT

THE YEAR 2002 BROUGHT MORE JOY TO THE ENTIRE LANGER family. At the Burlingame Community Hospital in Burlingame, California, a city south of San Francisco, Casey Langer Dow was born to Christine and Todd. The entire family was thrilled that Samantha Grace now had a younger brother.

Another somewhat radical change took place, when Al's long-time receptionist and bookkeeper left the company. He considered placing an ad for a new receptionist, but before he could do that, Irene volunteered for the position. When the company first began, everything had been done by hand and on paper: invoices, statements, accounts receivables and payables, accounting, correspondence, ledgers, and spreadsheets. Now, in the age of computerization, everything that applied to the business was taken care of by a series of computer programs, which were relatively simple to master. Al found the idea of working with Irene appealing, because it would give them more time together during the long commute to and from the shop.

Their work environment was considerably different from most others that Al had seen in his travels. Above the door of their reception area hung the classic picture of Jesus knocking on a door, conveying a clear message, to which many customers and visitors responded. The same picture was a favorite of Irene's, and she placed a smaller one on her desk. The pictures and their actions conveyed an atmosphere of Christian values in the shop and acted as an antidote against inappropriate behavior or displays, and foul or derogatory language. Without having to say it, their actions spoke loudly that this place of business was one that respected ethics and principles and had a strong moral fiber.

Irene became adept with the computer, and her pleasant and uplifting attitude with everyone—from their most valued customer to a delivery person—was refreshing and much appreciated. As a Cursillista herself, she was always more than willing to share her thoughts, feelings, and bliss with anyone who asked how she could so consistently be in such a good mood and have such a positive attitude.

On occasion, this attitude would diminish slightly during the evening drive back to Laguna Niguel. Seeing Al completely exhausted after working a ten-hour day, without taking time off for a break or even lunch, both saddened and concerned her. As the days, weeks, and months wore on, she could tell that his energy level was beginning to slowly diminish. Still, he gave her his standard response whenever she asked: "I'll retire when the time is right."

One event caused Al's energy level to return with monumental force—in 2004, at the John Muir Medical Center in Walnut Creek, California, Christine gave birth to Davis Bryant Dow. Samantha and Casey had a new baby brother. Todd and the grandparents once again beamed with enormous pride.

* * *

In May 2005, Al and Irene joined twenty-one fellow Cursillistas on an inspiring, enlightening, and highly spiritual pilgrimage to Medjugorje in Bosnia-Herzegovina, formerly known as Yugoslavia. Rev. Robert Puhlman, normally called Father Bob, from the La Virgin de Guadalupe parish in Mesquite, Nevada, led them. They flew from Los Angeles to Frankfurt, where they caught a connecting flight on Air Croatia to Split, Croatia. From there, they traveled by bus to Medjugorje. The long bus ride provided breathtaking sights of the deep green landscape, as they traveled along a high mountain road, overlooking the scenic vista of the Adriatic Coast while moving south toward Dubrovnik. Once they arrived in Medjugorje, the entire group stayed at a Pension, a large private home that had been converted into a bed-and-breakfast. The couple that owned the establishment greeted several of the group as family because they had stayed there previously.

The Cursillistas made this pilgrimage to Medjugorje because of the Visionaries of Our Lady. For nearly the past twenty years, Our Lady, the Blessed Virgin Mary, had appeared to six young parishioners in Medjugorje—simple people from the local area named Marija, Vicka, Ivan, Mirjana, Ivanka, and Jakov—confiding messages to them, which they, in turn, would share with the world. These visionaries had no special skills and, by their own account, had never asked for Our Lady to entrust them with such important messages for the world, yet they were blessed by daily apparitions that they recognized as Our Lady.

Al, Irene, and most of their group had the enormous privilege of watching as Vicka and Mirjana, on separate occasions, conveyed the messages they received. Vicka talked about the daily apparitions and the prayer intentions that Our Lady confided to her for the sick. Mirjana spoke about the yearly apparitions on March 18, during which Our Lady confided prayer intentions for nonbelievers—those who had not come to know the love of God. Each time, Al felt the presence of the Holy Spirit so strongly that it brought tears to his eyes.

Leaving Medjugorje by bus, their hearts were filled with joy from their experience. They returned to Split, a beautiful resort city on the Adriatic, and from there, they flew to Madrid, Spain, where they toured that vibrant and exciting city, and then went by bus to Avila and then Santiago de Compostela, also in Spain, where they spent one night. During their short visit they attended a Mass at the St. James Cathedral, where St. James the Apostle is buried in a tomb. It was here that Al had the privilege of giving the reading during the Mass, an honor he treasured deeply.

Their final destination was the city of Fatima, Portugal, where the group stayed in a hotel for three days. Their purpose was to attend the three days celebrating the feast day of Our Lady of Fatima on the May 13. They were within walking distance of the plaza, where over 100,000 worshippers came on an annual basis to witness the procession of the statue of Our Blessed Mother. Her apparitions appear in many forms and in many places throughout the world. In addition to Fatima, she has also made her presence known and delivered messages for the world as the Lady of Guadalupe in Mexico, the Lady of Lourdes in France, and Our Lady in Medjugorie.

Uplifted in spirit by the deeply religious pilgrimage, the group drove by bus to Lisbon, Portugal, where they boarded an airplane for their return to Los Angeles, eager and looking forward to relating their remarkable experience to family and friends.

* * *

Because of increased taxation, forced regulations, and incipient intrusions on his own and countless other small businesses, Al felt a growing sense of frustration with the political leadership in both California and Washington. He had the strong opinion, as did many others, that politicians at the highest level had lost touch with what they normally referred to as the common people. In order to correct what he felt was an unfair business atmosphere and an uneven playing field, his only option was to bring about change by voting new and different candidates into office, those who not only were more responsible but also were more business-friendly.

He often heard people complain that one man's vote wouldn't make a difference, but from his personal experience with Cursillo, he knew, without question, that was not true. Nevertheless, in order to vote, he must first become a citizen.

Al and Irene went to the Immigration and Naturalization Service office in Santa Ana, where they received applications to apply for citizenship and a study guide on the history of America that they were expected to learn. Following that, they were to make another appointment at the INS, where they would be questioned on what they'd read in the study guide.

After studying the fifty questions—everything from the color of the American flag to the three branches of government to who had the power to declare war—Al and Irene were completely familiar with them all. When they returned to the INS office and spoke with an official, Al explained, "I've lived in the United States for more than forty-five years and served in the California National Guard." He showed the official his discharge papers from the Guard.

The official smiled broadly and said, "I don't think there'll be any need for me to ask you any questions." He did, however, hand Al a pen and paper and told him write the words: "I will observe, abide, and live by the Constitution of the United States of America." The official smiled again and asked, "After all these years of living here, why, all of a sudden, do you want to become a citizen?"

Al simply replied, "Because I want to vote."

The official shook his hand and offered congratulations.

The swearing in ceremony took place on April 14, 2006, at the Los Angeles Convention Center. On that day, 3,800 people became citizens of the United States. They were given voter registration forms to fill out and also given a small American flag. Various officials stood behind a podium on a stage, with a huge screen behind them, and gave a few short speeches. Once that was completed, everyone was asked to stand, and loud speakers throughout the room played the "Star Spangled Banner," as a large picture of a waving flag appeared on the huge screen. This was followed by the classic song "God Bless the USA," sung eloquently by Lee Greenwood and turned up to full volume, as scenes of the United States from coast to coast were shown on the screen. The music was so loud, it appeared as if the room was shaking. It was an extremely powerful and highly emotional moment. At the conclusion of the song, there was barely a dry eye in the room. Without encouragement, the entire crowd erupted into wild applause and cheering as they waved their small flags. Once the cheering subsided, the multitude was asked to raise their right hands and together, they recited the Pledge of Allegiance.

Following the words, "with liberty and justice for all," the official beamed and said, "Congratulations. You are all now proud citizens of the United States of America." Amid more wild cheering, Al looked at Irene, and they both smiled. The words spoken had certainly been correct. They were indeed very, very proud.

* * *

The daily commute became more arduous, more difficult, and more painful. Al often felt like cutting down on his work schedule but realized that by doing so, he would be hurting the income of his employees. Many times during the long drive, he would lift himself up by pushing down on the seat with his left hand and steering with his right, supporting his weight with his elbow on the armrest. To a slight extent, this lessened the growing pain in his back. Even his physician, Dr. Homer Lew, regularly scolded him, "What language will it take for you to understand that the way you're going could land you in a wheelchair?" Irene continued to persistently suggest that he stop taking so many new orders and just live his life like a "normal person."

The dilemma Al faced was that he loved the work he knew so well and had been doing his entire life. He never had the slightest desire to do anything else. He also cared for his employees and the business in general. Many times he would reflect on the words his father had spoken to Herr Hartenstein, so very long ago, as they discussed the horses: "If you take care of them, they will take care of you." If it was possible, in several areas, Al cared too much.

He knew he was taking an enormous risk in running the company without having someone available to take over, should he become sick or unable to work. If that should occur, the shop would most unfortunately come to a standstill, the employees would be without pay, and the delivery of customers' dies would have to be delayed. But he was driven by the demand, seldom refusing anyone. He was still doing the same thing he'd been doing when he was thirty years younger—and the strain was taking its toll.

In February 2007, Doug Brown, one of his friendly competitors from Stellar Products, phoned with an emergency. He needed a rush job for one of his important customers. It turned out that his important customer was none other than Toby Keith, a famous country music singer. He had just recorded a new CD that needed to be packaged in a custom-made, vacuum-formed clamshell case, in order to be distributed to music stores and other outlets. To everyone's delight—but not surprise—Al managed to produce the tooling ahead of schedule, and Stellar Products produced the parts without any problems.

That work led to a dialogue in which Al finally asked Doug, "Would you and your father be interested in selling your steel rule-cutting die operation?" Al was just curious as to what the response would be.

To his surprise, Doug replied, "Actually I've spoken with my father about the possibility of purchasing Manhattan Die. In fact, we've had our eye on your company for quite some time."

Irene was completely in favor of accepting Stellar Products' offer. She tenderly suggested, "Al, you've been with the company for forty-six years. You're sixty-seven years old. Your doctor and I both think your health is being damaged. Perhaps now is the 'right time.'"

After seeking guidance from above and after eight months of below-the-radar and friendly negotiating, an agreement was struck. It was August 27, 2007. Stellar Products purchased only the intangible assets—the name "Manhattan Die," their customer list, and a non-compete clause from Al. To Al's great relief, they also agreed to hire all of Al's employees.

With bittersweet feelings and several days of thoughtful concern, Al composed and sent the following letter to all of his customers, informing them of the transaction:

August 27, 2007

> This is to announce that as of August 27, 2007, Stellar Products acquired Manhattan R.F. Die Company. Owners Bennett and Doug Brown have been friendly and respectful competitors, and I am pleased to turn over your account to them. Stellar Products has been a premier manufacturer of tooling, dies, and equipment to industries performing radio frequency heat-sealing and associated plastic converting and bonding processes since the late 1960s. I am confident that your orders will be in capable hands and will be handled with the utmost attention you deserve.

> Thank you for having given me the opportunity to serve you. I have tried to establish and maintain a personal relationship with you and your representatives in order to produce a top-quality product with fast turnaround time at the best possible cost.

> And now, after forty-six rewarding years of being in this business, I am looking forward to a new chapter in my life. I know I will miss the challenges, the daily grind, and uplifting rewards that came along with my hands-on ap-

proach of doing business. But most of all, I shall miss the personal contact with you, where I felt I was more than just a supplier of dies. I deeply appreciate the trust you have placed in me and my company, and thank you for being a loyal customer of Manhattan R.F. Die Company.

May you all be blessed with good health, happiness, and prosperity!

Al Langer

* * *

Within days of sending out the letter of notification, Al received a call from one of his largest long-time and loyal customers. Tommy Bath, owner of Domino Plastics in Bakersfield, California, phoned to inquire about the whereabouts of the equipment Al owned and had used so successfully over the years. He was pleased to learn the equipment was still in place and available for sale. Bath was also thrilled because if he owned the equipment, he would be able to make his own dies and increase his own profits. He made Al a very reasonable offer and purchased every piece of equipment in the entire shop, everything down to the last nut and bolt.

With his face blank but his heart heavy with emotion, Al watched as the last truck pulled out of the loading area, carrying away all the equipment and everything else that Tommy Bath had purchased. After a heavy sigh, he walked into the building—the shop where he had spent the majority of his life; the shop that had recently been filled with people and equipment, all working to manufacture some of the highest quality and precision dies in the entire country. And now, the large facility was an empty shell, nothing but a concrete floor and four blank walls.

As he slowly looked around the barren area, his mind filled with a rush of memories of other rooms and places he'd left in the past—Hermannstadt, after the soldiers made them leave their home at gunpoint, after they'd destroyed their blessed Maria Hilf Chapel, after they'd forced him to leave behind his loyal dog, Fritzl. Sleeping on straw mattresses in the gymnasium and the shoe factory, wondering when and from where their next meal was going to come, being treated as second-class citizens and outcasts by their fellow countrymen. Leaving the safety and comfort of their home in Selbitz to travel halfway across the world to begin a new life, a direct result of their being judged by their dialect rather than their competence or loyalty.

Throughout all the peril and hardships of Al's experience, he was always comforted by the faith and belief found in his parents' hearts, the same faith and beliefs they had instilled in his own. He smiled, remembering words his mother had often spoken: "God has a plan for all of us. There's no such thing as luck, fate, or coincidence. It is all actually part of God's plan. His will *will* be done."

As Al walked outside into the bright Southern California sunshine and closed the door behind him for the last time, he reiterated the thought, *God has a plan for all of us.* Prior to his Cursillo weekend, Al questioned that particular thought on numerous occasions. Was it luck that allowed their family to survive the cruel and inhuman treatment by the Czech Army? Was it fate that gave him the motivation and courage to leave his family and begin a new life, entrusted by his loving mother with the treasured family crucifix? Was it coincidence that inspired him, first with Hans and then alone, to continue to create and build such a successful company and provide for the needs of so many others?

Following his Cursillo weekend, he realized that his mother had been correct all along. Each life, no matter how apparently insignificant or seemingly unimportant, was an integral part of God's plan. Further, each of us is endowed with the free will to make choices—good or bad; right or wrong; with our eyes, souls, and hearts either lifted up to the heavens or down in defeat and despair.

Four remarkable days in the course of an entire lifetime had opened his eyes in ways he never imagined. It was if a veil had been lifted, and he could see clearly the meaning of life and his purpose for being here. He thought of the Irving Berlin song, "Count Your Blessings," and Al found it possible to relate completely.

He had been blessed with caring parents who instilled values that guided him throughout his life. Blessed with a loving and supporting wife, who never wavered in her encouragement. Blessed with a considerate, gentle daughter, a loving son-in-law, and three delightful grandchildren. Blessed with the opportunity of providing a comfortable living for his family doing that which he loved. But perhaps the greatest blessing of all was that he was able to share his knowledge, understanding, and faith with others. He had been transformed into a living example of one who would truly "walk the walk" with conviction and assurance, rather than one who would simply "talk the talk" with empty words and shallow beliefs.

The golden sun was slowly setting across the magnificence of the ocean as Al made his way home, comforted in the fact he had made the correct decision. He looked forward with great anticipation to a life that would, as God had ordained, continue to be blessed.

EPILOGUE

IRENE SEEMED TO BE RECEIVING AN UNUSUAL NUMBER OF phone calls, but Al paid little attention. Her birthday was approaching later that week, and he logically assumed the calls were from friends, wishing her well. His mind was preoccupied with the fact that Christine, Todd, and their children were coming down to join them for a celebratory dinner on Friday evening, October 19.

After they arrived and exchanged several hugs, kisses, and warm greetings, everyone piled into one car and drove to the Farantelli Restaurant in Dana Point. Upon entering the finely appointed establishment, the host greeted them politely and immediately directed them to a quiet table in the corner with a magnificent view. *Good*, Al thought. *This will be the ideal place for a quiet and enjoyable dinner with the kids.*

But a few moments later, the host reappeared. "I'm terribly sorry," he said, frowning to show his displeasure, "but I'm afraid this table has been reserved by another group. If you'll follow me, we have another table that will be equally acceptable."

Al was somewhat disappointed but quickly realized that the only important thing was that they were all together. Following a gentle nudge from Irene, they all rose and followed the host to the rear of the restaurant. As he opened the double doors to what proved to be a private room, Al froze where he stood, his mouth open, staring out at nearly seventy familiar and loving faces, who were staring back at him.

Irene led Al and Christine to a microphone in the front of the room, and after everyone finished a round of applause, she thanked them all for coming. The group was a mix of long-time neighbors, close friends who had also experienced their own Cursillo weekend, and others from their church. Following another round of applause, Christine stepped to the microphone, cleared her throat, and said with charm and dignity, "I'd like to say a few words about how proud I am of my dad and for all that he's accomplished.

"He began working in the tool and die industry over forty-six years ago and came to the United States from Germany, speaking barely any English. He was twenty-one years old when he left his family and friends behind to take a chance on a promising new job as an apprentice. His talent, hard work, and dedication to quality eventually earned him the position as owner and president of Manhattan Die Company.

"Not only has my dad worked very hard to fulfill his dreams, but he also earned himself an incredible reputation among his customers and competitors. They regard him as a businessman with great integrity and absolute dedication to quality, and a truly kind, fair human being.

"On a personal note, my dad's work ethic played a significant impact on my life. It pushed me to strive for great grades in school, go on to college, and then to graduate school. Yet in spite of his dedication to his job, he has always been there for me and my mom. He never missed my drill team practices or swim meets and always made our nightly family dinners a priority.

"So, for all that my dad has accomplished and to many relaxing years ahead, please raise your glasses to toast my dad, Al Langer."

"To Al!" the room responded in unison, as Christine led her father to center stage. He was genuinely humbled as he looked out at his friends and then offered a warm smile to his wife and daughter.

"As most of you know," Al began, "I'm definitely not very good as a speech maker." The opening line was greeted with much laughter. "But I would like to say that I am deeply honored that you would all take time out of your busy schedules to join me in celebrating Irene's birthday." There was even more laughter—everyone knew of the ruse of using Irene's birthday to get Al to the restaurant. He laughed with them, and then sobered.

"I only wish I had the words that are in my heart to thank you all for being such good friends over the years." He smiled knowingly. "And they've been such very good years." The crowd listened, enthralled by his words.

"I have been blessed with a wonderful wife, daughter, son-in-law, and three beautiful grandchildren. I have been blessed to have the opportunity of knowing each and every one of you gathered in this room. God has truly blessed me with more than I could ever possibly imagine. And for that, I honestly and sincerely thank both Him and you. Your presence in my life has made it considerably better. And even though one chapter of my life is now over, another one, even better, is just beginning. Again, as a living example, I must acknowledge that with God, all things are possible."

As the crowd rose to another round of applause, Al put his arms around Irene and Christine. He smiled, hoping that this new chapter of his life would continue to be blessed with true understanding, lasting satisfaction, and immeasurable joy.

ACKNOWLEDGEMENTS

I'D LIKE TO THANK MY MOM AND DAD FOR THEIR UNDYING support and love. The experiences of my childhood were often difficult, but my parents never let me forget that I was loved and that we could surmount all obstacles with faith and hard work. Thanks, too, go to Gary and Glenda Day, dear friends who encouraged me to develop my story into a book. Last but not least, my deep appreciation and thanks go to Gene Church, a gifted author whose writing skills helped to bring this project to life. Gene can be reached at genechurch@sbcglobal.net.